I0028828

DATA RESOURCE GUIDE

MANAGING THE
DATA RESOURCE DATA

MICHAEL H. BRACKETT

Published by:

Technics Publications, LLC
Post Office Box 161
Bradley Beach, NJ 07720 U.S.A.
www.technicspub.com

Cover design by Mark Brye

All rights reserved. No part of this book may be reproduced or transmitted in any form or by any means, electronic or mechanical, including photocopying, recording or by any information storage and retrieval system, without written permission from the publisher, except for the inclusion of brief quotations in a review.

The author and publisher have taken care in the preparation of this book, but make no expressed or implied warranty of any kind and assume no responsibility for errors or omissions. No liability is assumed for incidental or consequential damages in connection with or arising out of the use of the information or programs contained herein.

All trade and product names are trademarks, registered trademarks, or service marks of their respective companies, and are the property of their respective holders and should be treated as such.

This book is printed on acid-free paper.

Copyright © 2016 by Michael Brackett

ISBN, print ed.   978-1-6346210-0-7

First Printing 2016
Library of Congress Control Number: 2014945788

ATTENTION SCHOOLS AND BUSINESSES: Technics Publications books are available at quantity discounts with bulk purchase for educational, business, or sales promotional use. For information, please write to Technics Publications, PO Box 161, Bradley Beach, NJ 07090, or email Steve Hoberman, President of Technics Publications, at me@stevehoberman.com.

*Dedicated to those professionals desiring
to formally manage their Data Resource Data
with minimum effort.*

CONTENTS AT A GLANCE

CONTENTS

FIGURES

PREFACE

Thoroughly understanding all of the data that exist in an organization's data resource or are at an organization's disposal, and formally managing those data within a single organization-wide data architecture is mandatory if data are to be managed as a critical resource. When data are managed as a critical resource, equivalent to the human resource, financial resource, and real property, then the data resource fully supports the organization's business activities and the organization is more likely to be fully successful. When the data are not managed as a critical resource, the business activities suffer, and the organization is less likely to be fully successful.

Two Trilogies

The six books published with the current publisher form the Data Resource Simplexity series that helps organizations understand their data and manage those data as a critical resource of the organization. These six books provide all the concepts, principles, and techniques within the Common Data Architecture paradigm to formally manage the data resource. They also provide numerous examples about how to apply those concepts, principles, and techniques.

The six books in the Data Resource Simplexity Series form two very powerful trilogies.

The first Data Architecture Trilogy consists of *Data Resource Simplexity*, *Data Resource Integration*, and *Data Resource Design*. Collectively, these three books describe the need to build a simple and understandable data resource, the need to understand the existing disparate data and to develop a comparate data resource, and how to design and maintain a comparate data resource.

The second Data Understanding Trilogy consists of *Data Resource Data*, *Data Resource Understanding*, and *Data Resource Guide*. Collectively, these three books describe the need to create formal Data Resource Data to solve the meta-data fiasco, how to thoroughly understand the existing data through Data Resource Data, and how to develop and use a Data Resource Guide to manage those Data Resource Data.

Data Resource Guide

The Data Resource Guide is a repository for the Data Resource Data. Its primary purpose is to be the single repository for Data Resource Data as they are developed and to make those data readily available to any person in the organization that desires to thoroughly understand and use the organization's data resource.

The Data Resource Guide is a simple design. It is inexpensive to develop and maintain, and it is easy to use. It provides a powerful tool for understanding, documenting, and managing an organization's data resource. Any organization can develop its own Data Resource Guide with minimal effort and expense, compared to the effort and expense of acquiring and installing a commercial meta-data product and training people to use that product.

The Data Resource Guide can be developed incrementally. It provides an initial construct that an organization can grow into as it evolves to formally managing its data resource. It also provides a construct that can grow to support an organization's needs as that organization evolves toward better understanding and management of their data as a critical resource.

Intellectual Property

The first version of the current Data Resource Guide was developed in the late 1980s and early 1990s as a Meta-Data Warehouse to support the understanding and sharing of data between State agencies, Federal agencies, local government agencies, Indian Tribes, and private sector organizations. In the late 1990s a Data Resource Guide was developed to support the author's business clients. It was based on lessons learned from earlier data sharing efforts and was continually enhanced to support the specific needs of many and varied business clients. The current design that is presented in *Data Resource Guide* includes all of the lessons learned over a 30 year period working with a wide variety of public and private sector organizations.

From the late 1990s to 2015 the design of the Data Resource Guide was protected by Trade Secret Laws. During that time, several software vendors were approached about developing a commercial version of the Data Resource Guide. All vendors contacted declined with various reasons that ranged from the Data Resource Guide not being mainstream (meaning not supporting the meta-data hype) to it didn't fit within their existing product line (meaning not a substantial revenue stream).

With the author's retirement from active data resource management activities at the end of 2015, the design of the Data Resource Guide is being released into the public domain for the benefit of any organization that desires to develop their own Data Resource Guide to support formal management of their data as a critical resource. However, the author retains all intellectual property rights pertaining to the Data Resource Guide, the Data Resource Data that are stored in the Data Resource Guide, and the Common Data Architecture paradigm. Further, all material presented in the author's books and articles is copyrighted. The material may be used to support an organization's activities, but due credit needs to be given to the author.

Data Understanding Functions

The material in the current book is described according to the Data Understanding Functions as presented in *Data Resource Understanding*. The Data Understanding Functions are presented in the general sequence that they might be used by an organization to document and understand their data resource. However, an organization can use the Functions in any sequence that supports their need to document and understand their data resource, although some Functions must be performed before other functions. Also, an organization may decide not use all of the Functions presented or to add additional Functions.

Data Resource Guide contains the following Chapters oriented toward the Data Understanding Functions.

> Chapter 1 Managing the Data Resource describes the need to formally manage the data resource as a critical resource of the organization and the rules for presenting the Data Resource Guide design specifications.

> Chapter 2 Data Resource Guide provides the design specifications for the Data Resource Guide.

> Chapter 3 Data Responsibility provides the design specifications for the Data Responsibility Function.

> Chapter 4 Data Inventory provides the design specifications for the Data Inventory Function.

> Chapter 5 Common Data provides the design specifications for the Common Data Function.

> Chapter 6 Data Lexicon provides the design specifications for the Data Lexicon Function.

> Chapter 7 Data Cross-Reference provides the design specifications

for the Data Cross-Reference Function.

Chapter 8 Data Protection provides the design specifications for the Data Protection Function.

Chapter 9 Data Access provides the design specifications for the Data Access Function.

Chapter 10 Data Provenance provides the design specifications for the Data Provenance Function.

Chapter 11 Data Sharing provides the design specifications for the Data Sharing Function.

Chapter 12 Derived Data provides the design specifications for the Derived Data Function.

Chapter 13 Preferred Data provides the design specifications for the Preferred Data Function.

Chapter 14 Data Transformation provides the design specifications for the Data Transformation Function.

Chapter 15 Future Enhancements describes the future enhancements that could be made to the Data Resource Guide.

Chapter 16 Managing For Quality describes management of an organization's data resource to provide quality support to their business activities.

The Author's Challenges

The first challenge that the author faced in preparing *Data Resource Guide* was how to present the generic detailed design specifications for developing a Data Resource Guide without knowing anything about the specific operating environment of an organization, such as programming language, database management system, hardware, and so on, or knowing the standards and procedures of an organization. If those facts were known and were unique across all organizations, then specific detailed design specifications could be prepared. However, that situation doesn't exist and only generic detailed design specifications could be prepared. Each organization will need to adjust the generic detailed design specifications to specific detailed design specifications to meet their organization's operating environment, standards, and procedures.

The second challenge that the author faced in preparing *Data Resource Guide* was the page size. The current page size matches the previous books from the current publisher, which is a benefit to the publisher and the reader.

However, the outline format for the design specifications results in longer design specifications bunched on the right hand side of the page.

The problem could be resolved with a larger page size that provides more understandable design specifications. However, the larger page size produces a book that does not match the size of the previous books. The final resolution was to create a series of books that are physically the same size.

The third challenge that the author faced in preparing *Data Resource Guide* was the notation for presenting the generic detailed design specifications. The design specification notation used is an extension of the notation used for specifying data integrity rules, which includes commands that are described in Chapter 1.

The generic detailed design specifications in *Data Resource Guide* are not meant to be read like a novel. They are a reference for the design and development of a Data Resource Guide. Therefore, some of the design specifications may appear to be redundant or repetitive, but that approach allows a complete presentation of the design specifications for each particular Data Understanding Function.

Updated Versions

As with *Data Resource Data* and *Data Resource Understanding*, suggested revisions and additions to *Data Resource Guide* can be sent to the author at MHBDiscuss@aol.com or to the publisher. Updated versions of *Data Resource Data, Data Resource Understanding,* and *Data Resource Guide* may be published when sufficient enhancements have been made.

I sincerely hope that each public and private sector organization takes the initiative to manage their data as a critical resource, and to use the Common Data Architecture paradigm, the Data Resource Data design, and the Data Resource Guide construct as the foundations for that effort. The rewards will be monumental.

Best regards to all,

Michael Brackett
Olympic Mountains
August 2015

ACKNOWLEDGEMENTS

I thank all of the business professionals, data management professionals, professional friends, and personal friends that have a profound interest in understanding, documenting, managing, and fully utilizing an organization's data resource. They have provided many insights, thoughts, ideas, suggestions, and criticisms over the years that have improved the quality of the book and increased its usefulness.

I thank Steve Hoberman, yet again, for all of his support and encouragement through the development process and the publication process. He has remained a true professional friend as well as a close personal friend.

ABOUT THE AUTHOR

Mr. Brackett retired from the State of Washington in June 1996, where he was the State's Data Resource Coordinator. He was responsible for developing the State's common data architecture that spans multiple jurisdictions, such as state agencies, local jurisdictions, Indian tribes, public utilities, and Federal agencies, and includes multiple disciplines, such as water resource, growth management, and criminal justice. He is the founder of Data Resource Design and Remodeling and is a Consulting Data Architect specializing in developing integrated data resources.

Mr. Brackett has been in the data management field for over 50 years, during which time he developed many innovative concepts and techniques for designing applications and managing data resources. He is the originator of the Common Data Architecture paradigm, the Data Resource Management Framework, the data naming taxonomy and data naming vocabulary, the Five-Tier Five-Schema concept, the data rule concept, the Business Intelligence Value Chain, the Data Resource Data concept, the architecture-driven data model concept, the Data Resource Guide design, and many new techniques for understanding and integrating disparate data. Through is independent thinking and inquisitive mind he has evolved to a recognized thought leader, to a visionary thought leader, and has become a legend in data resource management.

Mr. Brackett has written eleven previous books on the topics of application design, data design, and common data architectures. *Data Sharing Using a Common Data Architecture* and *The Data Warehouse Challenge: Taming Data Chaos* describe the concept and uses of a common data architecture for developing an integrated data resource. *Data Resource Quality: Turning Bad Habits into Good Practices* describes how to stop the creation of disparate data. *Data Resource Simplexity: How Organizations Choose Data Resource Success or Failure* describes the approach to data resource management that avoids the creation of disparate data. *Data Resource Integration: Understanding and Resolving a Disparate Data Resource* describes how to permanently resolve an organization's disparate data. *Data Resource Design: Reality Beyond Illusion* describes how to formally design an organizations data resource. *Data Resource Data: A Comprehensive Data Resource Understanding* describes the data resource model for Data Resource Data. *Data Resource Understanding: Utilizing The Data Resource Data* describes how to use the Data Resource Data to thoroughly understand and formally manage an organizations data resource. He has written numerous articles, including monthly articles for Dataversity.net from 2012 through 2015. He is a well-known international author, speaker, and trainer on data resource management topics.

Mr. Brackett has a BS in Forestry (Forest Management) and a MS in Forestry (Botany) from the University of Washington, and a MS in Soils (Geology) from Washington State University. He was a charter member and is an active member of DAMA-PS, the Seattle Chapter of DAMA International established in 1985. He saw the formation of DAMA National in 1986 and DAMA International in 1988. He served as Vice President of Conferences for DAMA International, as the President of DAMA International from 2000 through 2003, and as Past President of DAMA International for 2004 and 2005. He was the founder and the first President of the DAMA International Foundation, an organization established for developing a formal data management profession, and served as Past President of the DAMA International Foundation through 2013. He was the Production Editor of the first DAMA-DMBOK released in April 2009.

Mr. Brackett received DAMA International's Lifetime Achievement Award in 2006 for his work in data resource management, the second person in the history of DAMA International to receive that award (Mr. Brackett presented the first award to John Zachman in 2003). He taught Data Design and Modeling in the Data Resource Management Certificate Program at the University of Washington and has been a member of the adjunct faculty at Washington State University and The Evergreen State College. He is listed in *Who's Who in the West*, *Who's Who in Education*, and *International Who's Who*.

Mr. Brackett is retired from formal data resource management activities and enjoys a variety of recreations activities, including back country hiking, cross-country skiing, snowshoeing, biking, kayaking, dancing, and writing children's books. He lives in a log home he built in the Olympic Mountains near Lilliwaup, Washington. He can be reached through the publisher.

Chapter 1

MANAGING THE DATA RESOURCE

The use of an organization's data resource to thoroughly understand and fully support its business activities is only limited by one's imagination. When the data resource is disparate and not well understood, that imagination is severely constrained and the business activities suffer. However, when the data resource is comparate and well understood, that imagination is limitless and the business activities support a successful organization.

Therefore, the best approach to a successful organization is to formally manage data as a critical resource of the organization, which has been a common theme through all of the Data Resource Books. When that critical data resource becomes comparate and is used by everyone in the organization to understand their business environment and to support their business activities, the organization has a much greater chance of being fully successful.

THE BOOK

Data Resource Data described *What* needs to be documented about an organization's data resource to provide the thorough understanding for properly managing data as a critical resource of the organization. *Data Resource Understanding* described *How* the Data Resource Data could be used to thoroughly understand and properly manage an organization's data resource, including a variety of business scenarios for using Data Resource Data.

The current *Data Resource Guide* provides the *Design* of the Data Resource Guide for storing and retrieving the Data Resource Data. It provides the generic detailed design specifications for the Data Resource Guide that are independent of an organization's standards and guidelines, programming languages, and database management systems. It does not describe *How* the Data Resource Guide is developed within a specific organization.

Data Resource Guide is organized by Data Understanding Functions, the same as *Data Resource Understanding* was organized. It is not organized by the data architecture as *Data Resource Data* was organized. However, all of the data structures, data definitions, and data integrity rules described in *Data Resource Data* apply to the generic detailed design specifications in *Data Resource Guide*. Those structures, definitions, and integrity rules will not be repeated in *Data Resource Guide*, but apply to all data entering the Data Resource Guide.

The generic detailed design specifications of the Data Resource Guide will be presented in the logical sequence of Data Understanding Functions. Each Data Understanding Function represents a cohesive portion of the Data Resource Data. However, the presentation sequence is not necessarily the sequence that the Data Resource Data might be entered or retrieved by an organization. The entry is usually driven by the availability of the Data Resource Data and any natural sequence for entry, such as Data Product Data and Common Data entry before Data Cross-Referencing. The retrieval is usually driven by the need of people in the organization to thoroughly understand the data resource.

The material provided in *Data Resource Integration* and *Data Resource Design* will not be repeated in *Data Resource Guide*. Those books can be consulted for detailed descriptions about integrating disparate data and designing a comparate data resource.

DATA RESOURCE GUIDE FEATURES

The basic features of the Data Resource Guide are described below, including data deletion, the meaning of organization specific, the meaning of business data, reports, calculations, formal data names, self-documentation, and access to the Data Resource Data from outside the Data Resource Guide.

Data Deletion

Deleting data occurrences is not allowed in the Data Resource Guide. All Data Resource Data are retained as historical documentation and become part of the data understanding process. Even obsolete Data Resource Data are never deleted. End dates and status codes show when a particular data occurrence became obsolete, but that data occurrence is never deleted.

However, mistakes sometimes do occur and bad data occurrences do enter the Data Resource Guide. Only the Data Resource Guide Administrator should have the authority to remove bad data occurrences from the Data Resource Guide. Business professionals and data management professionals with the authority to edit the Data Resource Data should not have the authority to delete any data occurrences.

Similarly, data definitions, descriptions, comments, and so on, are never deleted. They are also retained as part of the understanding process. Additional definition, description, and comment is added to the existing text when additional insight is gained. Each organization can decide whether textual statements are kept in chronological order or in reverse chronological order. Each sequence has advantages and disadvantages.

Organization Specific

The term 'organization specific' means the design details are up to the organization depending on their standards, guidelines and specific needs. For example, the window designs and report layouts are organization specific. The application language and database management system are organization specific. Therefore, the Data Resource Guide design specifications provide *What* needs to be done, not *How* it is done. Organizations can determine *How* the design specifications are implemented.

Organizations can also enhance the Data Resource Guide to meet their specific needs. Data Resource Data can be added or removed, reports and calculations can be added or removed, navigation between functions, processes, and routines can be adjusted, and so on. The basic construct of the Data Resource Guide is provided and organizations can make adjustments to that basic construct as needed.

Business Data

The Data Resource Guide contains Data Resource Data, not business data. One common misconception about the Data Resource Guide is that it contains the business data. For example, *Organization Unit* does not document the organizational structure of an organization, nor does *Data Steward* or *Business Process Steward* document the human resource data about those people. Those data are documented in business databases.

External links can be made from the Data Resource Guide to business databases for additional detail. For example, *Organization Unit* in the Data Resource Guide could have an external link to *Organization Unit* in another database which contains all of the data about organization units. Similarly, Data Steward and Business Process Steward in the Data Resource Guide could have external links to the human resource data in other business databases.

Having made that statement could lead to a philosophical discussion about whether or not the Data Resource Data are business data. Data Resource

3

Data are business data in the sense that management of the organization's data resource is a business function, and like other business functions must have data available for proper management of the data resource. However, the Data Resource Guide contains Data Resource Data supporting the data resource management business function, not data for the management of other business functions.

Reports

The report specifications that are shown at the end of each Chapter are basic reports that over the years have been found to be common to many organizations. Each organization can add or remove reports according to their specific needs. The basic construct of the Data Resource Guide allows for the addition and removal of reports.

All reports should have a report name and date, and any other organization specific data. However, these details are organization specific and are not shown on the report specifications. Each organization can add the details according to their policies and guidelines.

The report specifications provide details about what appears in a report. They are not examples of the Data Resource Data that could appear on a report. Nor are the report specifications application code for generating the reports, because of the differences in program languages, applications, and database management systems.

Over time in any organization the number of different report types tends to increase because organizations want to look at the Data Resource Data many different ways to understand and manage their data resource. However the number of printed reports tends to decrease substantially, because of the ready availability of the Data Resource Data through the Data Resource Guide. When the Data Resource Data are readily available, fewer reports are printed.

Also, over time in any organization more people begin talking quantitatively about their data resource and how to improve data resource understanding and quality. They begin to manage data as a critical resource of the organization. The ultimate benefit is better support for business activities.

Calculations

A few calculations are provided for viewing statistics about an organization's data resource. The calculations are in the form of reports that are listed at the end of each Chapter. Like other reports, only a few basic calculations are shown. However, an organization can add additional calculations to meet their specific needs.

As an organization becomes more familiar with understanding and managing their data resource through the Data Resource Data and the Data Resource Guide, more requests are made for additional types of calculations.

Formal Data Names

The data names used in the Data Resource Guide are the formal data names for the Data Resource Data. Those formal data names are readily accepted by business professionals, although they may not be readily accepted by data management professionals. Data management professionals tend to object to the formal data names because they are perceived to be too long, and take too much time and effort to type. However, over time in any organization the data management professionals tend to accept the formal data names because they provide better understanding, lead to a higher quality data resource, and ultimately reduce the problems that data management professionals need to resolve.

If data name abbreviations are desired, then formal data name word abbreviations and a formal data name abbreviation algorithm should be used to abbreviate the Data Resource Data. Random and informal data name abbreviations seriously impact understanding and lead to a lower quality data resource. The ultimate impact is on the quality of support provided to business processes.

Self-Documentation

The Data Resource Guide is self-documenting. The first data that should be placed in the Data Resource Guide are the Data Resource Data. That way the Data Resource Guide can be used to access, understand, and use the Data Resource Data to understand and manage the organization's data resource. The Data Resource Data are not privileged in any way and should be readily available to anyone in the organization desiring to understand and use the organizations data resource.

Access Outside the Data Resource Guide

The Data Resource Data can be accessed from outside the Data Resource Guide. They can be accessed by SQL or report generators for the preparation of special reports or calculations. However, if those reports or calculations could be beneficial to others, they should become part of the Data Resource Guide construct so they are readily available to anyone using the Data Resource Guide.

The Data Resource Data can also be accessed by business applications so that business professionals using those business applications can readily understand the data while using those business applications. That feature is seldom available from traditional data documentation applications, requiring a business professional to logon to another application to understand the data they are using. The Data Resource Data that are most useful to business professionals are the data definitions and data integrity rules.

PRESENTATION RULES

The following presentation rules apply throughout the current book and will not be repeated in each Chapter.

General Design Hierarchy

The highest level in the Data Resource Guide generic detailed design is Data Understanding Function, as described in *Data Resource Understanding*. Each Data Understanding Function has a formal name, such as Data Inventory Function.

The second level in the Data Resource Guide generic detailed design is Data Understanding Task. Each Data Understanding Task has a formal name, such as Data Product Steward Task within the Data Inventory Function.

The third level in the Data Resource Guide generic detailed design is Data Understanding Routine. Each Data Understanding Routine has a formal name, but the word 'Routine' does not appear in the name. For example, Organization Unit is a Data Understanding Routine within the Organization Unit Task.

The fourth level in the Data Resource Guide generic detailed design is composed of commands and actions, as described below.

General Design Navigation

The navigation between Data Understanding Functions, Data Understanding Tasks, and Data Understanding Routines is shown on a diagram containing boxes with lines between those boxes. The boxes represent the Functions, Tasks, or Routines, as shown by the name inside the box. The lines represent the navigation routes, and have no arrows because navigation can be either direction depending on the Commands and their actions.

General Design Logic

The Data Resource Guide generic detailed design is shown as nested (indented) sets. The generic detailed design may be as many as ten levels deep, depending on the detail that needs to be specified.

The generic detailed design could be shown as nested sets on hierarchy charts, but those charts would become quite large, exceed the page size, and result in considerable white space. Therefore, the nested (indented) set notation is used.

Data Hierarchy

The hierarchy of the Data Resource Data consists of nested data subjects, such as Data Product, Data Product Set, Data Product Unit, and Data Product Code, with the last three having one level of recursion for variations. Sometimes the data hierarchy can be four or five levels deep in the generic detailed design specifications. If the software an organization is using does not automatically handle data hierarchies with that many levels, then some form of additional programming is needed to show the data hierarchy indirectly.

Multiple Appearances of a Routine

A specific routine may appear in more than one place in the Data Resource Guide, such as Data Model Diagrams and Data Stewards. These routines, are defined once when they first appear in the book and subsequent appearances refer to that first appearance for the details.

When a specific routine is called from another routine, the [RETURN] Command Button returns control to the calling routine. Each organization needs to determine how to manage the navigation for calls and returns depending on the standards and guidelines, and programming language.

Command Buttons

Command Buttons are used throughout the Data Resource Guide for navigation. The name of the command is shown on the Command Button. The design and location of the Command Buttons on a window is organization specific, but should be consistent.

A Command Button that is available to anyone using the Data Resource Guide is shown as brackets with the name of the command in all caps within those brackets, such as [RETURN]. When the Command Button is clicked the operation by the name of the command is activated.

A Command Button that is available only to those authorized to add, update, or delete data in the Data Resource Guide is shown in parentheses with the name of the command in all caps within those parentheses, such as (NEW). These Command Buttons only appear on Edit and Update windows.

A Report Button that is available to anyone using the Data Resource Guide is shown as brackets with the name of the report capitalized within those brackets, such as [Selected Data Steward Detail]. The word 'Report' is not shown in the report name. Clicking the Report Button activates that report by the name shown on the Report Button.

The following Command Buttons are used in the Data Resource Guide.

[ACCEPT] means to accept the new data that has been entered in the data fields within the (NEW) command.

[BACK] means to display the previous data occurrence in the list. The action will not work for the first data occurrence in the list.

[CLOSE] means to Close the Data Resource Guide.

(DELETE) means to delete the selected data occurrence.

[DISPLAY] means to display data for viewing or editing.

[HELP] means to open the Help Window and display the Help Message with the same name as the window from which the [HELP] is initiated, such as:

   [HELP]
        Open Help Message Window
        Display Data Steward Help Message.

[NAME] means to Open a Window for a Function, Task, or Routine with the name shown, and transfer control to that window, such as:

   [DATA PRODUCT DATA TASK]
        Open Data Product Data Task

(NEW) means to display blank data fields for entering new data. It only appears on Edit windows. The word 'NEW' is used rather than 'ADD' because Add has two meanings. First it means adding additional material to material that already exists. Second it means adding something new that doesn't already exist. In the Data Resource Guide, 'Editing' means adding new material to material that already exists and 'New' means adding new material that doesn't already exist.

[NEXT] means to display the next data occurrence in the list. The action will not work for the last data occurrence in the list.

(NO) means to set the selected Indicator to 'No'

[PRINT] means to print the displayed data by sending to the appropriate printer. The printer details are organization specific.

[Report Name] means to open a report by the name shown in brackets. The detail for that report specifies the data that are shown on the report. The report name is capitalized, but not all capitals.

[RETURN] means to Close the window or report and Return to the parent Window. The return location is shown in the generic detailed design specifications, such as:

[RETURN]
Close the window and Return to Data Product Data Function.

(YES) means to set the selected Indicator to 'Yes'.

Data Names

Data names are italicized for ready identification, such as *Data Subject. Name Complete* or *Data Product.*

Terminology

The term 'window' is used rather than 'screen' since multiple windows can be opened and used at any time, while using only one physical screen. 'Window' is the logical display of data and actions, while 'screen' is the physical device where the windows are displayed.

The term 'Auto-Scroll List' means to provide a selection list of one data characteristic with a scroll bar for manual scrolling and a data field for entering text with automatic scrolling as the text is being entered. The data names displayed in an Auto-Scroll List should be in alphabetical order unless stated otherwise.

The term 'Scroll List' means to provide a selection list of more than one data characteristic with a scroll bar for manual scrolling, but no data field for entering text with automatic scrolling. The data names displayed in a Scroll List should be in alphabetical order for each data characteristic unless stated otherwise.

The term 'Display' means to display data in some form. When specific data are to be displayed, those data are specifically named, such as *Data Subject. Name Complete*. When multiple data are to be displayed, the grouping of those data is stated, such as *Data Subject Area* data.

The term 'Open' means open a window with the window name displayed and transfer control to that window, such as Open Help Message Reports.

The window can completely overlay the existing window from which it was opened, or it can be smaller than the existing window from which it was opened. Also, the originating window can either remain open or be closed. These decisions are organization specific. 'Open' is used rather than 'Call', 'Initiate', or similar words.

The term 'Close' means close a window or a report, such as Close <u>Help Message</u>.

The term 'Return' means to return control to the window specified, such as 'Return to <u>Data Steward Task</u>.' The name of the window is underscored.

The term 'Each' means that data for each data occurrence is displayed. For example, 'Display Each *Data Subject* data' means that data specified for each Data Subject is displayed.

The term 'Sort' means to sort the data specified in alphabetical order unless otherwise specified, such as 'Sort *Data Subject* by *Data Subject. Name Complete*.' A sequence of sorting is specified from major to minor with the up-caret, such as 'Sort *Data Subject. Name Complete ^ Data Characteristic. Name Complete*.'

The term 'Unique' applies to displaying sorted data and means to only display repetitive data once, with subordinate data displayed below.

The term 'Selected' means that the action is performed based on a previously selected data subject, such as "Display Each *Data Characteristic* within Selected *Data Subject*.'

The term 'from' means data are displayed from a specific data subject, such as 'Display Scroll List from *Business Glossary*.'

The term 'within' means 'subordinate to' or 'child of' a data subject, such as 'Display Each *Data Characteristic* within Selected *Data Subject*.'

The term 'with' means the display list includes the listed data characteristics, such as 'Display from Each *Data Product* with *Data Product. Name, Data Product. Definition*.'

Several terms may be combined within one actions, such as 'Display Auto-Scroll List from Each *Data Characteristic* within Selected *Data Subject* When *Common Data Status. Name* >< 'Preferred' with *Data Characteristic. Name Complete, Data Characteristic. Definition*.'

Conditional Logic

Conditional logic needs to be expressed in some situations. The When – Then notation is used to express that conditional logic, as explained in *Data*

Resource Data and *Data Resource Understanding*. The When – Then notation can be expressed in either of three ways.

First, it can be expressed with both words When and Then with no indentation, such as:

When Door is Open
Then Walk through Door

Note that the statements are not concatenated because they are difficult to understand, such as:

When Door is Open, Then Walk through Door

Second, it can be expressed without the word Then, but with an indentation for the Then action under the When statement, such as:

When Door is Open
    Walk through Door

Third, it can be expressed without a Then clause in a display command or action, such as:

Display from *Data Subject* When Com*mon Data Status. Name* ><
'Preferred' with *Data Subject. Name Complete*

Editing and Viewing Data

'Edit' means that new data can be entered and existing data can be changed. 'View' means that data can only be viewed; not entered or changed.

Data can be edited in the data fields where the data are displayed. However, that capability is only available on the Edit windows. Data cannot be edited on View windows.

When the data editing is complete, the [ACCEPT] command button is used to accepted the editing.

The editing and viewing task is described in more detail in the Data Resource Guide Edit/View Task section in the next Chapter.

System Identifiers

Most of the data subjects, except the data reference set data subjects, have a System Identifier as the primary key. Those System Identifiers are not visible to people using the Data Resource Guide, and most people using the Data Resource Guide are not even aware of what System Identifiers are or how they are used. Therefore, when displaying data in the Data Resource Guide, the System Identifier of a parent data subject is used to access that specific data occurrence in the parent data subject to obtain the Name, and then display that Name.

For example, *Data Product Set* has a parent *Data Product*. The foreign key to *Data Product* is *Data Product. System Identifier*. That System Identifier is used to access a specific *Data Product* data occurrence, the *Data Product. Name* is obtained, and that name is then displayed.

Chapter 2

DATA RESOURCE GUIDE

The Data Resource Guide overview is shown in Figure 2.1. The top two rows in the diagram represent administrative functions for opening the Data Resource Guide, determining the authority to use the Data Resource Guide, and actions to select the various Data Understanding Functions. The lower three rows in the diagram represent the twelve specific Data Understanding Functions that can be selected.

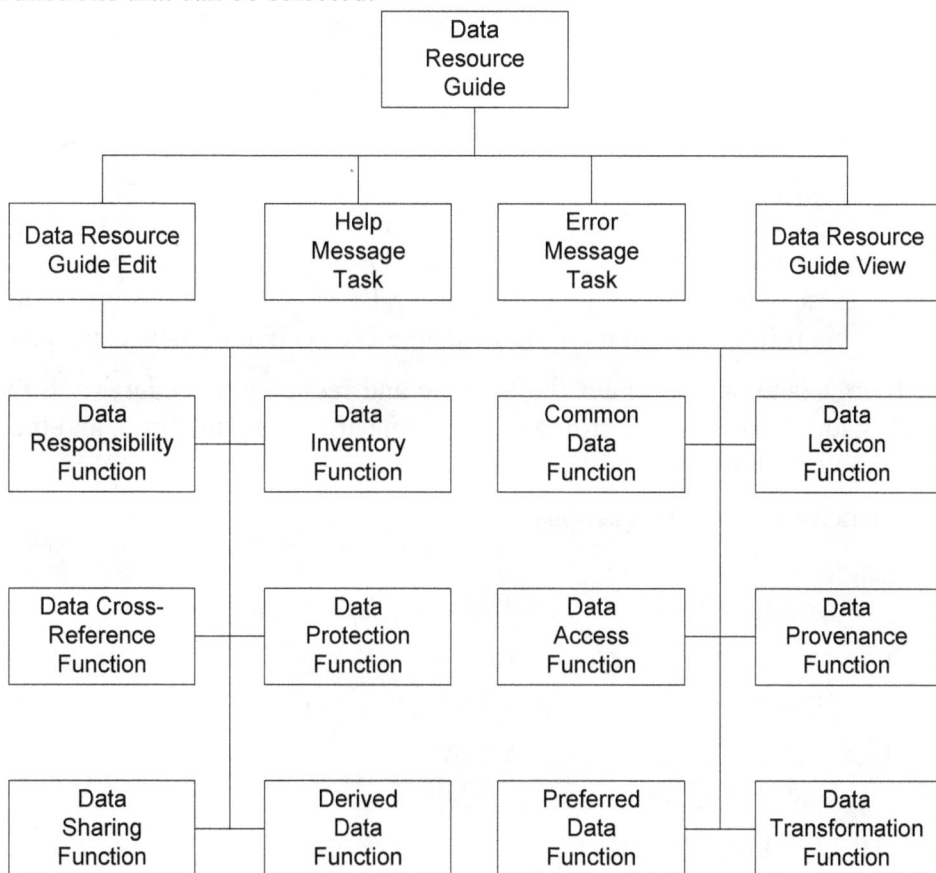

Figure 2.1. Data Resource Guide.

DATA RESOURCE GUIDE OVERVIEW

The Data Resource Guide is launched like any other application. The actions are organization specific. The opening window shows the login procedure that is also organization specific. Generally three levels of authorization are allowed for the Data Resource Guide.

The Data Resource Guide Administrator can enter and edit Help Messages, enter and edit Error Messages, delete records, and perform any other tasks related to operation of the Data Resource Guide and management of the Data Resource Data. Generally, only one or a very few people have administrative authority.

Edit capability allows a person to enter, change, and view the Data Resource Data. Generally that person is not allowed to Delete any data occurrences, however that option is organization specific. Some organizations allow those with edit capability to delete single data occurrences, while major deletes, such as cascade deletes, must be done by the Administrator. Generally, edit capability is reserved for anyone that is responsible for designing, developing, or documenting the organization's data resource.

View capability allows a person to view the Data Resource Data, but not enter any new Data Resource Data or make any changes to existing Data Resource Data. Generally, anyone in the organization that is interested in the Data Resource Data can have view capability.

Each organization determines the back-up and recovery procedures and the activity log procedures according to their standards and guidelines, and their operating environment.

The Data Resource Guide actions are:

Login
    Organization Specific Login/Authorization procedure.

[DATA RESOURCE GUIDE EDIT]
    Open Data Resource Guide Edit

[DATA RESOURCE GUIDE VIEW]
    Open Data Resource Guide View

[HELP MESSAGE TASK]
    Open Help Message Task

[ERROR MESSAGE TASK]
    Open Error Message Task

[CLOSE]
   Close Data Resource Guide

[HELP]
   Open <u>Help Message View</u>
   Display Data Resource Guide Help Message

DATA RESOURCE GUIDE EDIT / VIEW TASK

The Data Resource Guide Edit and Data Resource Guide View windows serve the same general purpose. They allow access to all of the Data Understanding Functions in the Data Resource Guide. The only difference between them is whether a person can add new data, change existing data, or delete existing data based on the Login Procedure.

Data Resource Guide Edit opens windows that have editing and delete capability, while Data Resource Guide View opens windows that do not have editing and delete capability. In other words, a person can access all the Data Understanding Functions, but may or may not be allowed to edit and delete data depending on their authorization.

The Tasks and Routines listed throughout the Data Resource Guide have both Edit and View capability. However, those Edit and View capabilities are not listed separately because the navigation would be redundant and would take considerable space. Instead, the editing and deletion capability is shown on each window with parenthesis, such as (NEW) and (DELETE), rather than with brackets, such as [RETURN] or [HELP].

Each organization can determine whether it wants to develop separate windows for Edit and View, or whether it wants to develop a single window and either enable or disable the edit and delete capabilities depending on a person's authorization.

Similarly, the Help Messages can be specific to Edit and View windows, or can be general to cover both the Edit and View capabilities depending on whether an organization develops separate Edit and View windows or single windows for editing and deleting.

The Error Messages only apply to the Edit windows since errors only occur when data are being entered or edited. They do not apply to the View windows.

The Data Resource Guide Edit / View actions are:

   [DATA RESPONSIBILITY FUNCTION]
      Open <u>Data Responsibility Function</u>

[DATA INVENTORY FUNCTION]
Open Data Inventory Function

[COMMON DATA FUNCTION]
Open Common Data Function

[DATA LEXICON FUNCTION]
Open Data Lexicon Function

[DATA CROSS-REFERENCE FUNCTION]
Open Data Cross-Reference Function

[DATA PROTECTION FUNCTION]
Open Data Protection Function

[DATA ACCESS FUNCTION]
Open Data Access Function

[DATA PROVENANCE FUNCTION]
Open Data Provenance Function

[DATA SHARING FUNCTION]
Open Data Sharing Function

[DERIVED DATA FUNCTION]
Open Derived Data Function

[PREFERRED DATA FUNCTION]
Open Preferred Data Function

[DATA TRANSFORMATION FUNCTION]
Open Data Transformation Function

[RETURN]
Close window and Return to Data Resource Guide Edit / View

[HELP]
Open Help Message View
Display Data Resource Guide Edit / View Help Message

HELP MESSAGE TASK

Help Messages provide specific instructions for each window in the Data Resource Guide. One Help Message is developed for each window in the Data Resource Guide. Help Messages are organization specific depending on how the organization decides to design, develop, and use the Data Resource Guide, and how it decides to develop and use the Data Resource Data. Generally, only the Data Resource Guide Administrator can add or change Help Messages.

Help Message Task contains Help Message View, Help Message Edit, and Help Message Reports, as shown in Figure 2.2. It is opened from Data Resource Guide.

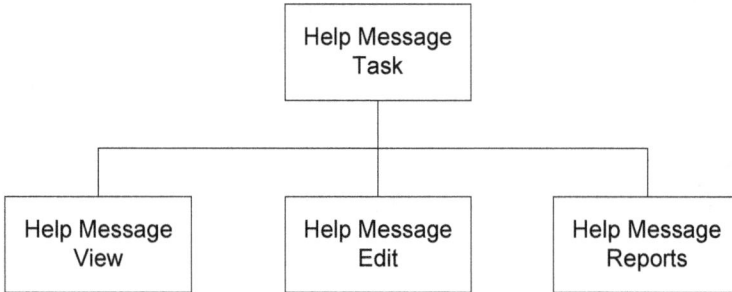

```
            ┌─────────────────┐
            │  Help Message   │
            │      Task       │
            └─────────────────┘
                     │
      ┌──────────────┼──────────────┐
┌───────────┐  ┌───────────┐  ┌───────────┐
│Help Message│  │Help Message│  │Help Message│
│   View     │  │   Edit     │  │  Reports   │
└───────────┘  └───────────┘  └───────────┘
```

Figure 2.2. Help Message Task.

The Help Message Task actions are:

[HELP MESSAGE VIEW]
    Open Help Message View

[HELP MESSAGE EDIT]
    Open Help Message Edit

[HELP MESSAGE REPORTS]
    Open Help Message Reports

[RETURN]
    Close window and Return to Data Resource Guide

[HELP]
    Open Help Message View
    Display Help Message Task Help Message

Help Message View

The Help Message View window can be opened on any window in the Data Resource Guide when [HELP] is clicked. The appropriate Help Message for that specific window is displayed in the Help Message View window. The Help Message View actions are:

[DISPLAY]
    Display Help Message with the same name as the window from
        which the Help Message View open was issued.

[CLOSE]

Close <u>Help Message View</u>

Help Message Edit

Help Message Edit is generally used only by the Administrator for creating and editing Help Messages. The Help Message Edit actions are:

[DISPLAY]
   Display Auto-Scroll List from *Help Message* with *Help Message.*
     Name
   Select *Help Message. Name*
   Display Selected *Help Message* data

      [PRINT]

      (DELETE)
         Delete Selected *Help Message* occurrence

(NEW)
   Display blank data fields for entry of new *Help Message* data.

   [ACCEPT]

[RETURN]
   Close window and Return to <u>Help Message Task</u>

[HELP]
   Open <u>Help Message Window</u>
   Display Help Message Edit Help Message

Help Message Reports

Help Message Reports contains reports for the Help Message Task. It is opened from Help Message Task. The specific reports and actions to obtain those reports are:

[Help Message Name]
   Display Each *Help Message. Name*

   [PRINT]

[Help Message Detail]
   Display Each *Help Message* data

   [PRINT]

[RETURN]
   Close report and Return to <u>Help Message Reports</u>

[HELP]
>Open Help Message Window
>Display Help Message Reports Help Message

HELP MESSAGE DATA ARCHITECTURE

The Help Message data architecture is shown below, including the data characteristic structure, data definitions, and data integrity rules. The Help Message data architecture is not part of the Data Resource Data architecture. It is part of the Data Resource Guide.

Help Message Data Structure

The Help Message data subject-relation diagram is shown in Figure 2.3. The data characteristic list is shown below the diagram.

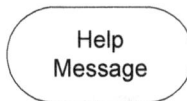

Help
Message

Figure 2.3. Help Message Data Structure.

Help Message

Primary Key:	Help Message. System Identifier
Alternate Key:	Help Message. Name

Data Characteristic List:
>Help Message. Name
>Help Message. System Identifier
>Help Message. Text

Help Message Data Definitions

The Help Message data subject and data characteristic definitions are listed below.

Help Message
Help Message provides instructions to a person using the Data Resource Guide. Each Help Message is relevant to a specific window and describes the actions that can be taken on that window.

>**Help Message. Name**
>The formal name of a Help Message, such as Business Glossary Edit or Data Steward View.

19

Help Message. System Identifier
The system-assigned identifier in the primary Data Resource Guide that uniquely identifies a Help Message.

Help Message. Text
The comprehensive text of the Help Message describing how the features on a window can be used.

Help Message Data Integrity Rules

The Help Message data integrity rules are listed below.

Help Message
Delete! Prevented
Proactive Update! Allowed
Retroactive Update! Allowed

Help Message. Name
Need! Required
Unique! Yes
Domain! 5 characters <= text <= 80 characters & first character <> ' '
Change! Allowed

Help Message. System Identifier
Need! Required
Unique! Yes
Domain! Long Integer
Change! Prevented

Help Message. Text
Need! Required
Unique! No
Domain! 5 characters <= text <= memo & first character <> ' '
Change! Allowed

ERROR MESSAGE TASK

Error Messages provide specific information about data edits that have been violated during the entry of new data or the editing of existing data. The data edits are based on the data integrity rules that become data edits during physical development of the Data Resource Guide. The data integrity rules are listed in *Data Resource Data*.

One Error Message is developed for each data edit that is performed in the Data Resource Guide. Error messages are partly specific to the Data Resource Data and partly specific to an organization's policies and guidelines. Generally, only the Data Resource Guide Administrator can add or change Error Messages.

The data edit violation notification is shown in the Error Message. The data edit violation action is that the requested data entry or data edit is not performed. In other words, no data are allowed into the Data Resource Guide that violate any of the data integrity rules for the Data Resource Data.

Error Message Task contains Error Message View, Error Message Edit, and Error Message Reports, as shown in Figure 2.4.

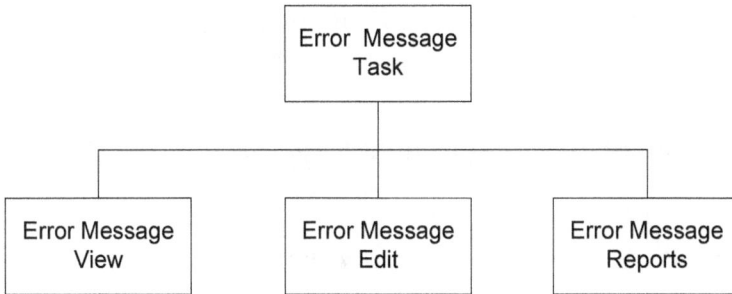

Figure 2.4. Error Message Task.

The Error Message Task actions are:

    [ERROR MESSAGE VIEW]
        Open Error Message View

    [ERROR MESSAGE EDIT]
        Open Error Message Edit

    [ERROR MESSAGE REPORTS]
        Open Error Message Reports

    [RETURN]
        Close window and Return to Data Resource Guide

    [HELP]
        Open Help Message View
        Display Error Message Task Help Message

Error Message View

The Error Message View window is opened on any edit window in the Data Resource Guide when a data edit has been violated. The appropriate Error Message that has been violated is displayed in that Error Message View window. The Error Message View actions are:

    [DISPLAY]

21

Display Error Message with the same name as the data edit that was violated.

[CLOSE]
Close <u>Error Message View</u>

Error Message Edit

Error Message Edit is generally used only by the Administrator for creating and editing Error Messages. The Error Message Edit actions are:

[DISPLAY]
Display Auto-Scroll List from *Error Message* with *Error Message. Name*
Select *Error Message. Name*
Display Selected *Error Message* data

[PRINT]

(DELETE)
Delete Selected *Error Message* occurrence

(NEW)
Display blank data fields for entry of new *Error Message* data.

[ACCEPT]

[RETURN]
Close window and Return to <u>Error Message Task</u>

[HELP]
Open <u>Help Message Window</u>
Display Error Message Edit Help Message

Error Message Reports

Error Message Reports contains reports for the Error Message Task. It is opened from Error Message Task. The specific reports and actions to obtain these reports are:

[Error Message Name]
Display Each *Error Message. Name*

[PRINT]

[Error Message Detail]
Display Each *Error Message* data

[PRINT]

[RETURN]
> Close report and Return to <u>Error Message Reports</u>

[HELP]
> Open <u>Help Message Window</u>
> Display Error Message Reports Help Message

ERROR MESSAGE DATA ARCHITECTURE

The Error Message data architecture is shown below, including the data characteristic structure, data definitions, and data integrity rules. The Error Message data architecture is not part of the Data Resource Data architecture. It is part of the Data Resource Guide.

Error Message Data Structure

The Error Message data subject-relation diagram is shown in Figure 2.5. The data characteristic list is shown below the diagram.

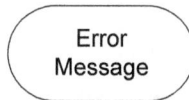

Figure 2.5. Error Message Data Structure.

Error Message

> Primary Key: Error Message. System Identifier

> Alternate Key: Error Message. Name

> Data Characteristic List:
> Error Message. Name
> Error Message. System Identifier
> Error Message. Text

Error Message Data Definitions

The Error Message data subject and data characteristic definitions are listed below.

Error Message
Error Message provides information to a person adding or editing data in the Data Resource Guide that a data edit has been violated. Each Error Message is relevant to a specific data edit and describes the data edit violation that has occurred.

Error Message. Name

The formal name of an Error Message, such as Data Subject Name Uniqueness Violated.

Error Message. System Identifier

The system-assigned identifier in the primary Data Resource Guide that uniquely identifies an Error Message.

Help Message. Text

The comprehensive text of the Error Message describing the data edit that has been violated.

Error Message Data Integrity Rules

The Error Message data integrity rules are listed below.

Error Message
Delete! Prevented
Proactive Update! Allowed
Retroactive Update! Allowed

Error Message. Name
Need! Required
Unique! Yes
Domain! 5 characters <= text <= 80 characters & first character <> ' '
Change! Allowed

Error Message. System Identifier
Need! Required
Unique! Yes
Domain! Long Integer
Change! Prevented

Error Message. Text
Need! Required
Unique! No
Domain! 5 characters <= text <= memo & first character <> ' '
Change! Allowed

Chapter 3

DATA RESPONSIBILITY

Data Responsibility Function includes Data Steward Task, Organization Unit Task, and Data Responsibility Reports, as shown in Figure 3.1. It is opened from Data Resource Guide Edit / View.

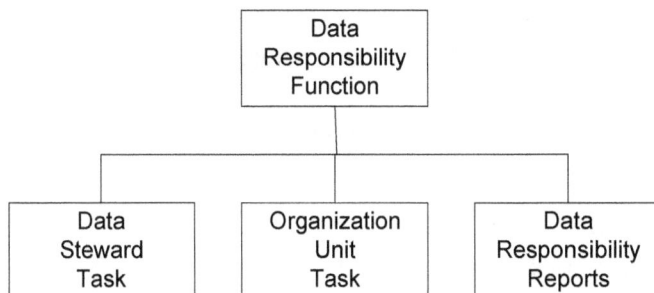

Figure 3.1. Data Responsibility Function.

The actions for Data Responsibility Function are:

[DATA STEWARD TASK]
   Open Data Steward Task

[ORGANIZATION UNIT TASK]
   Open Organization Unit Task

[DATA RESPONSIBILITY REPORTS]
   Open Data Responsibility Reports

[RETURN]
   Close window and Return to Data Resource Guide Edit / View

[HELP]
   Open Help Message View
   Display Data Responsibility Function Help Message

DATA STEWARD TASK

The Data Steward Task contains Data Steward, Data Steward Function, and Data Steward Level, as shown in Figure 3.2. It is opened from Data Responsibility Function. The assignments of Data Stewards to Data Products and Common Data are described in the Chapters where those assignments are relevant. Business Process Steward is described in the Data Access Chapter.

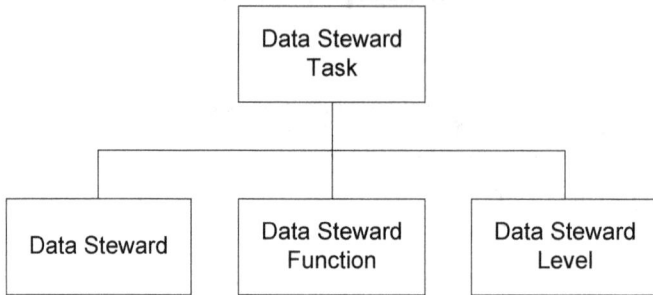

Figure 3.2. Data Steward Task

The actions for Data Steward Task are:

[DATA STEWARD]
Open <u>Data Steward</u>

[DATA STEWARD FUNCTION]
Open <u>Data Steward Function</u>

[DATA STEWARD LEVEL]
Open <u>Data Steward Level</u>

[RETURN]
Close window and Return to <u>Data Responsibility Function</u>

[HELP]
Open <u>Help Message View</u>
Display Data Steward Task Help Message

Data Steward

Data Steward can be opened from several different locations. The actions for Data Steward are:

[DISPLAY]
Display Auto-Scroll List from *Data Steward* with *Data Steward. Name Complete*
Select *Data Steward. Name Complete*
Display Selected *Data Steward* data

[PRINT]

(DELETE)
Delete Selected *Data Steward* occurrence

(NEW)
> Display blank data fields for entry of new *Data Steward* data
> Display Auto-Scroll List from *Organization Unit* with
>   *Organization Unit. Name*
> Select *Organization Unit. Name*

[ACCEPT]

[RETURN]
> When Opened from Data Steward Task
>   Close window and Return to <u>Data Steward Task</u>
> When Opened from Data Product Steward Task
>   Close window and Return to <u>Data Product Steward Task</u>
> When Opened from Common Data Steward Task
>   Close window and Return to <u>Common Data Steward Task</u>
> When Opened from Data Clearinghouse Item Task
>   Close window and Return to <u>Data Clearinghouse Item Task</u>
> When Opened from Data Project Task
>   Close window and Return to <u>Data Project Task</u>
> When Opened from Data Transformation Task
>   Close window and Return to <u>Data Transformation Task</u>

[HELP]
> Open <u>Help Message View</u>
> Display Data Steward Help Message

Data Steward Function

Data Steward Function is opened from several different locations. The actions for Data Steward Function are:

[DISPLAY]
> Display Auto-Scroll List from *Data Steward Function* with *Data
> Steward Function. Name*
> Select *Data Steward Function. Name*
> Display Selected *Data Steward Function* data

[PRINT]

(DELETE)
> Delete Selected *Data Steward Function* occurrence

(NEW)
> Display blank data fields for entry of new *Data Steward Function*
> data

27

[ACCEPT]

[RETURN]
>When Opened from Data Steward Task
>>Close window and Return to <u>Data Steward Task</u>
>When opened from Data Product Steward Task
>>Close window and Return to <u>Data Product Steward Task</u>
>When opened from Common Data Steward Task
>>Close window and Return to <u>Common Data Steward Task</u>

[HELP]
>Open <u>Help Message View</u>
>Display Data Steward Function Help Message

Data Steward Level

Data Steward Level is opened from several different locations. The actions for Data Steward Level are:

[DISPLAY]
>Display Auto-Scroll List from *Data Steward Level* with *Data Steward Level. Name*
>Select *Data Steward Level. Name*
>Display Selected *Data Steward Level* data

>[PRINT]

>(DELETE)
>>Delete Selected *Data Steward Level* occurrence

(NEW)
>Display blank data fields for entry of new *Data Steward Level* data

>[ACCEPT]

[RETURN]
>When Opened from Data Steward Task
>>Close window and Return to <u>Data Steward Task</u>
>When opened from Data Product Steward Task
>>Close window and Return to <u>Data Product Steward Task</u>
>When opened from Common Steward Task
>>Close window and Return to <u>Common Data Steward Task</u>

[HELP]
>Open <u>Help Message View</u>
>Display Data Steward Level Help Message

28

ORGANIZATION UNIT TASK

Organization Unit Task contains Organization Unit and Organization Unit Type, as shown in Figure 3.3. It is opened from Data Responsibility Function.

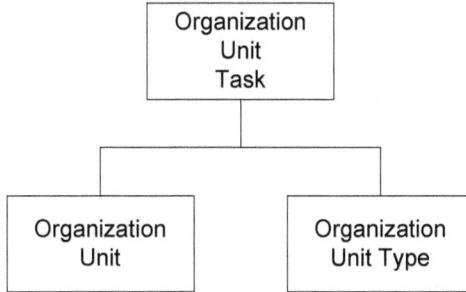

Figure 3.3. Organization Unit Task.

The actions for Organization Unit Task are:

[ORGANIZATION UNIT]
    Open Organization Unit

[ORGANIZATION UNIT TYPE]
    Open Organization Unit Type

[RETURN]
    Close window and Return to Data Responsibility Function

[HELP]
    Open Help Message View
    Display Organization Unit Task Help Message

Organization Unit

Organization Unit can be opened from several different locations. The actions for Organization Unit are:

[DISPLAY]
    Display Auto-Scroll List from *Organization Unit* with
        Organization Unit. Name
    Select *Organization Unit. Name*
    Display Selected *Organization Unit* data

[PRINT]

(DELETE)
    Delete Selected *Organization Unit* occurrence

(NEW)

    Display blank data fields for entry of new *Organization Unit* data

    Display Auto-Scroll List from *Organization Unit Type* with
      Organization Unit Type. Name

    Select *Organization Unit Type. Name*

    Display Auto-Scroll List from *Organization Unit* with
      Organization Unit. Name

    Select *"Parent" Organization Unit. Name*

    [ACCEPT]

[RETURN]

    When Opened from Organization Unit Task

      Close Window and Return to <u>Organization Unit Task</u>

    When Opened from Data Product Data Task

      Close window and Return to <u>Data Product Data Task</u>

    When Opened from Business Process Steward Task

      Close window and Return to <u>Business Process Steward Task</u>

    When Opened from Data Clearinghouse Item Task

      Close window and Return to <u>Data Clearinghouse Item Task</u>

    When Opened from Data Project Task

      Close window and Return to <u>Data Project Task</u>

    When Opened from Data Transformation Task

      Close window and Return to <u>Data Transformation Task</u>

[HELP]

    Open <u>Help Message View</u>

    Display Organization Unit Help Message

Organization Unit Type

Organization Unit Type is opened from Organization Unit Task. The actions for Organization Unit Type are:

[DISPLAY]

    Display Auto-Scroll List from *Organization Unit Type* with
      Organization Unit Type. Name

    Select *Organization Unit Type. Name*

    Display Selected *Organization Unit Type* data

[PRINT]

(DELETE)

    Delete Selected *Organization Unit Type* occurrence

(NEW)

>Display blank data fields for entry of new *Organization Unit Type*

[ACCEPT]

[RETURN]

>Close window and Return to <u>Organization Unit Task</u>

[HELP]

>Open <u>Help Message View</u>
>Display Organization Unit Type Help Message

DATA RESPONSIBILITY REPORTS

Data Responsibility Reports contains reports for the Data Responsibility Function. It is opened from Data Responsibility Function. Only a few examples of reports are shown. Many additional reports could be developed based on an organization's needs and added to the Data Resource Guide.

The specific reports and actions to obtain those reports are:

[Data Steward Name]

>Display Each *Data Steward. Name*

>[PRINT]

>[RETURN]

>>Close report and Return to <u>Data Responsibility Reports</u>

[Data Steward Detail]

>Display Each *Data Steward* data

>[PRINT]

>[RETURN]

>>Close report and Return to <u>Data Responsibility Reports</u>

[Selected Data Steward Detail]

>Display Auto-Scroll List from *Data Steward* with *Data Steward. Name*
>Select *Data Steward. Name*
>Display Selected *Data Steward* data

>[PRINT]

>[RETURN]

>>Close report and Return to <u>Data Responsibility Reports</u>

[Data Steward Function Detail]

31

Display Each *Data Steward Function* data

[PRINT]

[RETURN]
Close report and Return to <u>Data Responsibility Reports</u>

[Data Steward Level Detail]
Display Each *Data Steward Level* data

[PRINT]

[RETURN]
Close report and Return to <u>Data Responsibility Reports</u>

[Organization Unit Name]
Display Each *Organization Unit. Name*

[PRINT]

[RETURN]
Close report and Return to <u>Data Responsibility Reports</u>

[Organization Unit Detail]
Display Each *Organization Unit* data

[PRINT]

[RETURN]
Close report and Return to <u>Data Responsibility Reports</u>

[Selected Organization Unit Detail]
Display Auto-Scroll List from *Organization Unit* with
Organization Unit. Name
Select *Organization Unit. Name*
Display Selected *Organization Unit* data

[PRINT]

[RETURN]
Close report and Return to <u>Data Responsibility Reports</u>

[Organization Unit Type Detail]
Display Each *Organization Unit Type* data

[PRINT]

[RETURN]
Close report and Return to <u>Data Responsibility Reports</u>

[Organization Unit Name ^ Data Steward Name]
  Display Each *Organization Unit. Name*
    Display Each *Data Steward. Name*

  [PRINT]

  [RETURN]
    Close report and Return to <u>Data Responsibility Reports</u>

[Organization Unit Name ^ Data Steward Detail]
  Display Each *Organization Unit. Name*
    Display Each *Data Steward* data

  [PRINT]

  [RETURN]
    Close report and Return to <u>Data Responsibility Reports</u>

[Selected Organization Unit Detail ^ Data Steward Detail]
  Display Auto-Scroll List from *Organization Unit* with
    Organization Unit. Name
  Select *Organization Unit. Name*
  Display Selected *Organization Unit* data
    Display Each *Data Steward* data

  [PRINT]

  [RETURN]
    Close report and Return to <u>Data Responsibility Reports</u>

[RETURN]
  Close window and Return to <u>Data Responsibility Function</u>

[HELP]
  Open <u>Help Message View</u>
  Display Data Responsibility Reports Help Message

Chapter 4

DATA INVENTORY

Data Inventory Function includes Data Product Data Task, Data Product Key Task, Data Product Reference Set Task, Data Product Model Task, Data Product Steward Task, and Data Inventory Reports, as shown in Figure 4.1. It is opened from Data Resource Guide Edit / View.

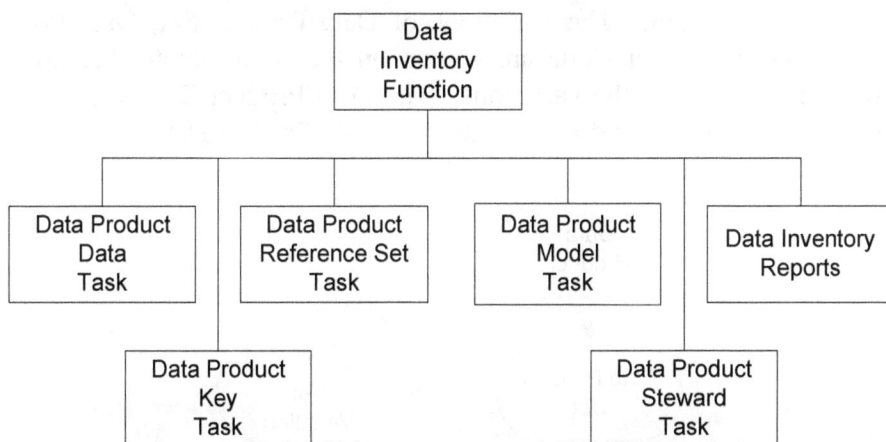

Figure 4.1. Data Inventory Function.

The actions for Data Inventory Function are:

[DATA PRODUCT DATA TASK]
 Open Data Product Data Task

[DATA PRODUCT KEY TASK]
 Open Data Product Key Task

[DATA PRODUCT REFERENCE SET TASK]
 Open Data Product Reference Set Task

[DATA PRODUCT MODEL TASK]
 Open Data Product Model Task

[DATA PRODUCT STEWARD TASK]
 Open Data Product Steward Task

[DATA INVENTORY REPORTS]

Open <u>Data Inventory Reports</u>

[RETURN]
Close window and Return to <u>Data Resource Guide Edit / View</u>

[HELP]
Open <u>Help Message View</u>
Display Data Inventory Function Help Message

The structure of the Data Product Data showing the relationships between Data Products, Data Product Sets, Data Product Units, and Data Product Codes, and their variations is shown in Figure 4.2. The primary components Data Product, Data Product Set, Data Product Unit, and Data Product Code are shown on the left. The variations of Data Product Set, Data Product Unit, and Data Product Code are shown on the right. Note that no data relations exist between the variations. The Data Product Data structure can be used to understand the documentation of Data Product Data.

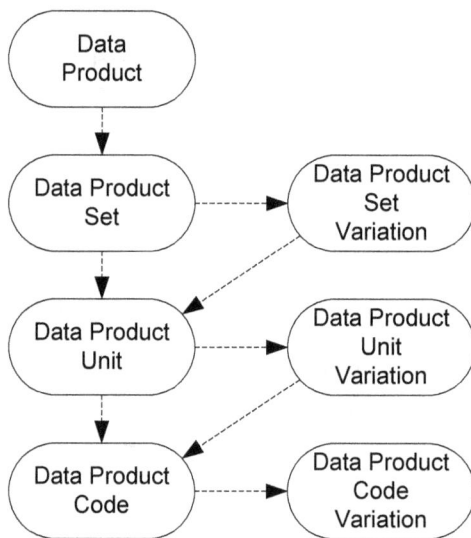

Figure 4.2. Data Product Data Structure

DATA PRODUCT DATA TASK

Data Product Data Task contains Data Product, Data Product Set, Data Product Unit, Data Product Code, Data Site, Organization Unit, and Data Name Abbreviation Scheme, as shown in Figure 4.3. It is opened from Data Inventory Function.

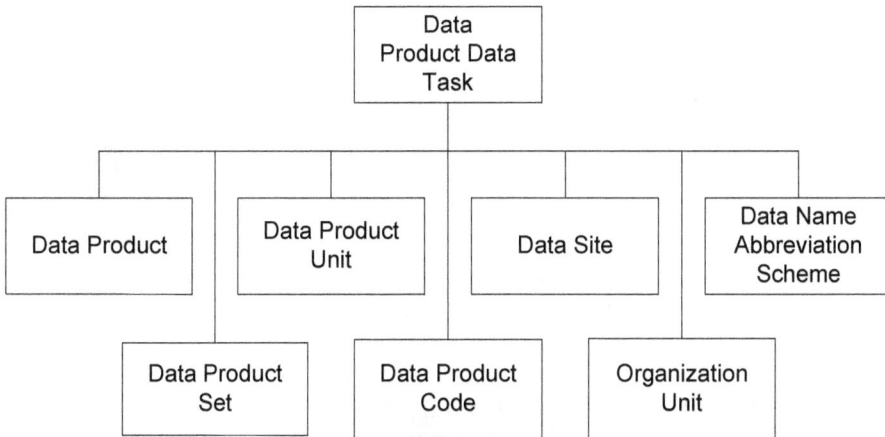

Figure 4.3. Data Product Data Task

The actions for Data Product Data Task are:

[DATA PRODUCT]
Open Data Product

[DATA PRODUCT SET]
Open Data Product Set

[DATA PRODUCT UNIT]
Open Data Product Unit

[DATA PRODUCT CODE]
Open Data Product Code

[DATA SITE]
Open Data Site

[ORGANIZATION UNIT]
Open Organization Unit

[DATA NAME ABBREVIATION SCHEME]
Open Data Name Abbreviation Scheme

[RETURN]
Close window and Return to Data Inventory Function

[HELP]
Open Help Message View
Display Data Product Data Task Help Message

Data Product

Data Product is opened from Data Product Data Task[1]. The actions for Data Product are:

[DISPLAY]
    Display Auto-Scroll List from *Data Product* with *Data Product. Name*
    Select *Data Product. Name*
    Display Selected *Data Product* data

[PRINT]
    Print Selected *Data Product* data

(DELETE)
    Delete *Data Product* occurrence

(NEW)
    Display blank data fields for entry of new *Data Product* data
    Display Auto-Scroll List from *Data Product Type* with *Data Product Type. Name*
    Select *Data Product Type. Name*

    Display Auto-Scroll List from *Data Site* with *Data Site. Name*
    Select *Data Site. Name*

    Display Auto-Scroll List from *Organization Unit* with *Organization Unit. Name*
    Select *Organization Unit. Name*

    [ACCEPT]

[RETURN]
    Close window and Return to Data Product Data Task

[HELP]
    Open Help Message View
    Display Data Product Help Message

Data Product Set

Data Product Set is opened from Data Product Data Task. Data Product Sets may or may not contain Data Product Set Variations. Cross-references from Data Product Set to Data Subject are described in the Data Cross-Reference

---

[1] Correction: On Page 22 of *Data Resource Understanding*, *Data Site. Name* needs to be added to the Data Characteristic List.

Chapter. The actions for Data Product Set are:

Display Auto-Scroll List from *Data Product* with *Data Product. Name*
Select *Data Product. Name*

Display Auto-Scroll List from *Data Product Set* within Selected *Data Product* with *Data Product Set. Name*
Select *Data Product Set. Name*

[DISPLAY]
Display Selected *Data Product Set* data

[PRINT]

(DELETE)
Delete Selected *Data Product Set* occurrence

(NEW)
Display blank data fields for entry of new *Data Product Set* data within Selected *Data Product*

Display Auto-Scroll List from *Data Name Abbreviation Scheme* with *Data Name Abbreviation Scheme. Name*
Select *Data Name Abbreviation Scheme. Name*

Display Auto-Scroll List from *Data Product Set Medium* with *Data Product Set Medium. Name*
Select *Data Product Set Medium. Name*

Display Auto-Scroll List from *Data Product Set Type* with *Data Product Set Type. Name*
Select *Data Product Set Type. Name*

[ACCEPT]

[DISPLAY VARIATION]
Display Auto-Scroll List from *Data Product Set Variation* within Selected *Data Product Set* with *Data Product Set Variation. Name*
Select *Data Product Set Variation*
Display Selected *Data Product Set Variation data*

[PRINT]

(DELETE)
Delete Selected *Data Product Set Variation* occurrence

(NEW VARIATION)

39

Display blank data fields for entry of new *Data Product Set Variation* data within Selected *Data Product Set*

Display Auto-Scroll List from *Data Name Abbreviation Scheme* with *Data Name Abbreviation Scheme. Name*
Select *Data Name Abbreviation Scheme. Name*

Display Auto-Scroll List from *Data Product Set Medium* with *Data Product Set Medium. Name*
Select *Data Product Set Medium. Name*

Display Auto-Scroll List from *Data Product Set Type* with *Data Product Set Type. Name*
Select *Data Product Set Type. Name*

[ACCEPT]

[RETURN]
Close window and Return to Data Product Data Task

[HELP]
Open Help Message View
Display Data Product Set Help Message

Data Product Unit

Data Product Unit is opened from Data Product Data Task. Data Product Unit may or may not have Data Product Unit Variations. Data Product Unit may be subordinate to a Data Product Set or a Data Product Set Variation. Cross-references from Data Product Unit to Data Characteristic Variation are described in the Data Cross-Reference Chapter. The actions for Data Product Unit are:

Display Auto-Scroll List from *Data Product* with *Data Product. Name*
Select *Data Product. Name*

Display Auto-Scroll List from *Data Product Set* within Selected *Data Product* with *Data Product Set. Name*
Select *Data Product Set. Name*

Display Scroll List from *Data Product Unit* within Selected *Data Product Set* with *Data Product Unit. Name*, *Data Product Unit. Mnemonic*
Select *Data Product Unit*

[SELECT SET VARIATION]

Display Auto-Scroll List from *Data Product Set Variation* within
Selected *Data Product Set* with *Data Product Set Variation.
Name*
Select *Data Product Set Variation. Name*

Display Scroll List from *Data Product Unit* within Selected *Data
Product Set Variation* with *Data Product Unit. Name*, Data
Product Unit. Mnemonic
Select *Data Product Unit*

[DISPLAY UNIT]
Display Selected *Data Product Unit* data

[PRINT]

(DELETE)
Delete Selected *Data Product Unit* occurrence

(NEW UNIT)
Display blank data fields for entry of new *Data Product Unit* data
Display Auto-Scroll List from *Data Format* with *Data Format.
Name*
Select *Data Format. Name*
"Inherit" Data Product Unit

[ACCEPT]

[DISPLAY UNIT VARIATION]
Display Scroll List from *Data Product Unit Variation* within
Selected *Data Product Unit* with *Data Product Unit Variation.
Name*, *Data Product Unit Variation.Mnemonic*
Select *Data Product Unit Variation*
Display Selected *Data Product Unit Variation* data

[PRINT]

(DELETE)
Delete Selected *Data Product Unit Variation* occurrence

(NEW UNIT VARIATION)
Display blank data fields for entry of new *Data Product Unit
Variation* data
Display Auto-Scroll List from *Data Format* with *Data Format.
Name*
Select *Data Format. Name*
"Inherit" Data Product Unit

41

[ACCEPT]

[RETURN]
Close window and Return to Data Product Data Task

[HELP]
Open Help Message View
Display Data Product Unit Help Message

Begin "Inherit" Data Product Unit
Display Auto-Scroll List from *Data Product* with *Data Product. Name*
Select *Data Product. Name*

Display Auto-Scroll List from *Data Product Set* within Selected *Data Product* with *Data Product Set. Name*
Select *Data Product Set. Name*

Display Scroll List from *Data Product Unit* within Selected *Data Product Set* with *Data Product Unit. Name, Data Product Unit. Mnemonic*
Select *"Inherit" Data Product Unit*

[SELECT SET VARIATION]
Display Auto-Scroll List from *Data Product Set Variation* within Selected *Data Product Set* with *Data Product Set Variation. Name*
Select *Data Product Set Variation. Name*

Display Scroll List from *Data Product Unit* within Selected *Data Product Set Variation* with *Data Product Unit. Name, Data Product Unit. Mnemonic*
Select *"Inherit" Data Product Unit*

[SELECT UNIT VARIATION]
Display Auto-Scroll List from *Data Product Unit Variation* within Selected Data *Product Unit* with *Data Product Unit Variation. Name, Data Product Unit Variation. Mnemonic*
Select *"Inherit" Data Product Unit*
End "Inherit" Data Product Unit

Data Product Code

Data Product Code is opened from Data Product Data Task. Data Product Code may or may not have Data Product Code Variations. Data Product

Code may be subordinate to Data Product Unit or Data Product Unit Variation. Cross-references from Data Product Code to Data Reference Set Variation are described in the Data Cross-Reference Chapter. The actions for Data Product Code are:

Display Auto-Scroll List from *Data Product* with *Data Product. Name*
Select *Data Product. Name*

Display Auto-Scroll List from *Data Product Set* within Selected *Data Product* with *Data Product Set. Name*
Select *Data Product Set. Name*

Display Scroll List from *Data Product Unit* within Selected *Data Product Set* with *Data Product Unit. Name, Data Product Unit. Mnemonic*
Select *Data Product Unit*

Display Scroll List from *Data Product Code* within Selected *Data Product Unit* with *Data Product. Name, Data Product Code. Value*
Select *Data Product Code*

[SELECT SET VARIATION]
Comment: Goes to *Data Product Set Variation* level.
Display Auto-Scroll List from *Data Product Set Variation* within Selected *Data Product Set* with *Data Product Set Variation. Name*
Select *Data Product Set Variation. Name*

Display Scroll List from *Data Product Unit* within Selected *Data Product Set Variation* with *Data Product Unit. Name*, Data *Product Unit. Mnemonic*
Select *Data Product Unit*

[SELECT UNIT VARIATION]
Display Scroll List from *Data Product Unit Variation* within Selected *Data Product Unit* with *Data Product Unit Variation. Name, Data Product Unit Variation. Mnemonic*
Select *Data Product Unit Variation*
Display Selected *Data Product Unit Variation* data

[DISPLAY CODE]
Display Scroll List from *Data Product* Code within Selected *Data Product Set* or *Data Product Set Variation* with *Data Product Code. Definition, Data Product Code. Name, Data Product Code. Value*

Select *Data Product Code*
Display Selected *Data Product Code* data

[PRINT]

(DELETE
    Delete Selected *Data Product Code* occurrence

(NEW CODE)
    Display blank data fields for entry of new *Data Product Code* data

[ACCEPT]

[DISPLAY CODE VARIATION]
    Display Scroll List from *Data Product Code Variation* within
        Selected *Data Product Code* with *Data Product Code Variation.*
        Definition, Data Product Code Variation. Name, Data Product
        Code Variation. Value
    Select *Data Product Code Variation*
    Display Selected *Data Product Code Variation* data

[PRINT]

(DELETE)
    Delete Selected *Data Product Code* occurrence

(NEW CODE VARIATION)
    Display blank data fields for entry of new *Data Product Code*
        Variation data

[ACCEPT]

[RETURN]
    Close window and Return to <u>Data Product Data Task</u>

[HELP]
    Open <u>Help Message View</u>
    Display Data Product Code Help Message

Data Site

Data Site is opened from Data Product Data Task. The actions for Data Site
are:

Display Auto-Scroll List from Data Site with *Data Site. Name*
Select *Data Site. Name*
Display *Data Site* data

[PRINT]

(NEW)
> Display blank data fields for entry of new *Data Site* data

[ACCEPT]

(DELETE)
> Delete Selected *Data Site* occurrence

[RETURN]
> Close window and Return to <u>Data Product Data Task</u>

[HELP]
> Open <u>Help Message View</u>
> Display Data Site Help Message

Organization Unit

Organization Unit is opened from Data Product Data Task. The actions for Organization Unit are provided in the Data Responsibility Chapter.

Data Name Abbreviation Scheme

Data Name Abbreviation Scheme is opened from Data Product Data Task. The actions for Data Name Abbreviation Scheme are provided in the Data Lexicon Chapter.

DATA PRODUCT KEY TASK

Data Product Key Task contains Data Product Primary Key, Data Product Foreign Key, and Data Relation Cardinality, as shown in Figure 4.4. It is opened from Data Inventory Function.

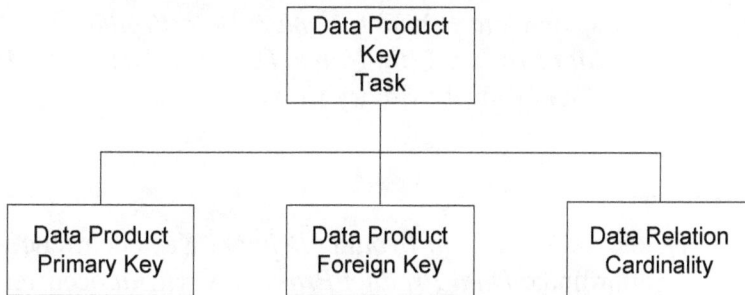

Figure 4.4. Data Product Key Task.

The actions for Data Product Key Task are:

[DATA PRODUCT PRIMARY KEY]
Open <u>Data Product Primary Key</u>

[DATA PRODUCT FOREIGN KEY]
Open <u>Data Product Foreign Key</u>

[DATA RELATION CARDINALITY]
Open <u>Data Relation Cardinality</u>

[RETURN]
Close window and Return to <u>Data Inventory Function</u>

[HELP]
Open <u>Help Message View</u>
Display Data Product Key Task Help Message

Data Product Primary Key

Data Product Primary Key is opened from Data Product Key Task. The actions for Data Product Primary Key are:

Display Auto-Scroll List from *Data Product* with *Data Product. Name*
Select *Data Product. Name*

Display Auto-Scroll List from *Data Product Set* within Selected *Data Product. Name* with *Data Product Set. Name*
Select *Data Product. Set. Name*

[DISPLAY]
Display Auto-Scroll List from *Data Product Primary Key* within Selected *Data Product Set* with *Data Product Primary Key. Comment*
Each *Data Product Primary Key Unit*
Display *Data Product. Name* ^ *Data Product Set. Name* ^ *Data Product Unit. Name*, *Data Product Unit. Mnemonic*
Select Data Product Primary Key

[PRINT]

(DELETE)
Delete Selected *Data Product Primary Key* occurrence and Subordinate *Data Product Primary Key Unit* occurrences

(NEW)
Display blank data fields for entry of new *Data Product Primary Key* data
Each *Data Product Primary Key Unit*

Display Auto-Scroll List from *Data Product* with *Data Product. Name*
Select *Data Product. Name*

Display Auto-Scroll List from *Data Product Set* within Selected *Data Product* with *Data Product Set. Name*
Select *Data Product Set. Name*

Display Scroll List from *Data Product Unit* within Selected *Data Product Set* with *Data Product Unit. Name, Data Product Unit. Mnemonic*
Select *Data Product Unit*

[ACCEPT]

[RETURN]
Close window and Return to <u>Data Product Key Task</u>

[HELP]
Open <u>Help Message View</u>
Display Data Product Primary Key Help Message

Data Product Foreign Key

Data Product Foreign Key is opened from Data Product Key Task.[2] The actions for Data Product Foreign Key are:

Display Auto-Scroll List from *Data Product* with *Data Product. Name*
Select *Data Product. Name*

Display Auto-Scroll List from *Data Product Set* within Selected *Data Product* with *Data Product Set. Name*
Select *Data Product. Set. Name* that is *"Local" Data Product Set*

[DISPLAY]
Display Auto-Scroll List from *Data Product Foreign Key* within Selected *Data Product Set* with *Data Product Foreign Key. Comment, Data Product Name* ^ *"Parent" Data Product Set. Name*
Each *Data Product Foreign Key* Unit
Display *Data Product. Name* ^ *Data Product Set. Name* ^ *Data Product Unit. Name, Data Product Unit. Mnemonic*
Select *Data Product Foreign Key*

---

[2] Correction: *Data Product. Foreign Key. System Identifier* should be removed at the bottom of Page 32 in *Data Resource Understanding*.

[PRINT]

(DELETE)

Delete Selected *Data Product Foreign Key* occurrence and subordinate *Data Product Foreign Key Unit* occurrences

(NEW)

Display blank data fields for entry of new *Data Product Foreign Key* data

Display Auto-Scroll List from *Data Product* with *Data Product. Name*
Select *Data Product. Name*

Display Auto-Scroll List from *Data Product Set* within Selected *Data Product* with *Data Product Set. Name*
Select *"Parent" Data Product Set. Name*

Display Auto-Scroll List from *Data Relation Cardinality* with *Data Relation Cardinality. Name*
Select *Data Relation Cardinality. Name*

[ACCEPT]

[RETURN]

Close window and Return to <u>Data Product Key Task</u>

[HELP]

Open <u>Help Message View</u>
Display Data Product Foreign Key Help Message

Data Relation Cardinality

Data Relation Cardinality is opened from Data Product Key Task. The actions for Data Relation Cardinality are:

[DISPLAY]

Display Auto-Scroll List from *Data Relation Cardinality* with *Data Relation Cardinality. Name*
Select *Data Relation Cardinality. Name*
Display Selected *Data Relation Cardinality* data

[PRINT]

(DELETE)

Delete Selected *Data Relation Cardinality* occurrence

(NEW)
>   Display blank data fields for entry of new *Data Relation Cardinality* data

>   [ACCEPT]

[RETURN]
>   Close window and Return to Data Product Key Task

[HELP]
>   Open Help Message View
>   Display Data Relation Cardinality Help Message

DATA PRODUCT REFERENCE SET TASK

Data Product Reference Set Task contains Data Product Type, Data Product Set Medium, Data Product Set Type, and Data Format, as shown in Figure 4.5. It is opened from Data Inventory Function.

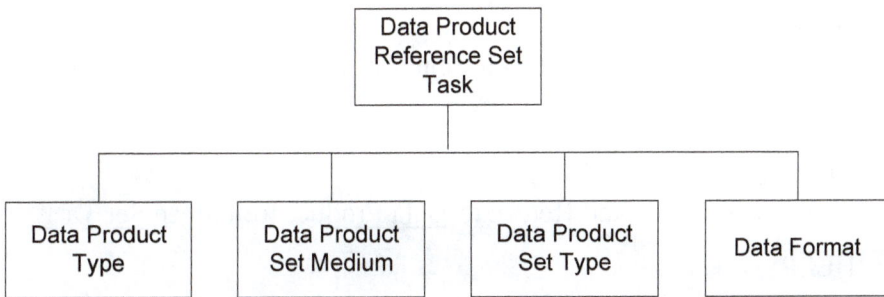

Figure 4.5. Data Product Reference Set Task.

The actions for Data Product Reference Set Task are:

[DATA PRODUCT TYPE]
>   Open Data Product Type

[DATA PRODUCT SET MEDIUM]
>   Open Data Product Set Medium

[DATA PRODUCT SET TYPE]
>   Open Data Product Set Type

[DATA FORMAT]
>   Open Data Format

[RETURN]
>   Close window and Return to Data Inventory Function

[HELP]

49

Open <u>Help Message View</u>
Display Data Product Reference Set Task Help Message

Data Product Type

Data Product Type is opened from Data Product Reference Set Task. The actions for Data Product Type are:

[DISPLAY]
Display Auto-Scroll List from *Data Product Type* with *Data Product Type. Name*
Select *Data Product Type. Name*
Display Selected *Data Product Type* data

[PRINT]

(DELETE)
Delete Selected *Data Product Type* occurrence

(NEW)
Display blank data fields for entry of new *Data Product Type* data

[ACCEPT]

[RETURN]
Close window and Return to <u>Data Product Reference Set Task</u>

[HELP]
Open <u>Help Message View</u>
Display Data Product Type Help Message

Data Product Set Medium

Data Product Set Medium is opened from Data Product Reference Set Task. The actions for Data Product Set Medium are:

[DISPLAY]
Display Auto-Scroll List from *Data Product Set Medium* with *Data Product Set Medium. Name*
Select *Data Product Set Medium. Name*
Display Selected *Data Product Set Medium* data

[PRINT]

(DELETE)
Delete Selected *Data Product Set Medium* occurrence

(NEW)

Display blank data fields for entry of new *Data Product Set Medium* data

[ACCEPT]

[RETURN]
Close window and Return to <u>Data Product Reference Set Task</u>

[HELP]
Open <u>Help Message View</u>
Display Data Product Set Medium Help Message

Data Product Set Type

Data Product Set Type is opened from Data Product Reference Set Task. The actions for Data Product Set Type are:

[DISPLAY]
Display Auto-Scroll List From *Data Product Set Type* with *Data Product Set Type. Name*
Select *Data Product Set Type. Name*
Display Selected *Data Product Set Type* data

[PRINT]

(DELETE)
Delete Selected *Data Product Set Type* occurrence

(NEW)
Display blank data fields for entry of new *Data Product Set Type* data

[ACCEPT]

[RETURN]
Close window and Return to <u>Data Product Reference Set Task</u>

[HELP]
Open <u>Help Message View</u>
Display Data Product Set Type Help Message

Data Format

Data Format is opened from Data Product Reference Set Task. The actions for Data Format are:

[DISPLAY]

Display Auto-Scroll List from *Data Format* with *Data Format.*
  Name
Select *Data Format. Name*
Display Selected *Data Format* data

[PRINT]

(DELETE)
    Delete Selected *Data Format* occurrence

(NEW)
    Display blank data fields for entry of new *Data Format* data

[ACCEPT]

[RETURN]
    Close window and Return to <u>Data Product Reference Set Task</u>

[HELP]
    Open <u>Help Message View</u>
    Display Data Format Help Message

DATA PRODUCT MODEL TASK

Data Product Model Task contains Data Product Model, Data Product Set Model, Data Model Diagram, and Data Model Diagram Type, as shown in Figure 4.6. It is opened from Data Inventory Function.

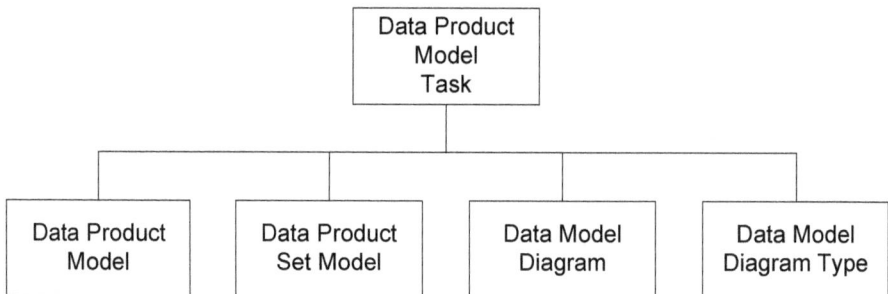

Figure 4.6. Data Product Model Task.

The actions for Data Produce Model Task are:

[DATA PRODUCT MODEL]
Open <u>Data Product Model</u>

[DATA PRODUCT SET MODEL]
Open <u>Data Product Set Model</u>

[DATA MODEL DIAGRAM]

Open <u>Data Model Diagram</u>

[DATA MODEL DIAGRAM TYPE]
Open <u>Data Model Diagram Type</u>

[RETURN]
 Close window and Return to <u>Data Inventory Function</u>

[HELP]
 Open <u>Help Message View</u>
 Display Data Product Model Task Help Message

Data Product Model

Data Product Model is opened from Data Product Model Task. The actions for Data Product Model are:

Display Auto-Scroll List from *Data Product* with *Data Product. Name*
Select *Data Product. Name*

[DISPLAY]
 Display Scroll List from *Data Product Model* within Selected *Data Product* with *Data Model Diagram. Name*
 Select *Data Product Model*
 Display Selected *Data Product Model* data

 [PRINT]

 (DELETE)
  Delete Selected *Data Product Model* occurrence

(NEW)
 Display blank data fields for entry of new *Data Product Model* data

 Display Auto-Scroll List from *Data Model Diagram* with *Data Model Diagram. Name*
 Select *Data Model Diagram. Name*

 [ACCEPT]

[RETURN]
 Close window and Return to <u>Data Product Model Task</u>

[HELP]
 Open <u>Help Message View</u>
 Display Data Product Model Help Message

Data Product Set Model

Data Product Set Model is opened from Data Product Model Task. The actions for Data Product Set Model are:

Display Auto-Scroll list from *Data Product* with *Data Product. Name*
Select *Data Product. Name*

Display Auto-Scroll List from *Data Product Set* within Selected *Data Product* with *Data Product Set. Name*
Select *Data Product Set*

[DISPLAY]
Display Scroll List from *Data Product Set Model* within Selected *Data Product Set* with *Data Product Set Model. Comment, Data Model Diagram. Name*
Select *Data Product Set Model*
Display Selected *Data Product Set Model* data

[PRINT]

(DELETE)
Delete Selected *Data Product Set Model* occurrence

(NEW)
Display blank data fields for entry of new *Data Product Set Model* data
Display Auto-Scroll List from *Data Model Diagram* with *Data Model Diagram. Name*
Select *Data Model Diagram. Name*

[ACCEPT]

[RETURN]
Close window and Return to Data Product Model Task

[HELP]
Open Help Message View
Display Data Product Set Model Help Message

Data Model Diagram

Data Model Diagram can be opened from several different locations. The actions for Data Model Diagram are:

[DISPLAY]
Display Auto-Scroll List from *Data Model Diagram* with *Data Model Diagram. Name*

Select *Data Model Diagram. Name*
Display Selected *Data Model Diagram* data

[PRINT]

(DELETE)
    Delete Selected *Data Model Diagram* occurrence

(NEW)
    Display blank data fields for entry of new *Data Model Diagram*
        data

[RETURN]
    When Opened from Data Product Model Task
        Close window and Return to <u>Data Product Model Task</u>
    When Opened from Common Data Model Task
        Close Window and Return to <u>Common Data Model Task</u>

    [HELP]
        Open <u>Help Message View</u>
        Display Data Model Diagram Help Message

Data Model Diagram Type

Data Model Diagram Type can be opened from several different locations.
The actions for Data Model Diagram Type are:

[DISPLAY]
    Display Auto-Scroll List from *Data Model Diagram Type* with
        Data Model Diagram Type. Name
    Select *Data Model Diagram Type. Name*
    Display Selected *Data Model Diagram Type* data

    [PRINT]

    (DELETE)
        Delete Selected *Data Model Diagram Type* occurrence

(NEW)
    Display blank data fields for entry of new *Data Model Diagram*
        Type data

    [ACCEPT]

[RETURN]
    When Opened from Data Product Model Task
        Close window and Return to <u>Data Product Model Task</u>

55

When Opened from Common Data Model Task
Close Window and Return to <u>Common Data Model Task</u>

[HELP]
Open <u>Help Message View</u>
Display Data Model Diagram Type Help Message

DATA PRODUCT STEWARD TASK

Data Product Steward Task contains Data Product Steward, Data Steward, Data Steward Function, and Data Steward Level, as shown in Figure 4.7. It is opened from Data Inventory Function.

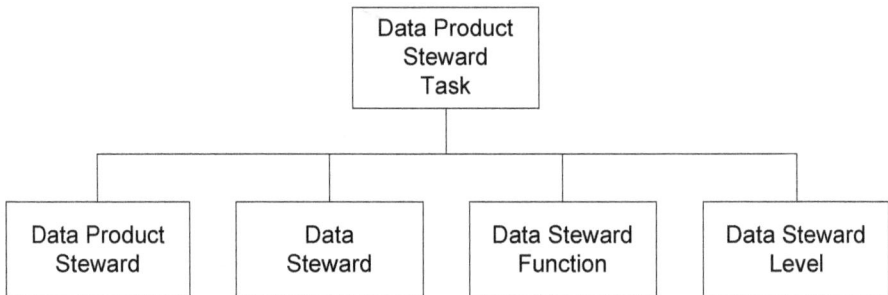

Figure 4.7. Data Product Steward Task.

The actions for Data Product Steward Task are:

[DATA PRODUCT STEWARD]
Open <u>Data Product Steward</u>

[DATA STEWARD]
Open <u>Data Steward</u>

[DATA STEWARD FUNCTION]
Open <u>Data Steward Function</u>

[DATA STEWARD LEVEL]
Open <u>Data Steward Level</u>

[RETURN]
Close window and Return to <u>Data Inventory Function</u>

[HELP]
Open <u>Help Message View</u>
Display Data Product Steward Task Help Message

Data Product Steward

Data Product Steward is opened from Data Product Steward Task. The actions for Data Product Steward are:

Display Auto-Scroll List from *Data Product* with *Data Product. Name*
Select *Data Product. Name*

[DISPLAY]
    Display Auto-Scroll List from *Data Product Steward* within
      Selected *Data Product* with *Data Product Steward. Name*
    Select *Data Product Steward. Name*
    Display Selected *Data Product Steward* data

    [PRINT]

    (DELETE)
      Delete Selected *Data Product Steward* occurrence

(NEW)
    Display blank data fields for entry of new *Data Product Steward*
      data

    Display Auto-Scroll List from *Data Steward* with *Data Steward.*
      Name Complete
    Select *Data Steward. Name Complete*

    Display Auto-Scroll List from *Data Steward Function* with *Data*
      Steward Function. Name
    Select *Data Steward Function. Name*

    Display Auto-Scroll List from *Data Steward Level* with *Data*
      Steward Level. Name
    Select *Data Steward Level. Name*

    [ACCEPT]

[RETURN]
    Close Window and Return to <u>Data Product Steward Task</u>

[HELP]
    Open <u>Help Message View</u>
    Display Data Model Diagram Type Help Message

Data Steward

Data Steward is opened from Data Product Steward Task. The actions for Data Steward are provided in the Data Responsibility Chapter.

Data Steward Function

Data Steward Function is opened from Data Product Steward Task. The actions for Data Steward Function are provided in the Data Responsibility Chapter.

Data Steward Level

Data Steward Level is opened from Data Product Steward Task. The actions for Data Steward Level are provided in the Data Responsibility Chapter.

DATA INVENTORY REPORTS

Data Inventory Reports contains reports for the Data Inventory Function. It is opened from Data Inventory Function. Only a few examples of reports are shown. Many additional reports could be developed based on an organization's needs and added to the Data Resource Guide.

The specific reports and actions to obtain those reports are:

    [Data Product Name]
        Display Each *Data Product. Name*

        [PRINT]

        [RETURN]
            Close report and Return to <u>Data Inventory Report</u>

    [Data Product Detail]
        Display Each *Data Product* data

        [PRINT]

        [RETURN]
            Close report and Return to <u>Data Inventory Reports</u>

    [Data Product Set Name]
        Display Each *Data Product. Name*
            Display Each *Data Product Set. Name*

        [PRINT]

        [RETURN]
            Close report and Return to <u>Data Inventory Reports</u>

    [Data Product Set Detail]
        Display Each *Data Product. Name*
            Display Each *Data Product Set* data

[PRINT]

[RETURN]
Close report and Return to <u>Data Inventory Reports</u>

[Selected Data Product Set Detail]
*Display Auto-Scroll List from Data Product with Data Product.
Name*
Select *Data Product. Name*
Display Each *Data Product Set* data within Selected *Data Product*

[PRINT]

[RETURN]
Close report and Return to <u>Data Inventory Reports</u>

[Data Product Set Variation Name]
Display Each *Data Product. Name*
Display Each *Data Product Set. Name*
Display Each *Data Product Set Variation. Name*

[PRINT]

[RETURN]
Close report and Return to <u>Data Inventory Reports</u>

[Data Product Set Variation Detail]
Display Each *Data Product. Name*
Display Each *Data Product Set. Name*
Display Each *Data Product Set Variation* data

[PRINT]

[RETURN]
Close report and Return to <u>Data Inventory Reports</u>

[Selected Data Product Set Variation Detail]
*Display Auto-Scroll List from Data Product with Data Product.
Name*
Select *Data Product. Name*
Display Each *Data Product Set. Name* within Selected *Data
Product*
Display Each *Data Product Set Variation* data

[PRINT]

[RETURN]
Close report and Return to <u>Data Inventory Reports</u>

[Data Product Unit Name]
> Display Each *Data Product. Name*
>> Display Each *Data Product Set. Name*
>>> Display Each *Data Product Unit. Name, Data Product Unit. Mnemonic*

[PRINT]

[RETURN]
> Close report and Return to <u>Data Inventory Reports</u>

[Data Product Unit Detail]
> Display Each *Data Product. Name*
>> Display Each *Data Product Set. Name*
>>> Display Each *Data Product Unit* data

[PRINT]

[RETURN]
> Close report and Return to <u>Data Inventory Reports</u>

[Selected Data Product Unit Detail]
> Display Auto-Scroll List from *Data Product* with *Data Product. Name*
> Select *Data Product. Name*
> Display Each *Data Product Set. Name* within Selected *Data Product*
>> Display *Each Data Product Unit* data

[PRINT]

[RETURN]
> Close report and Return to <u>Data Inventory Reports</u>

[Data Product Unit Variation Name]
> Display Each *Data Product. Name*
>> Display Each *Data Product Set. Name*
>>> Display Each *Data Product Set Variation. Name*
>>>> Display Each *Data Product Unit. Name, Data Product Unit. Mnemonic*
>>>>> Display Each *Data Product Unit Variation. Name, Data Product Unit Variation. Mnemonic*

[PRINT]

[RETURN]

Close report and Return to <u>Data Inventory Reports</u>

[Data Product Unit Variation Detail]
Display Each *Data Product. Name*
Display Each *Data Product Set. Name*
Display Each *Data Product Set Variation. Name*
Display Each *Data Product Unit. Name, Data Product Unit. Mnemonic*
Display Each *Data Product Unit Variation* data

[PRINT]

[RETURN]
Close report and Return to <u>Data Inventory Reports</u>

[Selected Data Product Unit Variation Detail]
Display Auto-Scroll List from *Data Product* with *Data Product. Name*
Select *Data Product. Name*
Display Each *Data Product Set. Name* within Selected *Data Product*
Display Each *Data Product Set Variation. Name*
Display Each *Data Product Unit. Name, Data Product Unit. Mnemonic*
Display Each *Data Product Unit Variation* data

[PRINT]

[RETURN]
Close report and Return to <u>Data Inventory Reports</u>

[Data Product Code Name]
Display Each *Data Product. Name*
Display Each *Data Product Set. Name*
Display Each *Data Product Unit. Name, Data Product Unit. Mnemonic*
Display Each *Data Product Code. Definition, Data Product Code. Name, Data Product Code. Value*

[PRINT]

[RETURN]
Close report and Return to <u>Data Inventory Reports</u>

[Data Product Code Detail]
Display Each *Data Product. Name*

61

Display Each *Data Product Set. Name*
Display Each *Data Product Unit. Name, Data Product Unit. Mnemonic*
Display Each *Data Product Code* data

[PRINT]

[RETURN]
Close report and Return to <u>Data Inventory Reports</u>

[Selected Data Product Code Name]
Display Auto-Scroll List from *Data Product* with *Data Product. Name*
Select *Data Product. Name*
Display Each *Data Product Set. Name* within Selected *Data Product*
Display Each *Data Product Unit. Name, Data Product Unit. Mnemonic*
Display Each *Data Product Code* data

[PRINT]

[RETURN]
Close report and Return to <u>Data Inventory Reports</u>

[Data Product Code Variation Name]
Display Each *Data Product. Name*
Display Each *Data Product Set. Name*
Display Each *Data Product Set Variation. Name*
Display Each *Data Product Unit. Name, Data Product Unit. Mnemonic*
Display Each *Data Product Unit Variation. Name, Data Product Unit Variation. Mnemonic*
Display Each *Data Product Code. Definition, Data Product Code. Name, Data Product Code. Value*
Display Each *Data Product Code Variation. Definition, Data Product Code Variation. Name, Data Product Code Variation. Value*

[PRINT]

[RETURN]
Close report and Return to <u>Data Inventory Reports</u>

[Data Product Code Variation Detail]
 Display Each *Data Product. Name*
  Display Each *Data Product Set. Name*
   Display Each *Data Product Set Variation. Name*
    Display Each *Data Product Unit. Name, Data Product Unit. Mnemonic*
     Display Each *Data Product Unit Variation. Name, Data Product Unit Variation* data
      Display each *Data Product Code Variation* data

 [PRINT]

 [RETURN]
  Close report and Return to <u>Data Inventory Reports</u>

[Selected Data Product Code Variation Detail]
 Display Auto-Scroll List from *Data Product* with *Data Product. Name*
 Select *Data Product. Name*
 Display Each *Data Product Set. Name* within Selected *Data Product*
  Display Each *Data Product Set Variation. Name*
   Display Each *Data Product Unit. Name, Data Product Unit. Mnemonic*
    Display Each *Data Product Unit Variation. Name, Data Product Unit Variation* data
     Display Each *Data Product. Code* data
      Display Each *Data Product Code Variation* data

 [PRINT]

 [RETURN]
  Close report and Return to <u>Data Inventory Reports</u>

[Data Site Name]
 Display Each *Data Site. Name*

 [PRINT]

 [RETURN]
  Close report and Return to <u>Data Inventory Reports</u>

[Data Site Detail]
 Display Each *Data Site* data

[PRINT]

[RETURN]
  Close report and Return to <u>Data Inventory Reports</u>

[Data Product Primary Key Detail]
  Display Each *Data Product. Name*
    Display Each *Data Product Primary Key* data
      Display Each *Data Product Primary Key Unit* data

[PRINT]

[RETURN]
  Close report and Return to <u>Data Inventory Reports</u>

[Selected Data Product Primary Key Detail]
  Display Auto-Scroll List from *Data Product* with *Data Product.
   Name*
  Select *Data Product. Name*
    Display Each *Data Product Primary Key* data within Selected
     Data Product. Name
      Display Each *Data Product Primary Key Unit* data

[PRINT]

[RETURN]
  Close report and Return to <u>Data Inventory Reports</u>

[Data Product Foreign Key Detail]
  Display Each *Data Product. Name*
    Display Each *Data Product Foreign Key* data When *"Local"*
     Data Product Name >< *"Parent" Data Product. Name*
      Display Each *Data Product Foreign Key Unit* data

[PRINT]

[RETURN]
  Close report and Return to <u>Data Inventory Reports</u>

[Selected Data Product Foreign Key Detail]
  Display Auto-Scroll List from *Data Product* with *Data Product.
   Name*
  Select *Data Product. Name*
  Display Each *Data Product Foreign Key* data within Selected *Data
   Product. Name* When *"Local" Data Product Set. Name* ><
   Selected *Data Product. Name*

[PRINT]

[RETURN]
> Close report and Return to <u>Data Inventory Reports</u>

[Data Relation Cardinality Name]
> Display Each *Data Relation Cardinality. Name*

[PRINT]

[RETURN]
> Close report and Return to <u>Data Inventory Reports</u>

[Data Relation Cardinality Detail]
> Display Each *Data Relation Cardinality* data

[PRINT]

[RETURN]
> Close report and Return to <u>Data Inventory Reports</u>

[Data Product Type Name]
> Display Each *Data Product Type. Name*

[PRINT]

[RETURN]
> Close report and Return to <u>Data Inventory Reports</u>

[Data Product Type Detail]
> Display Each *Data Product Type* data

[PRINT]

[RETURN]
> Close report and Return to <u>Data Inventory Reports</u>

[Data Product Set Medium Name]
> Display Each *Data Set Medium. Name*

[PRINT]

[RETURN]
> Close report and Return to <u>Data Inventory Reports</u>

[Data Product Set Medium Detail]
> Display Each *Data Set Medium* data

[PRINT]

[RETURN]

Close report and Return to <u>Data Inventory Reports</u>

[Data Product Set Type Name]
Display Each *Data Product Set Type. Name*

[PRINT]

[RETURN]
Close report and Return to <u>Data Inventory Reports</u>

[Data Product Set Type Detail]
Display Each *Data Product Set Type* data

[PRINT]

[RETURN]
Close report and Return to <u>Data Inventory Reports</u>

[Data Format Name]
Display Each *Data Format. Name*

[PRINT]

[RETURN]
Close report and Return to <u>Data Inventory Reports</u>

[Data Format Detail]
Display Each *Data Format* data

[PRINT]

[RETURN]
Close report and Return to <u>Data Inventory Reports</u>

[Data Product Model ^ Data Product]
Sort *Data Product Model* by *Data Model Diagram. Name ^ Data Product. Name*
Display from Sort Each Unique *Data Model Diagram. Name*
Display Each *Data Product. Name*

[PRINT]

[RETURN]
Close report and Return to <u>Data Inventory Reports</u>

[Data Product ^ Data Product Model]
Sort *Data Product Model* by *Data Product. Name ^ Data Model Diagram. Name*
Display from Sort Each Unique *Data Product. Name*

      Display Each *Data Model Diagram. Name*

[PRINT]

[RETURN]
      Close report and Return to <u>Data Inventory Reports</u>

[Data Product Set Model ^ Data Product]
      Sort *Data Product Set Model* by *Data Model Diagram. Name* ^
      Data Product Set. Name
      Display from Sort Each Unique *Data Model Diagram. Name*
          Display Each *Data Product Set. Name*

[PRINT]

[RETURN]
      Close report and Return to <u>Data Inventory Reports</u>

[Data Product ^ Data Product Set Model]
      Sort *Data Product Set Model* by *Data Product Set. Name* ^ *Data*
      Model Diagram. Name
      Display from Sort Each Unique *Data Product Set. Name*
          Display Each *Data Model Diagram. Name*

[PRINT]

[RETURN]
      Close report and Return to <u>Data Inventory Reports</u>

[Data Model Diagram Name]
      Display each *Data Model Diagram. Name*

[PRINT]

[RETURN]
      Close report and Return to <u>Data Inventory Reports</u>

[Data Model Diagram Detail]
      Display Each *Data Model Diagram* data

[PRINT]

[RETURN]
      Close report and Return to <u>Data Inventory Reports</u>

[Data Model Diagram Type Name]
      Display Each *Data Model Diagram Type. Name*

[PRINT]

[RETURN]
  Close report and Return to <u>Data Inventory Reports</u>

[Data Model Diagram Type Detail]
  Display Each *Data Model Diagram Type* data

[PRINT]

[RETURN]
  Close report and Return to <u>Data Inventory Reports</u>

[Data Product Steward Name ^ Data Product Name]
  Sort *Data Product Steward* by *Data Steward. Name Complete* ^
   Data Product. Name
  Display from Sort Each Unique *Data Steward. Name Complete*
   Display Each *Data Product. Name*

[PRINT]

[RETURN]
  Close report and Return to <u>Data Inventory Reports</u>

[Data Product Set Variability]
  Each *Data Product*
   Display *Data Product. Name*
   Each *Data Product Set*
    Count >< 0
    Each *Data Product Set Variation*
     Count + 1
    When Count > 0
     Display *Data Product Set. Name*, Count

[PRINT]

[RETURN]
  Close report and Return to <u>Data Inventory Reports</u>

[Data Product Unit Variability
  Each *Data Product*
   Display *Data Product. Name*
   Each *Data Product Set*
    Count >< 0
    Each *Data Product Unit*
     Each *Data Product Unit Variation*
     Count + 1
    Each *Data Product Set Variation*

68

Each *Data Product Unit*
  Each *Data Product Unit Variation*
   Count + 1
When Count > 1
 Display *Data Product Set. Name*, Count

[PRINT]

[RETURN]
 Close report and Return to <u>Data Inventory Reports</u>

[Data Product Code Variability]
 Each *Data Product*
  Display *Data Product. Name*
  Each *Data Product Set*
   Display *Data Product Set. Name*
   Each *Data Product Unit*
    Count >< 0
    Each *Data Product Code*
     Each *Data Product Code Variation*
      Count + 1
    When Count > 0
     Display *Data Product Unit. Name, Data Product Unit. Mnemonic*, Count
    Each *Data Product Unit Variation*
     Count >< 0
     Each *Data Product Code*
      Each *Data Product Code Variation*
       Count + 1
     When Count > 0
      Display *Data Product Unit Variation. Name, Data Product Unit. Mnemonic*, Count
   Each *Data Product Set Variation*
   Display *Data Product Set Variation. Name*
   Each *Data Product Unit*
    Count >< 0
    Each *Data Product Code*
     Each *Data Product Code Variation*
      Count + 1
    When Count > 0
     Display *Data Product Unit. Name, Data Product Unit. Mnemonic*, Count
    Each *Data Product Unit Variation*

Count >< 0
Each *Data Product Code*
Each *Data Product Code Variation*
Count + 1
When Count > 0
Display *Data Product Unit Variation.*
Name, Data Product Unit Variation.
Mnemonic, Count

[PRINT]

[RETURN]
Close report and Return to <u>Data Inventory Reports</u>

[RETURN]
Close window and Return to <u>Data Inventory Function</u>

[HELP]
Open Help Message View
Display Data Inventory Reports Help Message

Chapter 5

COMMON DATA

Common Data Function includes Common Data Task, Data Subject Area Task, Common Data Key Task, Common Data Reference Set Task, Common Data Model Task, Common Data Steward Task, and Common Data Reports, as shown in Figure 5.1. It is opened from Data Resource Guide Edit / View.

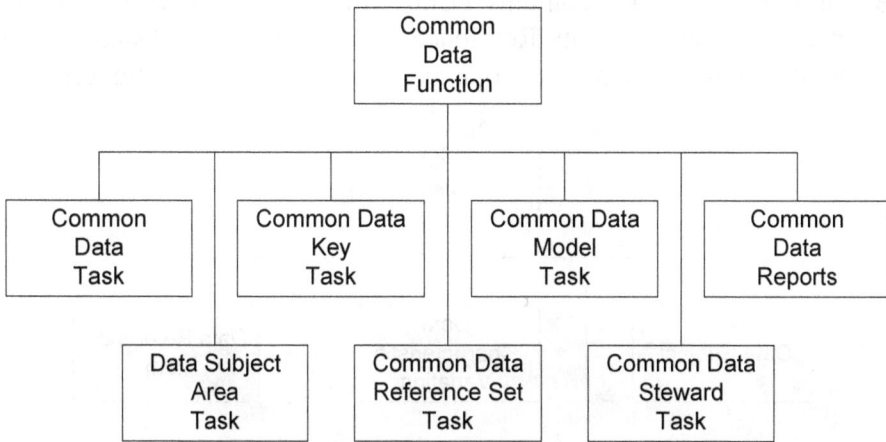

Figure 5.1. Common Data Function.

The actions for Common Data Function are:

[COMMON DATA TASK]
   Open <u>Common Data Task</u>

[DATA SUBJECT AREA TASK]
   Open <u>Data Subject Area Task</u>

[COMMON DATA KEY TASK]
   Open <u>Common Data Key Task</u>

[COMMON DATA REFERENCE SET TASK]
   Open <u>Common Data Reference Set Task</u>

[COMMON DATA MODEL TASK]
   Open <u>Common Data Model Task</u>

71

[COMMON DATA STEWARD TASK]
   Open <u>Common Data Steward Task</u>

[COMMON DATA REPORTS]
   Open <u>Common Data Reports</u>

[RETURN]
   Close window and Return to <u>Data Resource Guide Edit / View</u>

[HELP]
   Open <u>Help Message View</u>
   Display Common Data Function Help Message

COMMON DATA TASK

The Common Data Task contains Data Subject, Data Characteristic, Data Characteristic Variation, Data Reference Set Variation, and Data Reference Item, as shown in Figure 5.2 It is opened from Common Data Function.

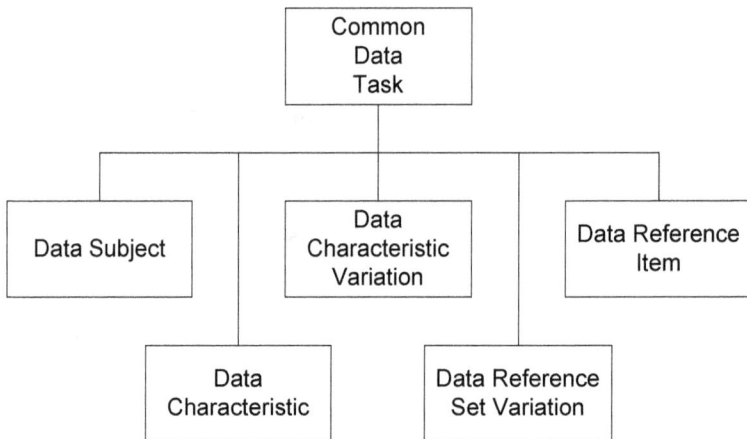

Figure 5.2. Common Data Task.

The actions for Common Data Task are:

[DATA SUBJECT]
   Open <u>Data Subject</u>

[DATA CHARACTERISTIC]
   Open <u>Data Characteristic</u>

[DATA CHARACTERISTIC VARIATION]
   Open <u>Data Characteristic Variation</u>

[DATA REFERENCE SET VARIATION]

Open <u>Data Reference Set Variation</u>

[DATA REFERENCE ITEM]
Open <u>Data Reference Item</u>

[RETURN]
Close window and Return to <u>Common Data Function</u>

[HELP]
Open <u>Help Message View</u>
Display Common Data Task Help Message

Data Subject

Data Subject can be opened from several different locations. The actions for Data Subject are:

[DISPLAY]
Display Auto-Scroll List from *Data Subject* with *Data Subject. Name Complete*
Select *Data Subject. Name Complete*
Display Selected *Data Subject* data

[PRINT]

(DELETE)
Delete Selected *Data Subject* occurrence

(NEW)
Display blank data fields for entry of new *Data Subject* data
Display Auto-Scroll List from *Data Subject* with *Data Subject. Name Complete*
Select *"Origin" Data Subject. Name Complete*

Display Auto-Scroll List from *Common Data Status* with *Common Data Status. Name*
Select *Common Data Status. Name*

[ACCEPT]

[RETURN]
When Opened from Common Data Task
Close window and Return to <u>Common Data Task</u>
When Opened from Data Product Set Cross-Reference
Close window and Return to <u>Data Product Set Cross-Reference</u>
When Opened from Data Product Unit Cross-Reference

Close window and Return to <u>Data Product Unit Cross-Reference</u>
When Opened from Data Product Code Cross-Reference
Close window and Return to <u>Data Product Code Cross-Reference</u>

[HELP]
Open <u>Help Message View</u>
Display Data Subject Help Message

Data Characteristic

Data Characteristic can be opened from several different locations. The actions for Data Characteristic are:

Display Auto-Scroll List from *Data Subject* with *Data Subject. Name Complete*
Select *Data Subject. Name Complete*

[DISPLAY]
Display Auto-Scroll List from *Data Characteristic* within Selected *Data Subject* with *Data Characteristic. Name Complete*
Select *Data Characteristic. Name Complete*
Display Selected *Data Characteristic* data

[PRINT]

(DELETE)
Delete Selected *Data Characteristic* occurrence

(NEW)
Display blank data fields for entry of new *Data Characteristic* data within Selected *Data Subject*

Display Auto-Scroll List from *Common Data Status* with *Common Data Status. Name*
Select *Common Data Status. Name*

[ACCEPT]

[RETURN]
When Opened from Common Data Task
Close window and Return to <u>Common Data Task</u>
When Opened from Data Product Unit Cross-Reference Task
Close window and Return to <u>Data Product Unit Cross-Reference Task</u>

[HELP]
>Open Help Message View
>Display Data Characteristic Help Message

Data Characteristic Variation

Data Characteristic Variation can be opened from several different locations. The actions for Data Characteristic Variation are:

>Display Auto-Scroll List from *Data Subject* with *Data Subject. Name Complete*
>Select *Data Subject. Name Complete*
>Display Auto-Scroll List from *Data Characteristic* within Selected *Data Subject* with *Data Characteristic. Name Complete*
>Select *Data Characteristic. Name Complete*

[DISPLAY]
>Display Auto-Scroll List from *Data Characteristic Variation* within selected *Data Characteristic* with *Data Characteristic Variation. Name Complete*
>Select *Data Characteristic Variation. Name Complete*
>Display Selected *Data Characteristic Variation* data

[PRINT]

(DELETE)
>Delete Selected *Data Characteristic Variation* occurrence

(NEW)
>Display blank data fields for entry of new *Data Characteristic Variation* data within Selected *Data Characteristic*

>Display Auto-Scroll List from *Common Data Status* with *Common Data Status. Name*
>Select *Common Data Status. Name*

[ACCEPT]

[RETURN]
>When Opened from Common Data Task
>>Close window and Return to Common Data Task
>When Opened from Data Product Unit Cross-Reference Task
>>Close window and Return to Data Product Unit Cross-Reference Task

[HELP]

Open Help Message View
Display Data Characteristic Variation Help Message

Data Reference Set Variation

Data Reference Set Variation can be opened from several different locations. The actions for Data Reference Set Variation are:

Display Auto-Scroll List from *Data Subject* with *Data Subject. Name Complete*
Select *Data Subject. Name*

[DISPLAY]

Display Auto-Scroll List from *Data Reference Set Variation* within Selected *Data Subject* with *Data Reference Set Variation. Name Complete*
Select *Data Reference Set Variation. Name Complete*
Display Selected *Data Reference Set Variation* data

[PRINT]

(DELETE)

Delete Selected *Data Reference Set Variation* occurrence

(NEW)

Display blank data fields for entry of new *Data Reference Set Variation*

Display Auto-Scroll List from *Common Data Status* with *Common Data Status. Name*
Select *Common Data Status. Name*

[ACCEPT]

[RETURN]

When Opened from Common Data Task
Close window and Return to Common Data Task
When Opened from Data Product Code Cross-Reference Task
Close window and Return to Data Product Code Cross-Reference Task

[HELP]

Open Help Message View
Display Data Reference Set Help Message

Data Reference Item

Data Reference Item is opened from Common Data Task. The actions for Data Reference Item are:

Display Auto-Scroll List from *Data Subject* with *Data Subject. Name Complete*
Select *Data Subject. Name Complete*

Display Auto-Scroll List from *Data Reference Set Variation* within Selected *Data Subject* with *Data Reference Set Variation. Name Complete*
Select *Data Reference Set Variation. Name Complete*

[DISPLAY]

Display Auto-Scroll List from *Data Reference Item* within Selected *Data Reference Set Variation* with *Data Reference Item. Name*
Select *Data Reference Item. Name*
Display Selected *Data Reference Item* data

[PRINT]

(DELETE)

Delete Selected *Data Reference Item* occurrence

(NEW)

Display blank data fields for entry of new *Data Reference Item*

Display Auto-Scroll List from *Common Data Status* with *Common Data Status. Name*
Select *Common Data Status. Name*

[ACCEPT]

[RETURN]
Close window and Return to Common Data Task

[HELP]
Open Help Message View window
Display Data Reference Item Help Message

COMMON DATA KEY TASK

Common Data Key Task contains Primary Key, Foreign Key, and Data Relation Cardinality, as shown in Figure 5.3. It is opened from Common Data Function.

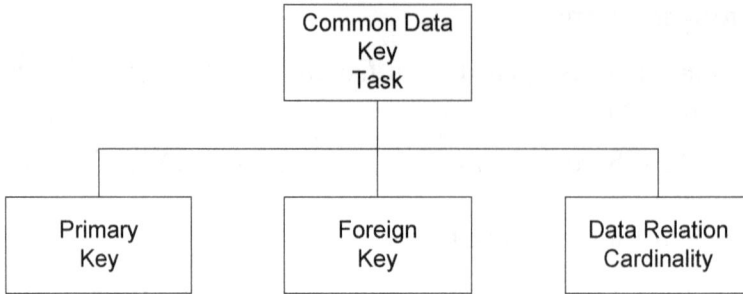

Figure 5.3. Common Data Key Task.

The actions for Common Data Key Task are:

[PRIMARY KEY]
 Open <u>Primary Key</u>

[FOREIGN KEY]
 Open <u>Foreign Key</u>

[DATA RELATION CARDINALITY]
 Open <u>Data Cardinality</u>

[RETURN]
 Close window and Return to <u>Common Data Key Task</u>

[HELP]
 Open <u>Help Message View</u>
 Display Common Data Key Task Help Message

Primary Key

Primary Key is opened from Common Data Key Task. The actions for Primary Key are:

Display Auto-Scroll List from *Data Subject* with *Data Subject. Name Complete*
Select *Data Subject. Name Complete*

[DISPLAY]
 Display Scroll List from *Primary Key* within Selected *Data Subject* with
   Each *Primary Key. Comment*
     Each *Primary Key Characteristic. Comment*, *Data Characteristic. Name Complete*
 Select *Primary Key*
 Display Selected *Primary Key* data

78

Display Each *Primary Key Characteristic. Comment, Data Characteristic. Name Complete*

[PRINT]

(DELETE)
Delete Selected *Primary Key* occurrence and subordinate *Primary Key Characteristic* occurrences

(NEW)
Display blank data fields for entry of new *Primary Key* data

Display Auto-Scroll List from *Common Data Status* with *Common Data Status. Name*
Select *Common Data Status. Name*

Display Auto-Scroll List from *Primary Key Composition* with *Primary Key Composition. Name*
Select *Primary Key Composition. Name*

Display Auto-Scroll List from *Primary Key Meaning* with *Primary Key Meaning. Name*
Select *Primary Key Meaning. Name*

Display Auto-Scroll List from *Primary Key Origin* with *Primary Key Origin. Name*
Select *Primary Key Origin. Name*

Display Auto-Scroll List rom *Primary Key Purpose* with *Primary Key Purpose. Name*
Select Primary *Key Purpose. Name*

Display Auto-Scroll List from *Primary Key Scope* with *Primary Key Scope. Name*
Select Primary *Key Scope. Name*

Each *Primary Key Characteristic*
Display Auto-Scroll List from *Data Subject* with *Data Subject. Name Complete*
Select *Data Subject. Name Complete*

Display Auto-Scroll List from *Data Characteristic* within Selected *Data Subject* with *Data Characteristic. Name Complete*
Select *Data Characteristic. Name Complete*

Display blank data field for entry of *Primary Key Characteristic. Comment*

[ACCEPT]

[RETURN]
Close window and Return to Common Data Key Task

[HELP]
Open Help Message View
Display Primary Key Help Message

Foreign Key

Foreign Key is opened from Common Data Key Task. The actions for Foreign Key are:

Display Auto-Scroll List from *Data Subject* with *Data Subject. Name Complete*
Select *Data Subject. Name Complete*

[DISPLAY]
Display Scroll List from *Foreign Key* with
Each *Foreign Key. Comment* within Selected *Data Subject* where *"Local" Data Subject* >< Selected *Data Subject*
Each *Foreign Key Characteristic. Comment, Data Characteristic. Name Complete*
Select *Foreign Key*
Display Selected *Foreign Key* data
Display Each *Foreign Key Characteristic. Comment, Data Characteristic. Name Complete*

[PRINT]

(DELETE)
Delete Selected *Foreign Key* occurrence and subordinate *Foreign Key Characteristic* occurrences

(NEW)
Display blank data fields for entry of new *Foreign Key* data

Display Auto-Scroll List from *Data Subject* with *Data Subject. Name Complete*
Select *"Parent" Data Subject. Name Complete*

Display Auto-Scroll List from *Common Data Status* with *Common Data Status. Name*

Select *Common Data Status. Name*

Display Auto-Scroll List from *Data Relation Cardinality* with *Data Relation Cardinality. Name*
Select *Data Relation Cardinality. Name*

Each *Foreign Key Characteristic*
    Display Auto-Scroll List from *Data Subject* with *Data Subject. Name Complete*
    Select *Data Subject. Name Complete*

    Display Auto-Scroll List from *Data Characteristic* within Selected *Data Subject* with *Data Characteristic. Name Complete*
    Select *Data Characteristic. Name Complete.*

    Display blank data fields for entry of *Foreign Key Characteristic* data

[ACCEPT]

[RETURN]
    Close window and Return to Common Data Key Task

[HELP]
    Open Help Message View
    Display Foreign Key Help Message

Data Relation Cardinality

Data Relation Cardinality is opened from Common Data Key Task. The actions for Data Relation Cardinality are:

[DISPLAY]
    Display Auto-Scroll List from *Data Relation Cardinality* with *Data Relation Cardinality. Name*
    Select *Data Relation Cardinality. Name*
    Display Selected *Data Relation Cardinality* data

[PRINT]

(DELETE)
    Delete Selected *Data Relation Cardinality* occurrence

(NEW)
    Display blank data fields for entry of new *Data Relation Cardinality* data

[ACCEPT]

[RETURN]
    Close window and Return to <u>Common Data Key Task</u>

[HELP]
    Open <u>Help Message View</u>
    Display Data Relation Cardinality Help Message

COMMON DATA REFERENCE SET TASK

The Common Data Reference Set Task contains Common Data Status, Primary Key Composition, Primary Key Meaning, Primary Key Origin, Primary Key Purpose, and Primary Key Scope, as shown in Figure 5.4. It is opened from Common Data Function.

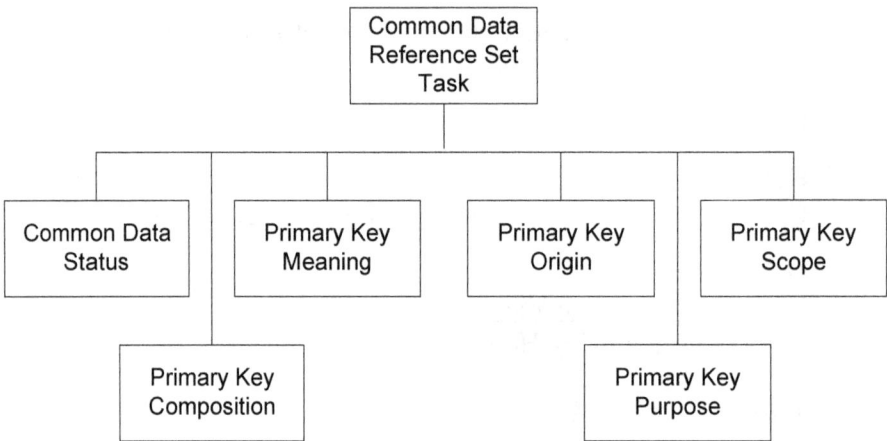

Figure 5.4. Common Data Reference Set Task.

The actions for Common Data Reference Set Task are:

[COMMON DATA STATUS]
    Open <u>Common Data Status</u>

[PRIMARY KEY COMPOSITION]
    Open <u>Primary Key Composition</u>

[PRIMARY KEY MEANING]
    Open <u>Primary Key Meaning</u>

[PRIMARY KEY ORIGIN]
    Open <u>Primary Key Origin</u>

[PRIMARY KEY PURPOSE]
    Open <u>Primary Key Purpose</u>

[PRIMARY KEY SCOPE]
    Open <u>Primary Key Scope</u>

[RETURN]
    Close window and Return to <u>Common Data Function</u>

[HELP]
    Open <u>Help Message View</u>
    Display Common Data Reference Set Task Help Message

Common Data Status

Common Data Status is opened from Common Data Reference Set Task. The actions for Common Data Status are:

[DISPLAY]
    Display Auto-Scroll List from *Common Data Status* with *Common Data Status. Name*
    Select *Common Data Status. Name*
    Display Selected *Common Data Status* data

    [PRINT]

    (DELETE)
        Delete Selected *Common Data Status* occurrence

(NEW)
    Display blank data fields for entry of new *Common Data Status* data

    [ACCEPT]

[RETURN]
    Close window and Return to <u>Common Data Reference Set Task</u>

[HELP]
    Open <u>Help Message View</u>
    Display Common Data Status Help Message

Primary Key Composition

Primary Key Composition is opened from Common Data Reference Set Task. The actions for Primary Key Composition are:

[DISPLAY]
    Display Auto-Scroll List from *Primary Key Composition* with *Primary Key Composition. Name*

Select *Primary Key Composition. Name*
Display Selected *Primary Key Composition* data

[PRINT]

(DELETE)
   Delete Selected *Primary Key Composition* occurrence

(NEW)
   Display blank data fields for entry of new *Primary Key*
      Composition data

[ACCEPT]

[RETURN]
   Close window and Return to <u>Common Data Reference Set Task</u>

[HELP]
   Open <u>Help Message View</u>
   Display Primary Key Composition Help Message

Primary Key Meaning

Primary Key Meaning is opened from Common Data Reference Set Task.
The actions for Primary Key Meaning are:

[DISPLAY]
   Display Auto-Scroll List from *Primary Key Meaning* with *Primary
      Key Meaning. Name*
   Select *Primary Key Meaning. Name*
   Display Selected *Primary Key Meaning* data

[PRINT]

(DELETE)
   Delete Selected *Primary Key Meaning* occurrence

(NEW)
   Display blank data fields for entry of new *Primary Key Meaning*
      data

[ACCEPT]

[RETURN]
   Close window and Return to <u>Common Data Reference Set Task</u>

[HELP]
   Open <u>Help Message View</u>

Display Primary Key Meaning Help Message

Primary Key Origin

Primary Key Origin is opened from Common Data Reference Set Task. The actions for Primary Key Origin are:

[DISPLAY]
Display Auto-Scroll List from *Primary Key Origin* with *Primary Key Origin. Name*
Select *Primary Key Origin. Name*
Display Selected *Primary Key Origin* data

[PRINT]

(DELETE)
Delete Selected *Primary Key Origin* occurrence

(NEW)
Display blank data fields for entry of new *Primary Key Origin* data

[ACCEPT]

[RETURN]
Close window and Return to Common Data Reference Set Task

[HELP]
Open Help Message View
Display Primary Key Origin Help Message

Primary Key Purpose

Primary Key Purpose is opened from Common Data Reference Set Task. The actions for Primary Key Purpose are:

[DISPLAY]
Display Auto-Scroll List from *Primary Key Purpose* with *Primary Key Purpose. Name*
Select *Primary Key Purpose. Name*
Display Selected *Primary Key Purpose* data

[PRINT]

(DELETE)
Delete Selected *Primary Key Purpose* occurrence

(NEW)

Display blank data fields for entry of new *Primary Key Purpose* data

[ACCEPT]

[RETURN]
Close window and Return to <u>Common Data Reference Set Task</u>

[HELP]
Open <u>Help Message View</u>
Display Primary Key Purpose Help Message

Primary Key Scope

Primary Key Scope is opened from Common Data Reference Set Task. The actions for Primary Key Scope are:

[DISPLAY]
Display Auto-Scroll List from *Primary Key Scope* with *Primary Key Scope. Name*
Select *Primary Key Scope. Name*
Display Selected *Primary Key Scope* data

[PRINT]

(DELETE)
Delete Selected *Primary Key Scope* occurrence

(NEW)
Display blank data fields for entry of new *Primary Key Scope* data

[ACCEPT]

[RETURN]
Close window and Return to <u>Common Data Reference Set Task</u>

[HELP]
Open <u>Help Message View</u>
Display Primary Key Scope Help Message

COMMON DATA STEWARD TASK

The Common Data Steward Task contains Data Subject Steward, Data Steward, Data Steward Function, and Data Steward Level, as shown in Figure 5.5. It is opened by Common Data Function.

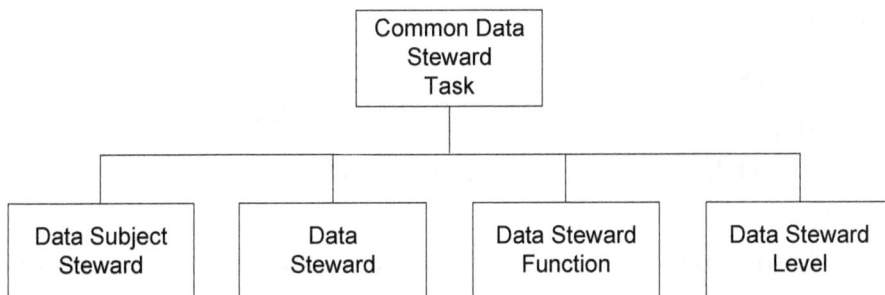

Figure 5.5. Common Data Steward Task.

The actions for Common Data Steward Task are:

[DATA SUBJECT STEWARD]
    Open <u>Data Subject Steward</u>

[DATA STEWARD]
    Open <u>Data Steward</u>

[DATA STEWARD FUNCTION]
    Open <u>Data Steward Function</u>

[DATA STEWARD LEVEL]
    Open <u>Data Steward Level</u>

[RETURN]
    Close window and Return to <u>Common Data Function</u>

[HELP]
    Open <u>Help Message View</u>
    Display Common Data Steward Task Help Message

Data Subject Steward

Data Subject Steward is opened from Common Data Steward Task. The actions for Data Subject Steward are:

[DISPLAY]
    Display Auto-Scroll List from *Data Subject* with *Data Subject.*
     Name Complete
    Select *Data Subject. Name Complete*

    Display Scroll List from *Data Subject Steward* within Selected
     Data Subject with *Data Subject Steward. Comment, Data*
     Steward. Name Complete
    Select *Data Subject Steward*

Display Selected *Data Subject Steward* data

[PRINT]

(DELETE)

Delete Selected *Data Subject Steward* occurrence

(NEW)

Display blank data fields for entry of new *Data Subject Steward* data

Display Auto-Scroll List from *Data Steward* with *Data Steward. Name Complete*
Select *Data Steward. Name Complete*

Display Auto-Scroll List from *Data Steward Function* with *Data Steward Function. Name*
Select *Data Steward Function. Name*

Display Auto-Scroll List from *Data Steward Level* with *Data Steward Level. Name*
Select *Data Steward Level. Name*

[ACCEPT]

[RETURN]

Close window and Return to Common Data Steward Task

[HELP]

Open Help Message View
Display Data Subject Steward Help Message

Data Steward

Data Steward is opened from Common Data Steward Task. The actions for Data Steward are provided in the Data Responsibility Chapter.

Data Steward Function

Data Steward Function is opened from Common Data Steward Task. The actions for Data Steward Function are provided in the Data Responsibility Chapter.

Data Steward Level

Data Steward Level is opened from Common Data Steward Task. The actions for Data Steward Level are provided in the Data Responsibility Chapter.

COMMON DATA MODEL TASK

Common Data Model Task contains Data Subject Model, Data Subject Area Model, Data Model Diagram, and Data Model Diagram Type, as shown in Figure 5.6. It is opened from Common Data Function.

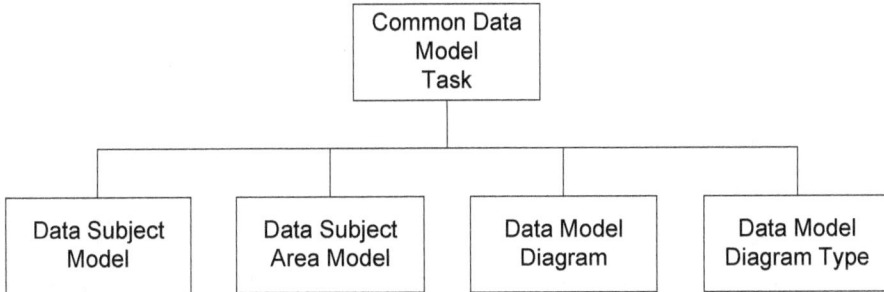

Figure 5.6. Common Data Model Task.

The actions for Common Data Model Task are:

[DATA SUBJECT MODEL]
Open Data Subject Model

[DATA SUBJECT AREA MODEL]
Open Data Subject Area Model

[DATA MODEL DIAGRAM]
Open Data Model Diagram

[DATA MODEL DIAGRAM TYPE]
Open Data Model Diagram Type

[RETURN]
Close window and Return to Common Data Function

[HELP]
Open Help Message View
Display Common Data Model Task Help Message

Data Subject Model

Data Subject Model is opened from Common Data Model Task. The actions for Data Subject Model are:

Display Auto-Scroll List with *Data Subject. Name Complete*
Select *Data Subject. Name Complete*

[DISPLAY]

Display Scroll List from *Data Subject Model* with *Data Subject Model. Comment, Data Model Diagram. Name* within Selected *Data Subject*
Select *Data Subject Model*
Display Selected *Data Subject Model* data

[PRINT]

(DELETE)
Delete Selected *Data Subject Model* occurrence

(NEW)
Display blank data fields for entry of new *Data Subject Model*

Display Auto-Scroll List from *Data Model Diagram* with *Data Model Diagram. Name*
Select *Data Model Diagram. Name*

[ACCEPT]

[RETURN]
Close window and Return to Common Data Model Task

[HELP]
Open Help Message View
Display Data Subject Model Help Message

Data Subject Area Model

Data Subject Area Model is opened from Common Data Model Task. The actions for Data Subject Area Model are:

Display Auto-Scroll List with *Data Subject Area. Name*
Select *Data Subject Area. Name*

[DISPLAY]
Display Scroll List from *Data Subject Area Model* within Selected *Data Subject Area* with *Data Subject Area Model. Comment, Data Model Diagram. Name*
Select *Data Subject Area Model*
Display Selected *Data Subject Area Model* data

[PRINT]

(DELETE)
Delete Selected *Data Subject Area Model* occurrence

(NEW)

Display blank data fields for entry of new *Data Subject Area Model*

Display Auto-Scroll List from *Data Model Diagram* with *Data Model Diagram. Name*
Select *Data Model Diagram. Name*

[ACCEPT]

[RETURN]
    Close window and Return to <u>Common Data Model Task</u>

[HELP]
    Open <u>Help Message View</u>
    Display Data Subject Area Model Help Message

Data Model Diagram

Data Model Diagram is opened from Common Data Model Task. Data Model Diagram actions are provided in the Data Inventory Chapter.

Data Model Diagram Type

Data Model Diagram Type is opened from Common Data Model Task. Data Model Diagram Type actions are provided in the Data Inventory Chapter.

DATA SUBJECT AREA TASK

Data Subject Area Task contains Data Subject Area, Data Subject Area Assignment, and Data Subject Area Purpose, as shown in Figure 5.7. It is opened from Common Data Function.

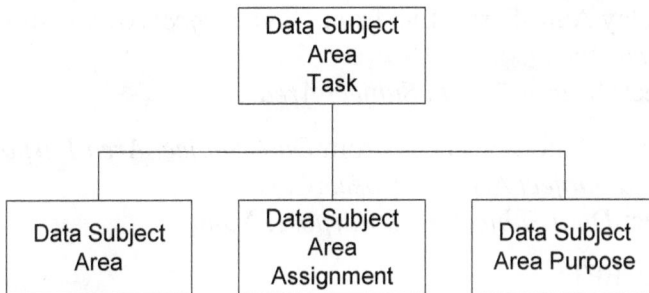

Figure 5.7. Data Subject Area Task.

The actions for Data Subject Area Task are:

[DATA SUBJECT AREA]
    Open <u>Data Subject Area</u>

[DATA SUBJECT AREA ASSIGNMENT]

91

Open <u>Data Subject Area Assignment</u>

[DATA SUBJECT AREA PURPOSE]
Open <u>Data Subject Area Purpose</u>

[RETURN]
Close window and Return to <u>Common Data Function</u>

[HELP]
Open <u>Help Message View</u>
Display Data Subject Area Task Help Message

Data Subject Area

Data Subject Are is opened from Data Subject Area Task. The actions for Data Subject Area are:

[DISPLAY]
Display Auto-Scroll List from *Data Subject Area* with *Data Subject Area. Name*
Select *Data Subject Area. Name*
Display Selected *Data Subject Area* data

[PRINT]

(DELETE)
Delete Selected *Data Subject Area* occurrence

(NEW)
Display blank data fields for entry of new *Data Subject Area*

Display Auto-Scroll List from *Data Subject Area* with *Data Subject Area. Name*
Select *"Parent" Data Subject Area*

Display Auto-Scroll List from *Data Subject Area Purpose* with *Data Subject Area Purpose. Name*
Select *Data Subject Area Purpose. Name*

[ACCEPT]

[RETURN]
Close window and Return to <u>Data Subject Area Task</u>

[HELP]
Open <u>Help Message View</u>
Display Data Subject Area Help Message

Data Subject Area Assignment

Data Subject Area Assignment is opened from Data Subject Area Task. The actions for Data Subject Area Assignment are:

[DISPLAY]
> Display Auto-Scroll List from *Data Subject Area* with *Data Subject Area. Name*
> Select *Data Subject Area. Name*
> Display Selected *Data Subject Area* data
>
> Display Scroll List from *Data Subject Area Assignment* within Selected *Data Subject Area* with *Data Subject Area Assignment. Comment, Data Subject. Name Complete*
> Select *Data Subject Area Assignment*
> Display Selected *Data Subject Area Assignment* data

[PRINT]

(DELETE)
> Delete Selected *Data Subject Area* occurrence

(NEW)
> Display blank data fields for entry of new *Data Subject Area Assignment*
>
> Display Auto-Scroll List from *Data Subject* with *Data Subject. Name Complete*
> Select *Data Subject. Name Complete*

[ACCEPT]

[RETURN]
> Close window and Return to <u>Data Subject Area Task</u>

[HELP]
> Open <u>Help Message View</u>
> Display Data Subject Area Assignment Help Message

Data Subject Area Purpose

Data Subject Area Purpose is opened from Data Subject Area Task. The actions for Data Subject Area Purpose are:

[DISPLAY]
> Display Auto-Scroll List from *Data Subject Area Purpose* with *Data Subject Area Purpose. Name*
> Display Selected *Data Subject Area Purpose* data

93

[PRINT]

(DELETE)
> Delete Selected *Data Subject Area Purpose* occurrence

(NEW)
> Display blank data fields for entry of new *Data Subject Area*
> *Purpose* data

[ACCEPT]

[RETURN]
> Close window and Return to <u>Data Subject Area Task</u>

[HELP]
> Open <u>Help Message View</u>
> Display Data Subject Area Purpose Help Message

COMMON DATA REPORTS

Common Data Reports contains the reports for the Common Data Function. It is opened from Common Data Function. Only a few examples of reports are shown. Many additional reports could be developed based on an organization's needs and added to the Data Resource Guide.

The specific reports and actions to obtain those reports are:

[Data Subject Name]
> Display Each *Data Subject. Name Complete*

[PRINT]

[RETURN]
> Close report and Return to <u>Common Data Reports</u>

[Data Subject Detail]

> Display Each *Data Subject* data

[PRINT]

[RETURN]
> Close report and Return to <u>Common Data Reports</u>

[Data Subject Name ^ Data Characteristic Name]

> Display Each *Data Subject. Name Complete*
> > Display Each *Data Characteristic. Name Complete*

[PRINT]

[RETURN]
> Close report and Return to <u>Common Data Reports</u>

[Data Subject Name ^ Data Characteristic Detail]

> Display Each *Data Subject. Name Complete*
> > Display Each *Data Characteristic* data

[PRINT]

[RETURN]
> Close report and Return to <u>Common Data Reports</u>

[Selected Data Subject Name ^ Data Characteristic Name]

> Display Auto-Scroll List from *Data Subject* with *Data Subject Name. Complete*
> Select *Data Subject. Name Complete*
> Display Each *Data Characteristic. Name Complete* within Selected *Data Subject*

[PRINT]

[RETURN]
> Close report and Return to <u>Common Data Reports</u>

[Selected Data Subject Name ^ Data Characteristic Detail]

> Display Auto-Scroll List from *Data Subject* with *Data Subject. Name Complete*
> Select *Data Subject. Name Complete*
> Display Each *Data Subject. Name Complete* within Selected *Data Subject*
> > Display Each *Data Characteristic* data

[PRINT]

[RETURN]
> Close report and Return to <u>Common Data Reports</u>

[Data Subject Name ^ Data Characteristic Name ^ Data Characteristic Variation Name]

> Display Each *Data Subject. Name Complete*
> > Display Each *Data Characteristic. Name Complete*
> > > Display Each *Data Characteristic Variation. Name Complete*

[PRINT]

[RETURN]
> Close report and Return to <u>Common Data Reports</u>

[Data Subject Name ^ Data Characteristic Name ^ Data Characteristic Variation Detail]

> Display Each *Data Subject. Name Complete*
>> Display Each *Data Characteristic. Name Complete*
>>> Display Each *Data Characteristic* data

[PRINT]

[RETURN]
> Close report and Return to <u>Common Data Reports</u>

[Selected Data Subject Name ^ Data Characteristic Name ^ Data Characteristic Variation Name]

> Display Auto-Scroll List from *Data Subject* with *Data Subject. Name Complete*
> Select *Data Subject. Name Complete*

> Display Each *Data Characteristic. Name Complete* within Selected *Data Subject*
>> Display Each *Data Characteristic Variation. Name Complete*

[PRINT]

[RETURN]
> Close report and Return to <u>Common Data Reports</u>

[Selected Data Subject Name ^ Data Characteristic Detail ^ Data Characteristic Variation Detail]

> Display Auto-Scroll List from *Data Subject* with *Data Subject. Name Complete*
> Select *Data Subject. Name Complete*

> Display Each *Data Characteristic* data within Selected *Data Subject*
>> Display Each *Data Characteristic Variation* data

[PRINT]

[RETURN]
> Close report and Return to <u>Common Data Reports</u>

[Selected Data Subject Name ^ Selected Data Characteristic Name ^ Data Characteristic Variation Detail]

    Display Auto-Scroll List from *Data Subject* with *Data Subject.*
      Name Complete
    Select *Data Subject. Name Complete*

    Display Auto-Scroll List from *Data Characteristic* within Selected
      Data Subject with *Data Characteristic. Name Complete*
    Select *Data Characteristic. Name Complete*

    Display Each *Data Characteristic Variation* data within Selected
      Data Characteristic

    [PRINT]

    [RETURN]
      Close report and Return to <u>Common Data Reports</u>

[Data Subject Name ^ Data Reference Set Variation Name]

    Display Each *Data Subject. Name Complete*
      Display Each *Data Reference Set Variation. Name Complete*

    [PRINT]

    [RETURN]
      Close report and Return to <u>Common Data Reports</u>

[Data Subject Name ^ Data Reference Set Variation Detail]

    Display Each *Data Subject. Name Complete*
      Display Each *Data Reference Set Variation* data

    [PRINT]

    [RETURN]
      Close report and Return to <u>Common Data Reports</u>

[Data Subject Name ^ Data Reference Set Variation Name ^ Data Reference Item Name]

    Display Each *Data Subject. Name Complete*
      Display Each *Data Reference Set Variation. Name Complete*
        Display Each *Data Reference Item. Name*

    [PRINT]

    [RETURN]
      Close report and Return to <u>Common Data Reports</u>

[Data Subject Name ^ Data Reference Set Variation Name ^ Data Reference Item Detail

    Display Each *Data Subject. Name Complete*
        Display Each *Data Reference Variation. Name Complete*
           Display Each *Data Reference Item* data

    [PRINT]

    [RETURN]
        Close report and Return to <u>Common Data Reports</u>

[Selected Data Subject Name ^ Data Reference Set Variation Detail ^ Data Reference Item Detail]

    Display Auto-Scroll List from *Data Subject* with *Data Subject. Name Complete*
    Select *Data Subject. Name Complete*

    Display *Data Reference Set Variation* data within Selected *Data Subject*
        Display Each *Data Reference Item* data

    [PRINT]

    [RETURN]
        Close report and Return to <u>Common Data Reports</u>

[Data Subject Name ^ Primary Key Detail]

    Display Each *Data Subject. Name Complete*
        Display Each *Primary Key* data

    [PRINT]

    [RETURN]
        Close report and Return to <u>Common Data Reports</u>

[Data Subject Name ^ Foreign Key Detail]

    Display Each *Data Subject. Name Complete*
        Display Each *Foreign Key* data

    [PRINT]

    [RETURN]
        Close report and Return to <u>Common Data Reports</u>

[Selected Data Subject Name ^ Primary Key Detail]

Display Auto-Scroll List from *Data Subject* with *Data Subject. Name Complete*
Select *Data Subject. Name Complete*

Display Each *Primary Key* data within Selected *Data Subject*

[PRINT]

[RETURN]
    Close report and Return to <u>Common Data Reports</u>

[Selected Data Subject Name ^ Foreign Key Detail]

Display Auto-Scroll List from *Data Subject* with *Data Subject. Name Complete*
Select *Data Subject. Name Complete*

Display Each *Foreign Key* data within Selected *Data Subject*

[PRINT]

[RETURN]
    Close report and Return to <u>Common Data Reports</u>

[Data Subject Name ^ Subordinate Data Subjects]

Display Each *Data Subject. Name Complete*
    Display Each Subordinate *Data Subject. Name Complete*

[PRINT]

[RETURN]
    Close report and Return to <u>Common Data Reports</u>

[Data Relation Cardinality Detail]

Display Each *Data Relation Cardinality* data

[PRINT]

[RETURN]
    Close report and Return to <u>Common Data Reports</u>

[Common Data Status Detail]

Display Each *Common Data Status* data

[PRINT]

[RETURN]
    Close report and Return to <u>Common Data Reports</u>

[Primary Key Composition Detail]

    Display Each *Primary Key Composition* data

    [PRINT]

    [RETURN]
        Close report and Return to <u>Common Data Reports</u>

[Primary Key Meaning Detail]

    Display Each *Primary Key Meaning* data

    [PRINT]

    [RETURN]
        Close report and Return to <u>Common Data Reports</u>

[Primary Key Origin Detail]

    Display Each *Primary Key Origin* data

    [PRINT]

    [RETURN]
        Close report and Return to <u>Common Data Reports</u>

[Primary Key Purpose Detail]

    Display Each *Primary Key Purpose* data

    [PRINT]

    [RETURN]
        Close report and Return to <u>Common Data Reports</u>

[Primary Key Scope Detail]

    Display Each *Primary Key Scope* data

    [PRINT]

    [RETURN]
        Close report and Return to <u>Common Data Reports</u>

[Data Subject Name ^ Data Steward Detail]

    Display Each *Data Subject. Name Complete*
        Display Each *Data Subject Steward* data

    [PRINT]

    [RETURN]

Close report and Return to <u>Common Data Reports</u>

[Data Steward Detail ^ Data Subject Names]

Display Each *Data Steward* data
Display Each *Data Subject. Name Complete*
Comment: Navigate through *Data Subject Steward* to find *Data Subject*

[PRINT]

[RETURN]
Close report and Return to <u>Common Data Reports</u>

[Data Steward Function Detail]

Display Each *Data Steward Function* data

[PRINT]

[RETURN]
Close report and Return to <u>Common Data Reports</u>

[Data Steward Level Detail]

Display Each *Data Steward Level* data

[PRINT]

[RETURN]
Close report and Return to <u>Common Data Reports</u>

[Data Subject Name ^ Data Subject Model Detail]

Display Each *Data Subject. Name Complete*
Display Each *Data Subject Model* data

[PRINT]

[RETURN]
Close report and Return to <u>Common Data Reports</u>

[Data Subject Model ^ Data Subject Name]

Sort *Data Subject Model* by *Data Model Diagram. Name ^ Data Subject. Name Complete*

Display from Sort Each Unique *Data Model Diagram. Name*
Display Each *Data Subject. Name Complete*

[PRINT]

[RETURN]
> Close report and Return to <u>Common Data Reports</u>

[Data Subject Name ^ Data Subject Area Model Detail]

> Sort *Data Subject Area Model* by *Data Subject. Name Complete ^ Data Model Diagram. Name*

> Display from Sort Each Unique *Data Subject. Name Complete*
> > Display Each *Data Subject Area Model* data

[PRINT]

[RETURN]
> Close report and Return to <u>Common Data Reports</u>

[Data Subject Area Model – Data Subject Name]

> Sort *Data Subject Area Model* by *Data Model Diagram. Name ^ Data Subject. Name Complete*

> Display from Sort Each Unique *Data Model Diagram. Name*
> > Display *Each Data Subject. Name Complete*

[PRINT]

[RETURN]
> Close report and Return to <u>Common Data Reports</u>

[Data Subject Area Name ^ Data Subject Name]

> Sort *Data Subject Area Assignment* by *Data Subject Area. Name ^ Data Subject. Name Complete*

> Display from Sort Each Unique *Data Subject Area. Name*
> > Display Each *Data Subject. Name Complete*

[PRINT]

[RETURN]
> Close report and Return to <u>Common Data Reports</u>

[Data Subject Name – Data Subject Area Detail]

> Sort *Data Subject Area Assignment* by *Data Subject . Name Completer ^ Data Subject Area. Name*

> Display from Sort Each Unique *Data Subject. Name Complete*
> > Display Each *Data Subject Area* data

[PRINT]

102

[RETURN]
   Close report and Return to <u>Common Data Reports</u>

[Data Subject Area Purpose Detail]

   Display Each *Data Subject Area Purpose* data

   [PRINT]

   [RETURN]
      Close report and Return to <u>Common Data Reports</u>

[Data Characteristic Variability]

   Each *Data Subject*
      Display *Data Subject. Name Complete*
      Each *Data Characteristic*
         Count >< 0
         Each *Data Characteristic Variation*
            Count + 1
         When Count > 0
            Display *Data Characteristic. Name Complete*, Count

   [PRINT]

   [RETURN]
      Close report and Return to <u>Common Data Reports</u>

[Data Reference Set Variability]

   Each *Data Subject*
      When *Data Subject. Data Reference Set Indicator* >< 'Yes'
         Count >< 0
         Each *Data Reference Set Variation*
            Count + 1
         When Count > 0
            Display *Data Subject. Name Complete*, Count

   [PRINT]

   [RETURN]
      Close report and Return to <u>Common Data Reports</u>

[RETURN]
   Close window and Return to <u>Common Data Function</u>

[HELP]
   Open <u>Help Message View</u>

Display Common Data Reports Help Message

Chapter 6

DATA LEXICON

Data Lexicon Function includes Common Word Task, Data Name Abbreviation Task, Data Subject Thesaurus Task, Business Term Task, and Data Lexicon Reports, as shown in Figure 6.1. It is opened from Data Resource Guide Edit / View.

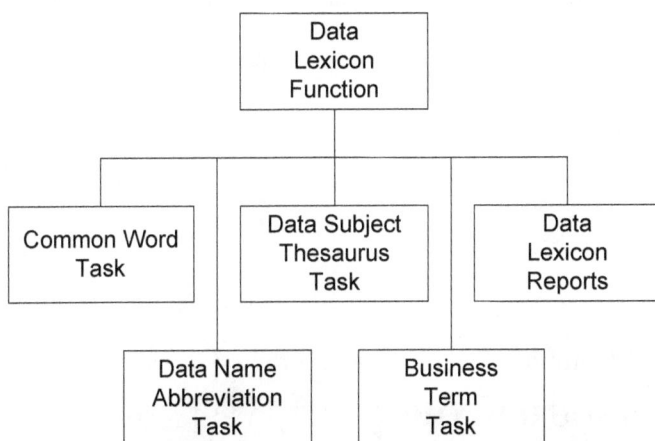

```
                    ┌─────────────┐
                    │    Data     │
                    │  Lexicon    │
                    │  Function   │
                    └─────────────┘
          ┌────────────────┼────────────────┐
  ┌──────────────┐ ┌──────────────┐ ┌──────────────┐
  │ Common Word  │ │ Data Subject │ │    Data      │
  │    Task      │ │  Thesaurus   │ │   Lexicon    │
  │              │ │    Task      │ │   Reports    │
  └──────────────┘ └──────────────┘ └──────────────┘
          ┌──────────────┐ ┌──────────────┐
          │  Data Name   │ │  Business    │
          │ Abbreviation │ │    Term      │
          │    Task      │ │    Task      │
          └──────────────┘ └──────────────┘
```

Figure 6.1. Data Lexicon Function..

The actions for Data Lexicon Function are:

[COMMON WORD TASK]
   Open Common Data Name Word Task

[DATA NAME ABBREVIATION TASK]
   Open Data Name Abbreviation Task

[DATA SUBJECT THESAURUS TASK]
   Open Data Subject Thesaurus Task

[BUSINESS TERM TASK]
   Open Business Term Task

[DATA LEXICON REPORTS]
   Open Data Lexicon Reports

[RETURN]

Close window and Return to <u>Data Resource Guide Edit / View</u>

[HELP]
Open <u>Help Message View</u>
Display Data Lexicon Function Help Message

COMMON WORD TASK

Data Common Word Task contains Data Resource Component Type, Data Name Common Word, and Data Name Common Word Thesaurus, as shown in Figure 6.2 It is opened from Data Lexicon Function.

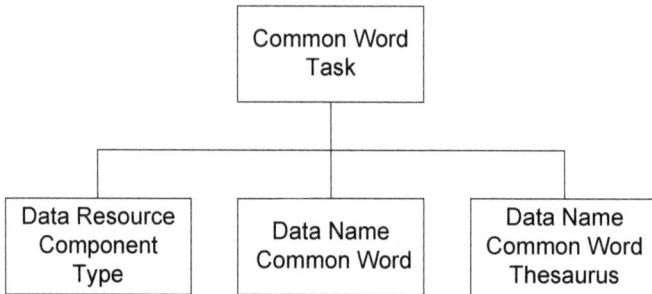

Figure 6.2. Common Word Task.

The actions for Common Data Name Word Task area:

[DATA RESOURCE COMPONENT TYPE]
Open <u>Data Resource Component Type</u>

[DATA NAME COMMON WORD]
Open <u>Data Name Common Word</u>

[DATA NAME COMMON WORD THESAURUS]
Open <u>Data Name Common Word Thesaurus</u>

[RETURN]
Close window and Return to <u>Data Lexicon Function</u>

[HELP]
Open <u>Help Message View</u>
Display Common Word Task Help Message

Data Resource Component Type

Data Resource Component Type is opened from Common Word Task. The actions for Data Resource Component Type are:

[DISPLAY]

Display Auto-Scroll List from *Data Resource Component Type*
with *Data Resource Component Type. Name*
Select *Data Resource Component Type. Name*
Display Selected *Data Resource Component Type* data

[PRINT]

(DELETE)
Delete Selected *Data Resource Component Type* occurrence

(NEW)
Display blank data fields to enter new *Data Resource Component
Type data*

[ACCEPT]

[RETURN]
Close window and Return to <u>Common Word Task</u>

[HELP]
Open <u>Help Message View</u>
Display Data Resource Component Type Help Message

Data Name Common Word

Data Name Common Word is opened from Common Word Task. The
actions for Data Name Common Word are:

[DISPLAY]
Display Auto-Scroll List from *Common Data Name Word* with
Data Name Common Word. Phrase
Select *Data Name Common Word. Phrase*
Display Selected *Data Name Common Word* data

[PRINT]

(DELETE)
Delete Selected *Data Name Common Word* occurrence

(NEW)
Display blank data fields for entry of new *Data Name Common
Word*

Display Auto-Scroll List from *Data Resource Component Type*
with *Data Resource Component Type. Name*
Select *Data Resource Component Type. Name*

[ACCEPT]

107

[RETURN]
> Close window and Return to Common Word Task

[HELP]
> Open Help Message View
> Display Data Name Common Word Help Message

Data Name Common Word Thesaurus

Data Name Common Word Thesaurus is opened from Common Word Task. The actions for Data Name Common Word Thesaurus are:

[DISPLAY]
> Display Auto-Scroll List from *Data Name Common Word Thesaurus* with *Data Name Common Word Thesaurus. Source Phrase*
> Select *Data Name Common Word Thesaurus. Source Phrase*
> Display Selected *Data Name Common Word Thesaurus* data

> [PRINT]

> (DELETE)
>> Delete Selected *Data Name Common Word Thesaurus* occurrence

(NEW)
> Display blank data fields for entry of new *Data Name Common Word Thesaurus* data
> Display Auto-Scroll List from *Data Name Common Word* with *Data Name Common Word. Phrase*
> Select *Data Name Common Word. Phrase*

> [ACCEPT]

[RETURN]
> Close window and Return to Common Word Task

[HELP]
> Open Help Message View
> Display Data Name Common Word Thesaurus Help Message

DATA NAME ABBREVIATION TASK

Data Name Abbreviation Task contains Data Name Word Set, Data Name Word, Data Name Abbreviation Algorithm, and Data Name Abbreviation Scheme, as shown in Figure 6.4. It is opened from Data Lexicon Function.

108

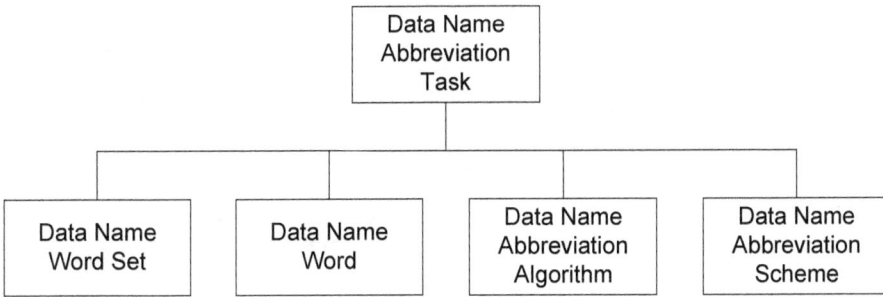

Figure 6.3. Data Name Abbreviation Task.

The actions for Data Name Abbreviation Task are:

[DATA NAME WORD SET]
Open <u>Data Name Word Set</u>

[DATA NAME WORD]
Open <u>Data Name Word</u>

[DATA NAME ABBREVIATION ALGORITHM]
Open <u>Data Name Abbreviation Algorithm</u>

[DATA NAME ABBREVIATION SCHEME]
Open D<u>ata Name Abbreviation Scheme</u>

[RETURN]
Close window and Return to <u>Data Lexicon Function</u>

[HELP]
Open <u>Help Message View</u>
Display Data Name Abbreviation Task Help Message

Data Name Word Set

Data Name Word Set is opened from Data Name Abbreviation Task. The actions for Data Name Word Set are:

[DISPLAY]
Display Auto-Scroll List from *Data Name Word Set* with *Data Name Word Set. Name*
Select *Data Name Word Set. Name*
Display Selected *Data Name Word Set* data

[PRINT]

(DELETE)
Delete Selected *Data Name Word Set* occurrence

(NEW)
>   Display blank data fields for entry of new *Data Name Word Set*
>   data

>   [ACCEPT]

[RETURN]
>   Close window and Return to <u>Data Name Abbreviation Task</u>

[HELP]
>   Open <u>Help Message View</u>
>   Display Data Name Word Set Help Message

Data Name Word

Data Name Word is opened from Data Name Abbreviation Task. The actions for Data Name Word are:

[DISPLAY]
>   Display Auto-Scroll List from *Data Name Word* with *Data Name
>   Word. Word Complete*
>   Select *Data Name Word. Word Complete*
>   Display Selected *Data Name Word* data

>   [PRINT]

>   (DELETE)
>>   Delete Selected *Data Name Word* occurrence

(NEW)
>   Display blank data fields for entry of new *Data Name Word* data

>   Display Auto-Scroll List from *Data Name Word Set* with *Data
>   Name Word Set. Name*
>   Select *Data Name Word Set. Name*

>   [ACCEPT]

[RETURN]
>   Close window and Return to <u>Data Name Abbreviation Task</u>

[HELP]
>   Open <u>Help Message View</u>
>   Display Data Name Word Help Message

Data Name Abbreviation Algorithm

Data Name Abbreviation Algorithm is opened from Data Name

110

Abbreviation Task. The actions for Data Name Abbreviation Algorithm are:

[DISPLAY]
>	Display Auto-Scroll List from *Data Name Abbreviation Algorithm*
>	with *Data Name Abbreviation Algorithm. Name*
>	Select *Data Name Abbreviation Algorithm. Name*
>	Display Selected *Data Name Abbreviation Algorithm* data

>	[PRINT]

>	(DELETE)
>>		Delete Selected *Data Name Abbreviation Algorithm* occurrence

(NEW)
>	Display blank data fields for entry of new *Data Name Abbreviation
>	Algorithm* data

>	[ACCEPT]

[RETURN]
>	Close window and Return to <u>Data Name Abbreviation Task</u>

[HELP]
>	Open <u>Help Message View</u>
>	Display Data Name Abbreviation Algorithm Set Help Message

Data Name Abbreviation Scheme

Data Name Abbreviation Scheme can be opened from several locations. The actions for Data Name Abbreviation Scheme are:

[DISPLAY]
>	Display Auto-Scroll List from *Data Name Abbreviation Scheme*
>	with *Data Name Abbreviation Scheme. Name*
>	Select *Data Name Abbreviation Scheme. Name*
>	Display Selected *Data Name Abbreviation Scheme* data

>	[PRINT]

>	(DELETE)
>>		Delete Selected *Data Name Abbreviation Scheme* occurrence

(NEW)
>	Display blank data fields for entry of new *Data Name Abbreviation
>	Scheme* data

>	Display Auto-Scroll List from *Data Name Word Set* with *Data
>	Name Word Set. Name*

111

Select *Data Name Word Set. Name*

Display Auto-Scroll List from *Data Name Abbreviation Algorithm*
with *Data Name Abbreviation Algorithm. Name*
Select *Data Name Abbreviation Algorithm. Name*

[ACCEPT]

[RETURN]
When opened from Data Name Abbreviation Task
Close window and Return to Data Name Abbreviation Task
When opened from Data Product Data Task
Close window and Return to Data Product Data Task

[HELP]
Open Help Message View
Display Data Name Abbreviation Scheme Help Message

DATA SUBJECT THESAURUS TASK

Data Subject Thesaurus Task contains Data Subject Thesaurus, as shown in Figure 6.4. It is opened from Data Lexicon Function.

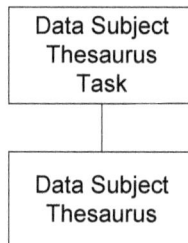

Figure 6.4. Data Subject Thesaurus Task.

The actions for Data Subject Thesaurus are:

[DATA SUBJECT THESAURUS]
Open Data Subject Thesaurus

[RETURN]
Close window and Return to Data Lexicon Function

[HELP[
Open Help Message View
Display Data Subject Thesaurus Task Help Message

112

Data Subject Thesaurus

Data Subject Thesaurus is opened from Data Subject Thesaurus Task. The actions for Data Subject Thesaurus are:

[DISPLAY SINGLE]

Sort *Data Subject Thesaurus* by *Data Subject Thesaurus. Source Phrase* ^ *Data Subject Thesaurus. Target Phrase* ^ *Data Subject. Name Complete*

Display Scroll List from Sort with *Data Subject Thesaurus. Source Phrase, Data Subject Thesaurus. Target Phrase, Data Subject Name Complete*
Select *Data Subject Thesaurus* occurrence

[PRINT]

[DELETE]

Delete *Data Subject Thesaurus* occurrence

(NEW)

Display blank data fields for entry of new *Data Subject Thesaurus* data

Display Auto-Scroll List from *Data Subject* with *Data Subject. Name Complete*

[ACCEPT]

[DISPLAY SOURCE ^ TARGET]

Sort *Data Subject Thesaurus* by *Data Subject Thesaurus. Source Phrase* ^ *Data Subject Thesaurus. Target Phrase*

Display Auto-Scroll List from Sort with Unique *Data Subject Thesaurus. Source Phrase*
Select *Data Subject Thesaurus. Source Phrase*
Display Each *Data Subject Thesaurus. Target Phrase*

[PRINT]

(NEW TARGETS)

Each new *Data Subject Thesaurus. Target Phrase* within Selected *Data Subject Thesaurus. Source Phrase*
Display blank data field for entry of new *Data Subject Thesaurus. Target Phrase*

[ACCEPT]

113

(NEW SOURCE ^ TARGETS)
> Display blank data field for entry of new *Data Subject Thesaurus. Source Phrase*
> Each new *Data Subject Thesaurus. Target Phrase*
>> Display blank data field for entry of new *Data Subject Thesaurus. Target Phrase*

> [ACCEPT]

[DISPLAY TARGET ^ SOURCE]
> Sort *Data Subject Thesaurus* by *Data Subject Thesaurus. Target Phrase ^ Data Subject Thesaurus. Source Phrase*

> Display Auto-Scroll List from Sort with Unique *Data Subject Thesaurus. Target Phrase*
> Select *Data Subject Thesaurus. Target Phrase*
>> Display Each *Data Subject Thesaurus. Source Phrase*

[PRINT]

(NEW SOURCES)
> Each new *Data Subject Thesaurus. Source Phrase* within
> Selected *Data Subject Thesaurus. Target Phrase*
>> Display blank data field for entry of new *Data Subject Thesaurus. Source Phrase*

> [ACCEPT]

(NEW TARGET ^ SOURCES)
> Display blank data field for entry of new *Data Subject Thesaurus. Target Phrase*
> Each new *Data Subject Thesaurus. Source Phrase*
>> Display blank data field for entry of new *Data Subject Thesaurus. Source Phrase*

> [ACCEPT]

[DISPLAY SUBJECT ^ SOURCE]
> Sort *Data Subject Thesaurus* by *Data Subject. Name Complete ^ Data Subject Thesaurus. Source Phrase*

> Display Auto-Scroll List from Sort with Unique *Data Subject. Name Complete*
> Select *Data Subject. Name Complete*
>> Display Each *Data Subject Thesaurus. Source Phrase*

[PRINT]

114

(NEW SOURCES)
>Each new *Data Subject Thesaurus. Source Phrase* within
>>Selected *Data Subject. Name Complete*
>>>Display blank data field for entry of new *Data Subject Thesaurus. Source Phrase*

>[ACCEPT]

(NEW SUBJECT ^ SOURCES)
>Display Auto-Scroll List from *Data Subject* with *Data Subject. Name Complete*
>Select *Data Subject. Name Complete*
>Each new *Data Subject Thesaurus. Source Phrase*
>>Display blank data field for entry of new *Data Subject Thesaurus. Source Phrase*

>[ACCEPT]

[DISPLAY SOURCE ^ SUBJECT]
>Sort *Data Subject Thesaurus* by *Data Subject Thesaurus. Source Phrase* ^ *Data Subject. Name Complete*

>Display Auto-Scroll List from Sort with Unique *Data Subject Thesaurus. Source Phrase*
>Select *Data Subject Thesaurus. Source Phrase*
>>Display Each *Data Subject. Name Complete*

[PRINT]

(NEW SUBJECTS)
>Each new *Data Subject* within Selected *Data Subject Thesaurus. Source Phrase*
>>Display Auto-Scroll List from *Data Subject* with *Data Subject. Name Complete*
>>Select *Data Subject. Name Complete*

>[ACCEPT]

(NEW SOURCE ^ SUBJECTS)
>Display blank data fields for entry of new *Data Subject Thesaurus. Source Phrase*
>Each new *Data Subject*
>>Display Auto-Scroll List from *Data Subject* with *Data Subject. Name Complete*
>>Select *Data Subject. Name Complete*

115

[ACCEPT]

[RETURN]
Close window and Return to <u>Data Subject Thesaurus Task</u>

[HELP]
Open <u>Help Message View</u>
Display Data Subject Thesaurus Help Message

BUSINESS TERM TASK

Business Term Task includes Business Glossary and Business Glossary Item, as shown in Figure 6.5. It is opened from Data Lexicon Function.

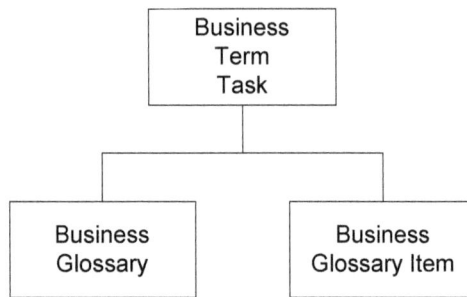

Figure 6.5. Business Term Task.

The actions for Business Term Task are:

[BUSINESS GLOSSARY]
Open <u>Business Glossary</u>

[BUSINESS GLOSSARY ITEM]
Open <u>Business Glossary Item</u>

[RETURN]
Close window and Return to <u>Data Lexicon Function</u>

[HELP]
Open <u>Help Message View</u>
Display Business Term Task Help Message

Business Glossary

Business Glossary is opened from Business Term Task. The actions for Business Glossary are:

[DISPLAY]

Display Auto-Scroll List from *Business Glossary* with *Business Glossary. Name*
Select *Business Glossary. Name*
Display Selected *Business Glossary* data

[PRINT]

(DELETE)
    Delete Selected *Business Glossary* occurrence

(NEW)
    Display blank data fields for entry of new *Business Glossary* data

    [ACCEPT]

[RETURN]
    Close window and Return to <u>Business Term Task</u>

[HELP]
    Open <u>Help Message View</u>
    Display Business Glossary Help Message

Business Glossary Item

Business Glossary Item is opened from Business Term Task. The actions for Business Glossary Item are:

Display Auto-Scroll List from *Business Glossary* with *Business Glossary. Name*
Select *Business Glossary. Name*

[DISPLAY]

    Display Auto-Scroll List from *Business Glossary Item* within Selected *Business Glossary* with *Business Glossary Item. Phrase*
    Select *Business Glossary Item. Phrase*

    Display Selected *Business Glossary Item* data

    [PRINT]

    (DELETE)
        Delete Selected *Business Glossary Item* occurrence

(NEW)
    Display blank data fields for entry of new *Business Glossary Item* data

Display Auto-Scroll List from *Business Glossary Item* within
   Selected Business Glossary with *Business Glossary Item. Phrase*
Select *"Reference" Business Glossary Item. Phrase*

   [ACCEPT]

[RETURN]
   Close window and Return to <u>Business Term Task</u>

[HELP]
   Open <u>Help Message View</u>
   Display Business Glossary Item Help Message

DATA LEXICON REPORTS

Data Lexicon Reports contains the reports for the Data Lexicon Function. It is opened from Data Lexicon Function. Only a few examples of reports are shown. Many additional reports could be developed based on an organization's needs and added to the Data Resource Guide.

The specific reports and actions to obtain those reports are:

   [Data Resource Component Type]
      Display Each *Data Resource Component Type* data

      [PRINT]

      [RETURN]
         Close report and Return to <u>Data Lexicon Reports</u>

   [Data Name Common Word Detail]
      Display Each *Data Name Common Word* data

      [PRINT]

      [RETURN]
         Close report and Return to <u>Data Lexicon Reports</u>

   [Data Resource Component Type ^ Data Name Common Word Detail]
      Display Each *Data Resource Component Type. Name*
         Display Each *Data Name Common Word* data

      [PRINT]

      [RETURN]
         Close report and Return to <u>Data Lexicon Reports</u>

   [Data Name Common Word ^ Data Name Common Word Thesaurus]
      Display Each *Data Name Common Word* data

Display Each *Data Name Common Word Thesaurus. Source Phrase*

[PRINT

[RETURN]
Close report and Return to <u>Data Lexicon Reports</u>

[Selected Data Name Common Word ^ Data Name Common Word Thesaurus]
Display Auto-Scroll List with *Data Name Common Word. Phrase*
Select *Data Name Common Word. Phrase*
Display Each *Data Name Common Word Thesaurus. Source Phrase* within Selected *Data Name Common Word*

[PRINT]

[RETURN]
Close report and Return to <u>Data Lexicon Reports</u>

[Data Name Word Set Detail]
Display Each *Data Name Word* Set data

[PRINT]

[RETURN]
Close report and Return to <u>Data Lexicon Reports</u>

[Data Name Word Detail]
Display Each *Data Name Word* data

[PRINT]

[RETURN]
Close report and Return to <u>Data Lexicon Reports</u>

[Data Name Word Set ^ Data Name Word Detail]
Display *Each Data Name Word Set* data
Display Each *Data Name Word* data

[PRINT]

[RETURN]
Close report and Return to <u>Data Lexicon Reports</u>

[Data Name Abbreviation Algorithm Detail]
Display Each *Data Name Abbreviation Algorithm* data

[PRINT]

[RETURN]
> Close report and Return to <u>Data Lexicon Reports</u>

[Data Name Abbreviation Scheme Detail]
> Display Each *Data Name Abbreviation Scheme* data

[PRINT]

[RETURN]
> Close report and Return to <u>Data Lexicon Reports</u>

[Data Name Word Set ^ Data Name Abbreviation Scheme]
> Display Each *Data Name Word Set* data
>> Display Each *Data Name Abbreviation Scheme* data

[PRINT]

[RETURN]
> Close report and Return to <u>Data Lexicon Reports</u>

[Data Name Abbreviation Algorithm ^ Data Name Abbreviation Scheme]
> Display Each *Data Name Abbreviation Algorithm* data
>> Display Each Data Name Abbreviation Scheme data

[PRINT]

[RETURN]
> Close report and Return to <u>Data Lexicon Reports</u>

[Data Subject Thesaurus Source Phrase ^ Target Phrase]
> Sort *Data Subject Thesaurus* by *Data Subject Thesaurus. Source Phrase ^ Data Subject Thesaurus. Target Phrase*
>
> Display from Sort Each Unique *Data Subject Thesaurus. Source Phrase*
>> Display Each *Data Subject Thesaurus. Target Phrase*

[PRINT]

[RETURN]
> Close report and Return to <u>Data Lexicon Reports</u>

[Data Subject Thesaurus Target Phrase ^ Source Phrase]
> Sort *Data Subject Thesaurus* by *Data Subject Thesaurus. Target Phrase ^ Data Subject Thesaurus. Source Phrase*
>
> Display from Sort Each Unique *Data Subject Thesaurus. Target Phrase*

Display Each *Data Subject Thesaurus. Source Phrase*

[PRINT]

[RETURN]
Close report and Return to <u>Data Lexicon Reports</u>

[Data Subject Thesaurus Source Phrase ^ Data Subject]
Sort *Data Subject Thesaurus* by *Data Subject Thesaurus. Source Phrase* ^ *Data Subject . Name Complete*

Display from Sort Each Unique *Data Subject Thesaurus. Source Phrase*
Display Each *Data Subject. Name Complete*

[PRINT]

[RETURN]
Close report and Return to <u>Data Lexicon Reports</u>

[Data Subject ^ Data Subject Thesaurus Source Phrase]
Sort *Data Subject Thesaurus* by *Data Subject. Name Complete* ^ *Data Subject Thesaurus. Source Phrase*

Display from Sort Each Unique *Data Subject. Name Complete*
Display Each *Data Subject Thesaurus. Source Phrase*

[PRINT]

[RETURN]
Close report and Return to <u>Data Lexicon Reports</u>

[Business Glossary Name]
Display Each *Business Glossary. Name*

[PRINT]

[RETURN]
Close report and Return to <u>Data Lexicon Reports</u>

[Business Glossary Detail]
Display Each *Business Glossary* data

[PRINT]

[RETURN]
Close report and Return to <u>Data Lexicon Reports</u>

[Business Glossary Name ^ Business Glossary Item Name
Display Each *Business Glossary. Name*

Display Each *Business Glossary Item. Phrase*

[PRINT]

[RETURN]
Close report and Return to <u>Data Lexicon Reports</u>

[Business Glossary Name ^ Business Glossary Item Detail]
Display Each *Business Glossary. Name*
Display Each *Business Glossary Item* data

[PRINT]

[RETURN]
Close report and Return to <u>Data Lexicon Reports</u>

[Selected Business Glossary Name ^ Business Glossary Item Detail]
Display Auto-Scroll List from *Business Glossary* with *Business Glossary. Name*
Select *Business Glossary. Name*

Display Each *Business Glossary Item* data within Selected *Business Glossary*

[PRINT]

[RETURN]
Close report and Return to <u>Data Lexicon Reports</u>

[RETURN]
Close window and Return to <u>Data Lexicon Function</u>

[HELP]
Open <u>Help Message View</u>
Display Data Lexicon Reports Help Message

Chapter 7

DATA CROSS-REFERENCE

The Data Cross-Reference Function includes Data Cross-Reference Task and Data Cross-Reference Reports, as shown in Figure 7.1. It is opened from Data Resource Guide Edit / View.

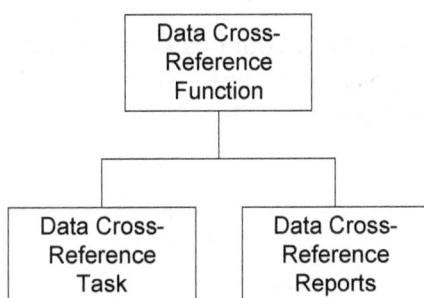

Figure 7.1. Data Cross-Reference Function.

The actions for Data Cross-Reference Function are:

[DATA CROSS-REFERENCE TASK]
    Open <u>Data Cross-Reference Task</u>

[DATA CROSS-REFERENCE REPORTS]
    Open <u>Data Cross-Reference Reports</u>

[RETURN]
    Close window and Return to <u>Data Resource Guide Edit / View</u>

[HELP]
    Open <u>Help Message View</u>
    Display Data Cross-Reference Function Help Message

DATA CROSS-REFERENCE TASK

Data Cross-Reference Task is only for those people with authorization to edit the Data Resource Data. Therefore, only Edit windows need to be created for the Data Cross-Reference Tasks. View windows do not need to be created. The viewing can be done through the View windows described in the Data Inventory Chapter.

123

Data Cross-References are created as described in the Data Cross-Reference routines below. Data Cross-References cannot be created as described in the Data Inventory Chapter.

The Data Cross-Reference routines only display data relative to making the data cross-references. All of the data inventory data are not displayed in the Data Cross-Reference routines, but can be viewed as described in the Data Inventory Chapter.

The Data Cross-Reference Reports only contain data relative to the data cross-references. All of the data inventory data are not displayed in the Data Cross-Reference Reports, but can be displayed in the Data Inventory Reports described the Data Inventory Chapter.

The Data Cross-Reference Task contains Data Product Set Cross-Reference, Data Product Unit Cross-Reference, and Data Product Code Cross-Reference as shown in Figure 7.2. It is opened from Data Cross-Reference Function.

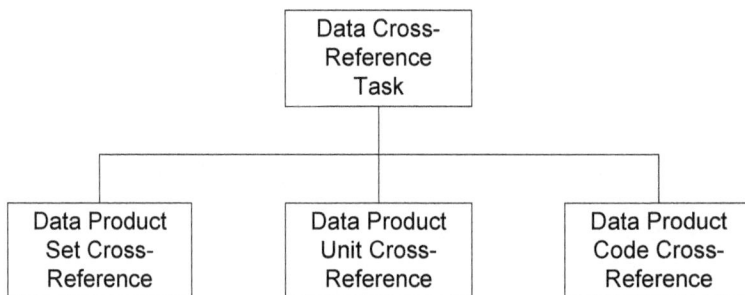

Figure 7.2. Data Cross-Reference Task.

The actions for the Data Cross-Reference Task are:

[DATA PRODUCT SET CROSS-REFERENCE]
   Open Data Product Set Cross-Reference

[DATA PRODUCT UNIT CROSS-REFERENCE]
   Open Data Product Unit Cross-Reference

[DATA PRODUCT CODE CROSS-REFERENCE]
   Open Data Product Code Cross-Reference

[RETURN]
   Close window and Return to Data Cross-Reference Function.

[HELP]
   Open Help Message View
   Display Data Cross-Reference Task Help Message

The data structure of Data Product Data, Common Data, and the cross-references between Data Product Data and Common Data is shown in Figure 7.3. The Data Product Data are shown on the left and the Common Data are shown on the right. The three data cross-references are shown between the Data Product Data and the Common Data. The data structure can be used to understand the data cross-referencing actions.

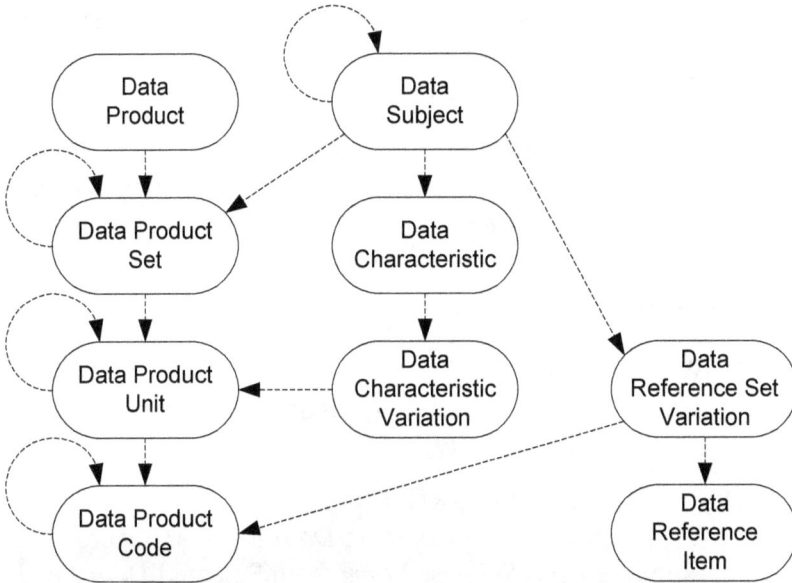

Figure 7.3. Data Product Data Structure.

Data Product Set Cross-Reference

Data Product Sets can be cross-referenced to Data Subjects under certain conditions described in *Data Resource Data* and *Data Resource Understanding*.

Data Product Set may have one level of subordinate Data Product Set Variation, as explained in *Data Resource Data* and *Data Resource Understanding*. When a subordinate Data Product Set Variation exists, it can be cross-referenced to a Data Subject and the parent Data Product Set cannot be cross-referenced to a Data Subject. When a subordinate Data Product Set Variation does not exist, the parent Data Product Set can be cross-referenced to a Data Subject.

The actions for Data Product Set Cross-Reference are:

Display Auto-Scroll List from *Data Product* with *Data Product. Name*
Select *Data Product. Name*

Display Auto-Scroll List from *Data Product Set* within Selected *Data Product* with *Data Product Set. Name*
Select *Data Product Set. Name*

[DISPLAY SET]
  Comment: *Data Product Set* cross-referencing.
  Display from Selected *Data Product Set* with *Data Product Set. Name, Data Product Set. Cross-Reference Comment, Data Subject. Name Complete*

  (CROSS-REFERENCE SET)
    Comment: Cross-reference *Data Product Set* to *Data Subject.*
    Display Auto-Scroll List from *Data Subject* with *Data Subject. Name Complete*
    Select *Data Subject. Name Complete*

    [ACCEPT]

  (NEW DATA SUBJECT)
    Comment: Create a new *Data Subject* for cross-referencing.
    Open <u>Data Subject Edit</u>

  (DELETE SET CROSS-REFERENCE)
    Comment: Remove existing *Data Product Set* cross-reference.
    Remove *Data Subject. Name* from Selected *Data Product Set*

    [ACCEPT]

[DISPLAY SET VARIATION]
  Comment: *Data Product Set Variation* cross-referencing.
  Display Auto-Scroll List from *Data Product Set Variation* within Selected *Data Product Set* with *Data Product Set Variation. Name*
  Select *Data Product Set Variation. Name*
  Display Selected *Data Product Set Variation. Name, Data Product Set Variation. Cross-Reference Comment, Data Subject. Name Complete*

  (CROSS-REFERENCE SET VARIATION)
    Comment: Cross-reference *Data Product Set Variation* to *Data Subject.*
    Display Auto-Scroll List from *Data Subject* with *Data Subject. Name Complete*
    Select *Data Subject. Name Complete*

[ACCEPT]

(NEW DATA SUBJECT)
Comment: Create a new *Data Subject* for cross-referencing.
Open <u>Data Subject Edit</u>

(DELETE VARIATION CROSS-REFERENCE)
Comment: Remove existing *Data Product Set Variation* cross-reference.
Remove *Data Subject. Name Complete* from Selected *Data Product Set Variation*

[ACCEPT]

[RETURN]
Close window and Return to <u>Data Cross-Reference Task</u>

[HELP]
Open <u>Help Message View</u>
Display Data Product Set Cross-Reference Help Message

Data Product Unit Cross-Reference

Data Product Unit can be cross-referenced to Data Characteristic Variation. Data Product Unit may have one level of subordinate Data Product Unit Variation, as explained in *Data Resource Data* and *Data Resource Understanding*. When a subordinate Data Product Unit Variation exists, it can be cross-referenced to a Data Characteristic Variation and the parent Data Product Unit cannot be cross-referenced to a Data Characteristic Variation. When a subordinate Data Product Unit Variation does not exist, the parent Data Product Unit can be cross-referenced to a Data Characteristic Variation.

The actions for Data Product Unit Cross-References are:

Display Auto-Scroll List from *Data Product Unit* with *Data Product. Name*
Select *Data Product. Name*

Display Auto-Scroll List from *Data Product Set* within Selected *Data Product* with *Data Product Set. Name*
Select *Data Product Set. Name*

[SELECT SET VARIATION]
Comment: Select *Data Product Set Variation* within *Data Product Set.* When in *Data Product Set Variation*, must return and re-

open the routine to cancel the selected *Data Product Set Variation*.

Display Auto-Scroll List from *Data Product Set Variation* within Selected *Data Product Set* with *Data Product Set Variation. Name Complete*

Select *Data Product Set Variation*

Display Scroll List from *Data Product Unit* within Selected {*Data Product Set* | *Data Product Set Variation*}with *Data Product Unit. Name, Data Product Unit. Mnemonic*

Select *Data Product Unit*

[DISPLAY UNIT]

Comment: Display *Data Product Unit* for cross-referencing.

Display Selected *Data Product Unit. Name, Data Product Unit. Mnemonic, Data Product Unit. Cross-Reference Comment, Data Characteristic Variation. Name Complete*

(CROSS-REFERENCE UNIT)

Comment: Cross-reference *Data Product Unit* to *Data Characteristic Variation*

Display Auto-Scroll List from *Data Subject* with *Data Subject. Name Complete*

Select *Data Subject. Name Complete*

Display Auto-Scroll List from *Data Characteristic* within Selected *Data Subject* with *Data Characteristic. Name Complete*

Select *Data Characteristic. Name Complete*

Display Auto-Scroll List from *Data Characteristic Variation* within Selected *Data Characteristic* with *Data Characteristic Variation. Name Complete*

Select *Data Characteristic Variation. Name Complete*

[ACCEPT]

(NEW CHARACTERISTIC VARIATION)

Comment: Create new *Data Characteristic Variation*. New *Data Subject* and new *Data Characteristic* can be created as described in the Common Data Chapter.

Open Data Characteristic Variation Edit

(DELETE UNIT CROSS-REFERENCE)

Comment: Remove existing *Data Product Unit* cross-
reference.

Remove *Data Characteristic Variation. Name Complete* from
Selected *Data Product Unit.*

[ACCEPT]

[DISPLAY UNIT VARIATION]
Comment: *Data Product Unit Variation* cross-referencing.

Display Scroll List from *Data Product Unit Variation* within
Selected *Data Product Unit* with *Data Product Unit Variation.*
Name, Data Product Unit Variation. Mnemonic
Select *Data Product Unit Variation*

Display Selected *Data Product Unit Variation. Name, Data
Product Unit Variation. Mnemonic, Data Product Unit Variation.
Cross-Reference Comment, Data Characteristic Variation. Name
Complete*

(CROSS-REFERENCE UNIT)
Comment: Cross-reference *Data Product Unit Variation* to
Data Characteristic Variation.

Display Auto-Scroll List from *Data Subject* with *Data Subject.*
Name Complete
Select *Data Subject. Name Complete*

Display Auto-Scroll List from *Data Characteristic* within
Selected *Data Subject* with *Data Characteristic. Name
Complete*
Select *Data Characteristic. Name Complete*

Display Auto-Scroll List from *Data Characteristic Variation*
within Selected *Data Characteristic* with *Data Characteristic
Variation. Name Complete*
Select *Data Characteristic Variation. Name Complete*

[ACCEPT]

(NEW CHARACTERISTIC VARIATION)
Comment: Create new *Data Characteristic Variation.*
Open Data Characteristic Variation Edit

(DELETE VARIATION CROSS-REFERENCE)
Comment: Remove existing *Data Product Unit Variation*
cross-reference.

129

Remove *Data Characteristic Variation. Name Complete* from Selected *Data Product Unit Variation*

[ACCEPT]

[RETURN]
Close window and Return to <u>Data Cross-Reference Task</u>

[HELP]
Open *Help Message View*
Display Data Product Unit Cross-Reference Help Message

Data Product Code Cross-Reference

Data Product Code can be cross-referenced to Data Reference Set Variation. Data Product Code may have one level of subordinate Data Product Code Variation, as explained in *Data Resource Data* and *Data Resource Understanding*. When a subordinate Data Product Code Variation exists, the parent Data Product Code cannot be cross-referenced to a Data Reference Set Variation. When a subordinate Data Product Code Variation does not exist, the parent Data Product Code can be cross-referenced to a Data Reference Set Variation.

The actions for Data Product Code Cross-References are:

Display Auto-Scroll List from *Data Product* with *Data Product. Name*
Select *Data Product. Name*

Display Auto-Scroll List from *Data Product Set* within Selected *Data Product* with *Data Product Set. Name*
Select *Data Product Set. Name*

[SELECT SET VARIATION]
Comment: Select *Data Product Set Variation* within *Data Product Set*. When in *Data Product Set Variation*, must return and re-open the routine to cancel the selected *Data Product Set Variation*.

Display Auto-Scroll List from *Data Product Set Variation* within Selected *Data Product Set* with *Data Product Set Variation. Name*
Select *Data Product Set Variation. Name*

Display Scroll List from *Data Product Unit* within Selected {*Data Product Set | Data Product Set Variation*} with *Data Product Unit. Name, Data Product Unit. Mnemonic*
Select *Data Product Unit*

130

[SELECT UNIT VARIATION]
> Comment: Select *Data Product Unit Variation* within Selected *Data Product Unit*. When in *Data Product Unit Variation*, must return and re-open the routine to cancel the selected *Data Product Unit Variation*.
>
> Display Scroll List from *Data Product Unit Variation* within Selected *Data Product Unit* with *Data Product Unit Variation. Name, Data Product Unit Variation. Mnemonic*

[DISPLAY CODE}
> Comment: *Data Product Code* cross-referencing.
> Display Scroll List from *Data Product Code* within Selected {*Data Product Unit | Data Product Unit Variation*} with *Data Product Code. Definition, Data Product Code. Name, Data Product Code. Value*
> Select *Data Product Code*

(CROSS-REFERENCE CODE
> Comment: Cross-reference *Data Product Code* to *Data Reference Set Variation*
> Display Auto-Scroll List from *Data Subject* with *Data Subject. Name Complete* When *Data Subject. Data Reference Set Indicator >< 'Yes'*
> Select *Data Subject. Name Complete*
>
> Display Auto-Scroll List from *Data Reference Set Variation* within Selected *Data Subject* with *Data Reference Set Variation. Name Complete*
> Select *Data Reference Set Variation. Name Complete*
>
> [ACCEPT]

(NEW REFERENCE SET)
> Comment: Create new *Data Reference Set Variation* within Selected *Data Subject*.
> Open <u>Data Reference Set Variation Edit</u>

(DELETE CODE CROSS-REFERENCE)
> Comment: Remove existing *Data Product Code* cross-reference.
> Remove *Data Reference Set Variation. Name Complete* from *Data Product Code*
>
> [ACCEPT]

[DISPLAY CODE VARIATION]
> Comment: *Data Produce Code Variation* cross-referencing.
> Display Scroll List from *Data Product Code Variation* within
>   Selected *Data Product Code* with *Data Product Code Variation.*
>   *Definition, Data Product Code Variation. Name, Data Product*
>   *Code Variation. Value*
> Select *Data Product Code Variation*

> (CROSS-REFERENCE CODE VARIATION)
> > Comment: Cross-reference *Data Product Code Variation* to
> >   *Data Reference Set Variation.*
> > Display Auto-Scroll List from *Data Subject* with *Data Subject.*
> >   *Name Complete* When *Data Subject. Data Reference Set*
> >   *Indicator* >< 'Yes'
> > Select *Data Subject. Name Complete*

> > Display Auto-Scroll List from *Data Reference Set Variation*
> >   within Selected *Data Subject* with *Data Reference Set*
> >   *Variation. Name Complete*
> > Select *Data Reference Set Variation. Name Complete*

> > [ACCEPT]

> (NEW REFERENCE SET)
> > Comment: Create new *Data Reference Set Variation* within
> >   Selected *Data Subject.*
> > Open Data Reference Set Variation Edit

> (DELETE VARIATION CROSS-REFERENCE)
> > Comment: Remove existing *Data Product Code Variation*
> >   cross-reference.
> > Remove *Data Reference Set Variation. Name Complete* from
> >   *Data Product Code Variation*

> > [ACCEPT]

[RETURN]
> Close window and Return to Data Cross-Reference Task

[HELP]
> Open Help Message View
> Display Data Product Code Cross-Reference Help Message

DATA CROSS-REFERENCE REPORTS

Data Cross-Reference Reports contains reports for Data Cross-Reference Function. It is opened from Data Cross-Reference Function. Only a few examples of reports are shown. Many additional reports could be developed based on an organization's needs and added to the Data Resource Guide.

Data Product Set can have one level of subordinate Data Product Set Variation, Data Product Unit can have one level of subordinate Data Product Unit Variation, and Data Product Code can have one level of subordinate Data Product Code Variation as described in *Data Resource Data* and *Data Resource Understanding*.

All Data Cross-Reference Reports display only data relative to data cross-references between Data Product Data and Common Data. Otherwise the reports could show large quantities of data that are not relevant to any cross-referencing. Each organization can change the Data Cross-Reference Report specifications to meet their needs.

All Data Cross-Reference Reports select a specific Data Product for the Data Product Data and a specific Data Subject for the Common Data. Otherwise the reports could be exceptionally long and difficult to interpret. Each organization can change the Data Cross-Reference Report specifications to meet their need.

The specific reports and actions to obtain those reports are:

[Data Product Set To Data Subject}
    Comment: Displays *Data Product Set* and *Data Product Set Variation* within a Selected *Data Product* that are cross-referenced to *Data Subject* with cross-reference comments.

    Display Auto-Scroll List from *Data Product* with *Data Product. Name*
    Select *Data Product. Name*
    Display *Data Product. Name*

    Each *Data Product Set* within Selected *Data Product*
        Data Product Set Display >< 'No'
        When *Data Subject. Name Complete* <> ' '
            Display *Data Product Set. Name, Data Subject. Name Complete, Data Product Set. Cross-Reference Comment*

        Each *Data Product Set Variation*
            When *Data Subject. Name Complete* <> ' '
                When Data Product Set Display >< 'No'

Display *Data Product Set. Name*
Data Product Set Display >< 'Yes'
Display *Data Product Set Variation. Name, Data
Subject. Name Complete, Data Product Set
Variation. Cross-Reference Comment*

[PRINT]

[RETURN]
Close report and Return to <u>Data Cross-Reference Reports</u>

[Data Product Unit To Data Characteristic Variation}
Comment: Displays *Data Product Unit* and *Data Product Unit
Variation* within Selected *Data Product* that are cross-referenced
to *Data Characteristic Variation* with cross-reference comments.

Display Auto-Scroll List from *Data Product* with *Data Product.
Name*
Select *Data Product. Name*
Display *Data Product. Name*

Each *Data Product Set* within Selected *Data Product*
Data Product Set Name Display >< 'No'

Each *Data Product Unit*
Data Product Unit Name Display >< 'No'
When *Data Characteristic Variation. Name Complete* <>
' '

When Data Product Set Name Display >< 'No'
Display *Data Product Set. Name*
Data Product Set Name Display >< 'Yes'
Display *Data Product Unit. Name, Data Product
Unit. Mnemonic, Data Product Unit. Cross-
Reference Comment*

Each *Data Product Unit Variation*
When *Data Characteristic Variation. Name Complete*
>< ' '
When Data Product Set Name Display >< 'No'
Display Data Product Set. Name
Data Product Set Name Display >< 'Yes'
When Data Product Unit Name Display >< 'No'
Display *Data Product Unit. Name, Data
Product Unit. Mnemonic*
Data Product Unit Name Display >< 'Yes'

Display *Data Product Unit Variation. Name,*
Data Product Unit Variation. Mnemonic, Data
Product Unit Variation. Cross-Reference
Comment

Each *Data Product Set Variation*
Data Product Set Variation Name Display >< 'No'

Each *Data Product Unit*
Data Product Unit Name Display >< 'No'

When *Data Characteristic Variation. Name Complete*
<> ' '
When Data Product Set Name Display >< 'No'
Display *Data Product Set. Name*
Data Product Set Name Display >< 'Yes'
When Data Product Set Variation Name Display
>< 'No'
Display *Data Product Set Variation. Name*
Data Product Set Variation Name Display ><
'Yes'
Display *Data Product Unit. Name, Data Product*
Unit. Mnemonic, Data Product Unit. Cross-
Reference Comment

Each *Data Product Unit Variation*
When *Data Characteristic Variation. Name*
Complete >< ' '
When Data Product Set Name Display ><
'No'
Display *Data Product Set. Name*
Data Product Set Name Display ><
'Yes'
When Data Product Set Variation Name
Display >< 'No'
Display *Data Product Set Variation.*
Name
Data Product Set Variation Name
Display >< 'Yes'
When Data Product Unit Name Display ><
'No'
Display *Data Product Unit. Name, Data*
Product Unit. Mnemonic

135

Display *Data Product Unit Variation. Name, Data Product Unit Variation. Mnemonic, Data Reference Set Variation. Name, Data Product Unit Variation. Cross-Reference Comment*

[PRINT]

[RETURN]
Close report and Return to <u>Data Cross-Reference Reports</u>

[Data Product Code To Data Reference Set Variation]
Comment: Displays *Data Product Code* and *Data Product Code Variation* within Selected *Data Product* that are cross-referenced to *Data Reference Set Variation* with cross-reference comments.

Display Auto-Scroll List from *Data Product* with *Data Product. Name*
Select *Data Product. Name*
Display *Data Product. Name*
Data Product Code Hit >< 'No'
Each *Data Product Set* within Selected *Data Product*
    Each *Data Product Unit*
        Each *Data Product Code*
            When *Data Reference Set Variation. Name Complete* <> ' '
                Save to *Hold* File with *Data Product Set. Name* ^ *Data Product Set Variation. Name* >< ' ' ^ *Data Product Unit. Name, Data Product Unit. Mnemonic* ^ *Data Product Unit Variation. Name* >< ' ', *Data Product Unit Variation. Mnemonic* >< ' ' ^ *Data Product Code. Name, Data Product Code. Value, Data Product Code. Definition, Data Reference Set Variation. Name Complete, Data Product Code. Cross-Reference Comment* ^ *Data Product Code Variation. Name* >< ' ', *Data Product Code Variation. Value* >< ' ', *Data Reference Set Variation. Name Complete* >< ' ', *Data Product Code Variation. Cross-Reference Comment* >< ' '

            Each *Data Product Code Variation*
                When *Data Reference Set Variation. Name Complete* <> ' '

Save to Hold File with *Data Product Set. Name ^ Data Product Set Variation. Name >< ' ' ^ Data Product Unit. Name, Data Product Unit. Mnemonic ^ Data Product Unit Variation. Name >< ' ', Data Product Unit Variation. Mnemonic >< ' ' ^ Data Product Code. Name, Data Product Code. Value, Data Product Code. Definition, Data Reference Set Variation. Name Complete, Data Product Code. Cross-Reference Comment ^ Data Product Code Variation. Name, Data Product Code Variation. Value, Data Reference Set Variation. Name Complete, Data Product Code Variation. Cross-Reference Comment*

Each *Data Product Unit Variation*
Each *Data Product Code*
When *Data Reference Set Variation. Name Complete* <> ' '

Save to Hold File with *Data Product Set. Name ^ Data Product Set Variation. Name ^ Data Product Unit. Name, Data Product Unit. Mnemonic ^ Data Product Unit Variation. Name, Data Product Unit Variation. Mnemonic ^ Data Product Code. Name, Data Product Code. Value, Data Product Code. Definition, Data Reference Set Variation. Name Complete, Data Product Code. Cross-Reference Comment ^ Data Product Code Variation. Name, Data Product Code Variation. Value,* Data Reference Set Variation. Name Complete, *Data Product Code Variation. Cross-Reference Comment*

Each *Data Product Code Variation*
When *Data Reference Set Variation. Name Complete* <> ' '

Save to Hold File with *Data Product Set. Name ^ Data Product Set Variation. Name >< ' ' ^ Data Product Unit.*

137

Name, *Data Product Unit. Mnemonic ^
Data Product Unit Variation. Name,
Data Product Unit Variation.
Mnemonic ^ Data Product Code.
Name, Data Product Code. Value,
Data Product Code. Definition, Data
Reference Set Variation. Name
Complete, Data Product Code. Cross-
Reference Comment ^ Data Product
Code Variation. Name, Data Product
Code Variation. Value, Data Reference
Set Variation. Name Complete, Data
Product Code Variation. Cross-
Reference Comment*

Each *Data Product Set Variation*
   Each *Data Product Unit*
      Each *Data Product Code*
         When *Data Reference Set Variation. Name
            Complete* <> ' '
            Save to Hold File with *Data Product Set.
              Name ^ Data Product Set Variation. Name
              ^ Data Product Unit. Name, Data Product
              Unit. Mnemonic ^ Data Product Unit
              Variation. Name >< ' ', Data Product Unit
              Variation. Mnemonic >< ' ' ^ Data Product
              Code. Name, Data Product Code. Value,
              Data Product Code. Definition, Data
              Reference Set Variation. Name Complete,
              Data Product Code. Cross-Reference
              Comment ^ Data Product Code Variation.
              Name >< ' ', Data Product Code
              Variation. Value >< ' ', Data Reference Set
              Variation. Name Complete >< ' ', Data
              Product Code Variation. Cross-Reference
              Comment >< ' '*

         Each *Data Product Code Variation*
            When *Data Reference Set Variation. Name
              Complete* <> ' '
              Save to *Hold File* with *Data Product
                Set. Name ^ Data Product Set*

Variation. Name ^ Data Product Unit. Name, Data Product Unit. Mnemonic ^ Data Product Unit Variation. Name >< ' ', Data Product Unit Variation. Mnemonic >< ' ' ^ Data Product Code. Name, Data Product Code. Value, Data Product Code. Definition, Data Reference Set Variation. Name Complete, Data Product Code. Cross-Reference Comment ^ Data Product Code Variation. Name, Data Product Code Variation. Value, Data Reference Set Variation. Name Complete, Data Product Code Variation. Cross-Reference Comment

Each *Data Product Unit Variation*
  Each *Data Product Code*
    When *Data Reference Set Variation. Name Complete <> ' '*
      Save to Hold File with *Data Product Set. Name ^ Data Product Set Variation. Name ^ Data Product Unit. Name, Data Product Unit. Mnemonic ^ Data Product Unit Variation. Name, Data Product Unit Variation. Mnemonic ^ Data Product Code. Name, Data Product Code. Value, Data Product Code. Definition, Data Reference Set Variation. Name Complete, Data Product Code. Cross-Reference Comment ^ Data Product Code Variation. Name >< ' ', Data Product Code Variation. Value >< ' ', Data Reference Set Variation. Name Complete >< ' ', Data Product Code Variation. Cross-Reference Comment >< ' '*

  Each *Data Product Code Variation*
    When *Data Reference Set Variation. Name Complete <> ' '*

139

Save to Hold File with *Data Product Set. Name ^ Data Product Set Variation. Name ^ Data Product Unit. Name, Data Product Unit. Mnemonic ^ Data Product Unit Variation. Name, Data Product Unit Variation. Mnemonic ^ Data Product Code. Name, Data Product Code. Value, Data Product Code. Definition, Data Reference Set Variation. Name Complete, Data Product Code. Cross-Reference Comment ^ Data Product Code Variation. Name, Data Product Code Variation. Value, Data Product Code Variation. Definition, Data Reference Set Variation. Name Complete, Data Product Code Variation. Cross-Reference Comment*

When Data Product Code Hit >< 'Yes'

Sort *Hold File* by *Data Product Set. Name, Data Product Set Variation. Name, Data Product Unit. Name, Data Product Unit. Mnemonic, Data Product Unit Variation. Name, Data Product Unit. Mnemonic, Data Product Code. Name, Data Product Code. Value, Data Product Code. Definition, Data Product Code Variation. Name, Data Product Code Variation. Value, Data Product Code Variation. Definition*

Display from Sort

Each Unique *Data Product Set. Name*

Each Unique *Data Product Set Variation. Name*

Each Unique *Data Product Unit. Name*

Each Unique *Data Product Unit Variation. Name*

Each Unique *Data Product Code. Name, Data Product Code. Value, Data Product Code. Definition, Data Reference Set Variation. Name*

140

Complete, Data Product Code. Cross-Reference Comment
     Each *Data Product Code Variation. Name, Data Product Code Variation. Value, Data Product Code Variation. Definition, Data Reference Set Variation. Name Complete, Data Product Code Variation. Cross-Reference Comment*

[PRINT]

[RETURN]
     Close report and Return to <u>Data Cross-Reference Reports</u>

[Data Product Set From Data Subject]
     Display Auto-Scroll List from *Data Subject* with *Data Subject. Name Complete*
     Select *Data Subject. Name Complete*
     Display *Data Subject. Name Complete*
     Subordinate Hit >< 'No'
     Each *Data Product Set* I *Data Product Set Variation* v Selected *Data Subject*
          Subordinate Hit >< 'Yes'

          When *Data Product Set Variation* v *Data Subject*
               Save to Hold File with *Data Product. Name* ^ *Data Product Set. Name, Data Product Set. Cross-Reference Comment* >< ' ' ^ *Data Product Set Variation. Name, Data Product Set Variation. Cross-Reference Comment*

          When *Data Product Set* v *Data Subject*
               Save to Hold File with *Data Product. Name* ^ *Data Product Set. Name, Data Product Set. Cross-Reference Comment* ^ *Data Product Set Variation. Name* >< ' ', *Data Product Set Variation. Cross-Reference Comment* >< ' '

     When Subordinate Hit >< 'Yes'
          Sort *Hold File* by *Data Product. Name* ^ *Data Product Set. Name* ^ *Data Product Set Variation. Name*
          Display from Sort
               Each Unique *Data Product. Name*

141

Each Unique *Data Product Set. Name, Data Product
Set. Cross-Reference Comment*
Each *Data Product Set Variation. Name, Data
Product Set Variation. Cross-Reference
Comment*

[PRINT]

[RETURN]
Close report and Return to <u>Data Cross-Reference Reports</u>

[Data Product Unit From Data Characteristic Variation]
Display Auto-Scroll List from *Data Subject* When *Data Subject.
Reference Set Indicator* >< 'Yes' with *Data Subject. Name
Complete*
Select *Data Subject. Name Complete*
Display *Data Subject. Name Complete*
Each *Data Characteristic* within Selected *Data Subject*
Each *Data Characteristic Variation*
Subordinate Hit >< 'No'
Each *Data Product Unit* | *Data Product Unit Variation* ∨
Data Characteristic Variation
Subordinate Hit >< 'Yes'

When *Data Product Unit Variation* ∨ *Data
Characteristic Variation*

When *Data Product Set Variation* ^ *Data
Product Unit* ^ *Data Product Unit Variation*
Save to Hold File with *Data Product. Name,
^ Data Product Set. Name ^ Data Product
Set Variation. Name ^ Data Product Unit.
Name, Data Product Unit. Mnemonic, Data
Product Unit. Cross-Reference Comment*
>< ' ', *Data Product Unit Variation. Name,
Data Product Unit Variation. Mnemonic,
Data Product Unit Variation. Cross-
Reference Comment*

When *Data Product Set* ^ *Data Product Unit* ^
Data Product Unit Variation
Save to Hold File with *Data Product. Name,
^ Data Product Set. Name ^ Data Product
Set Variation. Name* >< ' ' ^ *Data Product*

142

Unit. Name, Data Product Unit. Mnemonic, Data Product Unit. Cross-Reference Comment >< ' ', *Data Product Unit Variation. Name, Data Product Unit Variation. Mnemonic, Data Product Unit Variation. Cross-Reference Comment*

When *Data Product Unit* ∨ *Data Characteristic Variation*

When *Data Product Set Variation* ∧ *Data Product Unit*

Save to Hold File with *Data Product. Name,* ∧ *Data Product Set. Name* ∧ *Data Product Set Variation. Name* ∧ *Data Product Unit. Name, Data Product Unit. Mnemonic, Data Product Unit. Cross-Reference Comment* ∧ *Data Product Unit Variation. Name* >< ' ' *Data Product Unit Variation. Mnemonic* >< ' ', *Data Product Unit Variation. Cross-Reference Comment* >< ' '

When *Data Product Set* ∧ *Data Product Unit*

Save to Hold File with *Data Product. Name,* ∧ *Data Product Set. Name* ∧ *Data Product Set Variation. Name* >< ' ' ∧ *Data Product Unit. Name, Data Product Unit. Mnemonic, Data Product Unit. Cross-Reference Comment* ∧ *Data Product Unit Variation. Name* >< ' ' *Data Product Unit Variation. Mnemonic* >< ' ', *Data Product Unit Variation. Cross-Reference Comment* >< ' '

When Subordinate Hit >< 'Yes'

Sort *Hold File* by *Data Product. Name* ∧ *Data Product Set. Name* ∧ *Data Product Set Variation. Name, Data Product Unit. Name, Data Product Unit. Mnemonic* ∧ *Data Product Unit Variation. Name, Data Product Unit. Mnemonic*

Display from Sort

Each Unique *Data Product. Name*

Each Unique *Data Product Set. Name*

Each Unique *Data Product Set Variation. Name*

Each Unique *Data Product Unit. Name, Data Product Unit. Mnemonic, Data Product Unit. Cross-Reference Comment*

Each *Data Product Unit. Name Variation. Name, Data Product Unit Variation. Mnemonic, Data Product Unit Variation. Cross-Reference Comment*

[PRINT]

[RETURN]

Close report and Return to <u>Data Cross-Reference Reports</u>

[Data Product Code From Data Reference Set Variation]

Display Auto-Scroll List from *Data Subject* When *Data Subject. Reference Set Indicator* >< 'Yes' with *Data Subject. Name Complete*

Select *Data Subject. Name Complete*

Display *Data Subject. Name Complete*

Each *Data Reference Set* within Selected *Data Subject*

Subordinate Hit >< 'No'

Each *Data Product Code* | *Data Product Code Variation* v Selected *Data Reference Set Variation*

Subordinate Hit >< 'Yes'

When *Data Reference Set Variation* ^ *Data Product Code* ^ *Data Product Code Variation*

When *Data Product Unit Variation* ^ *Data Product Code* ^ *Data Product Code Variation*

When *Data Product Set Variation* ^ *Data Product Unit*

Save to Hold File with *Data Product. Name* ^ *Data Product Set. Name* ^ *Data Product Set Variation. Name* ^ *Data Product Unit. Name, Data Product Unit. Mnemonic* ^ *Data Product Unit Variation. Name, Data Product Unit Variation. Mnemonic* ^ *Data Product Code. Name, Data Product Code. Value, Data Product Code. Definition,*

144

*Data Product Code. Cross-Reference
Comment ^ Data Product Code Variation.
Name, Data Product Code Variation.
Value, Data Product Code Variation.
Definition, Data Product Code Variation.
Cross-Reference Comment*

When *Data Product Set ^ Data Product Unit*
Save to Hold File with *Data Product. Name
^ Data Product Set. Name ^ Data Product
Set Variation. Name >< ' ' ^ Data Product
Unit. Name, Data Product Unit. Mnemonic
^ Data Product Unit Variation. Name, Data
Product Unit Variation. Mnemonic ^ Data
Product Code. Name, Data Product Code.
Value, Data Product Code. Definition,
Data Product Code. Cross-Reference
Comment ^ Data Product Code Variation.
Name, Data Product Code Variation.
Value, Data Product Code Variation.
Definition, Data Product Code Variation.
Cross-Reference Comment*

When *Data Product Unit ^ Data Product Code ^
Data Product Code Variation*
When *Data Product Set Variation ^ Data
Product Unit*
Save to Hold File with *Data Product. Name
^ Data Product Set. Name ^ Data Product
Set Variation. Name ^ Data Product Unit.
Name, Data Product Unit. Mnemonic ^
Data Product Unit Variation. Name >< ' ',
Data Product Unit Variation. Mnemonic
>< ' ' ^ Data Product Code. Name, Data
Product Code. Value, Data Product Code.
Definition, Data Product Code. Cross-
Reference Comment ^ Data Product Code
Variation. Name, Data Product Code
Variation. Value, Data Product Code
Variation. Definition, Data Product Code
Variation. Cross-Reference Comment*

When *Data Product Set ^ Data Product Unit*

145

Save to Hold File with *Data Product. Name
^ Data Product Set. Name ^ Data Product
Set Variation. Name* >< ' '^ *Data Product
Unit. Name, Data Product Unit. Mnemonic
^ Data Product Unit Variation. Name* >< '
', *Data Product Unit Variation. Mnemonic*
>< ' ' ^ *Data Product Code. Name, Data
Product Code. Value, Data Product Code.
Definition, Data Product Code. Cross-
Reference Comment ^ Data Product Code
Variation. Name, Data Product Code
Variation. Value, Data Product Code
Variation. Definition, Data Product Code
Variation. Cross-Reference Comment*

When *Data Reference Set Variation ^ Data Product Code*
When *Data Product Unit Variation ^ Data Product
Code*
When *Data Product Set Variation ^ Data
Product Unit*
Save to Hold File with *Data Product. Name
^ Data Product Set. Name ^ Data Product
Set Variation. Name ^ Data Product Unit.
Name, Data Product Unit. Mnemonic ^
Data Product Unit Variation. Name, Data
Product Unit Variation. Mnemonic ^ Data
Product Code. Name, Data Product Code.
Value, Data Product Code. Definition,
Data Product Code. Cross-Reference
Comment ^ Data Product Code Variation.
Name* >< ' ', *Data Product Code
Variation. Value* >< ' ', *Data Product
Code Variation. Definition* >< ' ', *Data
Product Code Variation. Cross-Reference
Comment* >< ' '

When *Data Product Set ^ Data Product Unit*
Save to Hold File with *Data Product. Name
^ Data Product Set. Name ^ Data Product
Set Variation. Name* >< ' ' ^ *Data Product
Unit. Name, Data Product Unit. Mnemonic
^ Data Product Unit Variation. Name, Data*

146

Product Unit Variation. Mnemonic ^ Data Product Code. Name, Data Product Code. Value, Data Product Code. Definition, Data Product Code. Cross-Reference Comment ^ Data Product Code Variation. Name >< ' ' >< ' ', Data Product Code Variation. Value >< ' ', Data Product Code Variation. Definition >< ' ', Data Product Code Variation. Cross-Reference Comment >< ' '

When *Data Product Unit ^ Data Product Code*
When *Data Product Set Variation ^ Data Product Unit*

Save to Hold File with *Data Product. Name ^ Data Product Set. Name ^ Data Product Set Variation. Name ^ Data Product Unit. Name, Data Product Unit. Mnemonic ^ Data Product Unit Variation. Name >< ' ', Data Product Unit Variation. Mnemonic >< ' ' ^ Data Product Code. Name, Data Product Code. Value, Data Product Code. Definition, Data Product Code. Cross-Reference Comment ^ Data Product Code Variation. Name >< ' ', Data Product Code Variation. Value >< ' ', Data Product Code Variation. Definition >< ' ', Data Product Code Variation. Cross-Reference Comment >< ' '*

When *Data Product Set ^ Data Product Unit*
Save to Hold File with *Data Product. Name ^ Data Product Set. Name ^ Data Product Set Variation. Name >< ' ' ^ Data Product Unit. Name, Data Product Unit. Mnemonic ^ Data Product Unit Variation >< ' '. Name, Data Product Unit Variation. Mnemonic >< ' ' ^ Data Product Code. Name, Data Product Code. Value, Data Product Code. Definition, Data Product Code. Cross-Reference Comment ^ Data Product Code Variation. Name >< ' ',*

Data Product Code Variation. Value >< '
', *Data Product Code Variation. Definition*
>< ' ', *Data Product Code Variation.*
Cross-Reference Comment >< ' '

When Subordinate Hit >< 'Yes'

Sort Hold File by *Data Product Name, Data Product Set.*
Name, Data Product Set Variation. Name, Data Product
Unit. Name, Data Product Unit. Mnemonic, Data
Product Unit Variation. Name, Data Product Unit
Variation. Mnemonic, Data Product Code. Name, Data
Product Code. Value, Data Product Code Definition,
Data Product Code Variation. Name, Data Product Code
Variation. Value, Data Product Code Variation.
Definition

Display from Sort

Each Unique *Data Product. Name*

Each Unique *Data Product Set. Name*

Each Unique *Data Product Set Variation. Name*

Each Unique *Data Product Unit. Name, Data*
Product Unit. Mnemonic

Each Unique *Data Product Unit*
Variation. Name, Data Product Unit
Variation. Mnemonic

Each Unique *Data Product Code.*
Name, Data Product Code. Value,
Data Product Code. Definition,
Data Product Code. Cross-
Reference Comment

Each *Data Product Code*
Variation. Name, Data
Product Code Variation.
Value, Data Product Code
Variation. Definition, Data
Product Code Variation.
Cross-Reference Comment

[PRINT]

[RETURN]

Close report and Return to <u>Data Cross-Reference Reports</u>

[Data Subject Cross-Reference Variability]

Each *Data Subject*
    Count >< 0
    Each ∨ {*Data Product Set* | *Data Product Set Variation*}
        Count + 1
    When Count > 0
        Display *Data Subject. Name Complete,* Count

[PRINT]

[RETURN]
    Close report and Return to <u>Data Cross-Reference Reports</u>

[Data Characteristic Cross-Reference Variability]

Each *Data Subject*
    Display *Data Subject. Name Complete*
    Each *Data Characteristic*
        Count >< 0
        Each *Data Characteristic Variation*
            Each ∨ {*Data Product Unit* | *Data Product Unit Variation*}
                Count + 1
        When Count > 0
            Display *Data Characteristic Variation. Name Complete*, Count

[PRINT]

[RETURN]
    Close report and Return to <u>Data Cross-Reference Reports</u>

[Data Reference Set Cross-Reference Variability]

Each *Data Subject*
    When *Data Subject. Data Reference Set Indicator* >< 'Yes'
        Display *Data Subject. Name Complete*
        Each *Data Reference Set Variation*
            Count >< 0
            Each ∨ {*Data Product Code* | *Data Product Code Variation*}
                Count + 1
            When Count > 0
                Display *Data Reference Set Variation. Name Complete*, Count

[PRINT]

[RETURN]
   Close report and Return to <u>Data Cross-Reference Reports</u>

[RETURN]
   Close window and Return to <u>Data Cross-Reference Function</u>

[HELP]
   Open <u>Help Message View</u>
   Display Data Cross-Reference Reports Help Message

Chapter 8

DATA PROTECTION

Data Protection Function includes Data Protection Regulation Task, Data Protection Reference Set Task, and Data Protection Reports, as shown in Figure 8.1. It is opened from Data Resource Guide Edit / View.

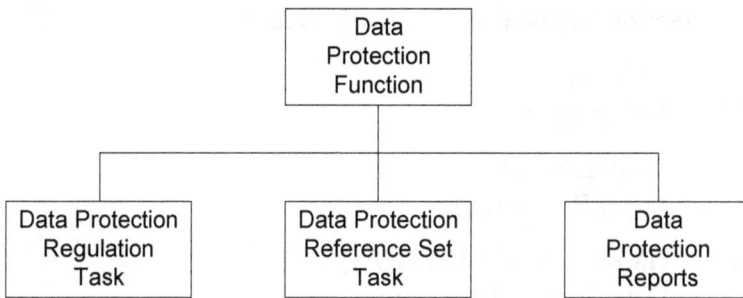

Figure 8.1. Data Protection Function.

The actions for Data Protection Function are:

[DATA PROTECTION REGULATION TASK]
Open Data Protection Regulation Task

[DATA PROTECTION REFERENCE SET TASK]
Open Data Protection Reference Set Task

[DATA PROTECTION REPORTS]
Open Data Protection Reports

[RETURN]
Close window and Return to Data Resource Guide Edit / View

[HELP]
Open Help Message View
Display Data Protection Function Help Message

DATA PROTECTION REGULATION TASK

Data Protection Regulation Task includes Jurisdiction, Legal Regulation, and Data Privacy Regulation, as shown in Figure 8.2. It is opened from Data

Protection Function.

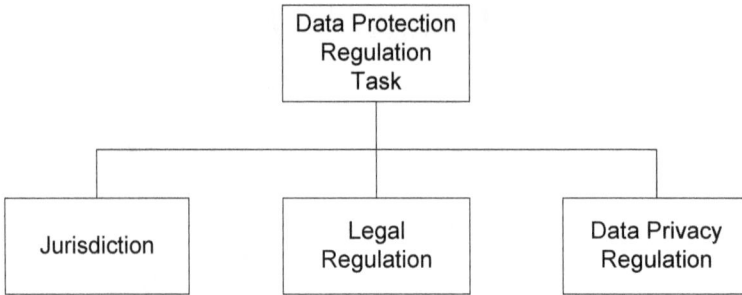

Figure 8.2. Data Protection Regulation Task.

The Data Protection Regulation Task actions are:

[JURISDICTION]
Open <u>Jurisdiction</u>

[LEGAL REGULATION]
Open <u>Legal Regulation</u>

[DATA PRIVACY REGULATION]
Open <u>Data Privacy Regulation</u>

[RETURN
Close window and Return to <u>Data Protection Function</u>

[HELP]
Open <u>Help Message View</u>
Display Data Protection Regulation Task Help Message

Jurisdiction

Jurisdiction is opened from Data Protection Regulation Task. The actions for Jurisdiction are:

[DISPLAY]
Display Auto-Scroll List from *Jurisdiction* with *Jurisdiction. Legal Name*
Select *Jurisdiction. Legal Name*
Display Selected *Jurisdiction* data

[PRINT]

(DELETE)
Delete Selected *Jurisdiction* occurrence

(NEW)

Display blank data fields for entry of new *Jurisdiction* data

Display Auto-Scroll List from *Jurisdiction Type* with *Jurisdiction Type. Name*
Select *Jurisdiction Type. Name*

[ACCEPT]

[RETURN]
Close Window and Return to Data Protection Regulation Task

[HELP]
Open Help Message View
Display Jurisdiction Help Message

Legal Regulation

Legal Regulation is opened from Data Protection Regulation Task. The actions for Legal Regulation are:

Display Auto-Scroll List from *Jurisdiction* with *Jurisdiction. Legal Name*
Select *Jurisdiction. Legal Name*

[DISPLAY]
Display Auto-Scroll List from *Legal Regulation* within Selected *Jurisdiction* with *Legal Regulation. Name*
Select *Legal Regulation. Name*
Display Selected *Legal Regulation* data

[PRINT]

(DELETE)
Delete Selected *Legal Regulation* occurrence

(NEW)
Display blank data fields for entry of new *Legal Regulation* data

Display Auto-Scroll List from *Legal Regulation* with *Legal Regulation. Title*
Select *"Parent" Legal Regulation. Title*

Display Auto-Scroll List from *Legal Regulation Type* with *Legal Regulation Type. Name*
Select *Legal Regulation Type. Name*

[ACCEPT]

[RETURN]
> Close Window and Return to <u>Data Protection Regulation Task</u>

[HELP]
> Open <u>Help Message View</u>
> Display Legal Regulation Help Message

Data Privacy Regulation

Data Privacy Regulation is opened from Data Protection Regulation Task. The actions for Data Privacy Regulation are:

> Display Auto-Scroll List from *Jurisdiction* with *Jurisdiction. Legal Name*
> Select *Jurisdiction. Legal Name*

> Display Auto-Scroll List from *Legal Regulation* within Selected *Jurisdiction* with *Legal Regulation. Title*
> Select *Legal Regulation. Title*

[DISPLAY]
> Display Scroll List from *Data Privacy Regulation* within Selected *Legal Regulation* with *Legal Regulation. Title, Data Subject. Name Complete, Data Characteristic. Name Complete*
> Select *Data Privacy Regulation*
> Display Selected *Data Privacy Regulation* data

[PRINT]

(DELETE)
> Delete Selected *Data Privacy Regulation* occurrence

(NEW)
> Display blank data fields for entry of new *Data Privacy Regulation* data

> Display Auto-Scroll List from *Data Subject* with *Data Subject. Name Complete*

> When *Data Privacy Regulation* v *Data Subject*
> Select *Data Subject. Name Complete*

> When *Data Privacy Regulation* v *Data Characteristic*
> Display Auto-Scroll List from *Data Characteristic* within Selected *Data Subject* with *Data Characteristic. Name Complete*
> Select *Data Characteristic. Name Complete*

[ACCEPT]

[RETURN]
    Close Window and Return to <u>Data Protection Regulation Task</u>

[HELP]
    Open <u>Help Message View</u>
    Display Data Privacy Regulation Help Message

DATA PROTECTION REFERENCE SET TASK

Data Protection Reference Set Task includes Jurisdiction Type and Legal Regulation Type, as shown in Figure 8.3. It is opened from Data Protection Function

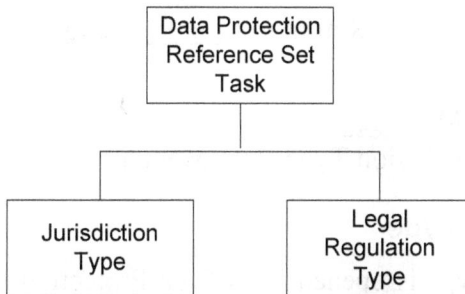

Figure 8.3. Data Protection Reference Set Task.

The Data Protection Regulation Task actions are:

[JURISDICTION TYPE]
    Open <u>Jurisdiction Type</u>

[LEGAL REGULATION TYPE]
    Open <u>Legal Regulation Type</u>

[RETURN
    Close window and Return to <u>Data Protection Function</u>

[HELP]
    Open <u>Help Message View</u>
    Display Data Protection Reference Set Task Help Message

Jurisdiction Type

Jurisdiction Type is opened from Data Protection Reference Set Task. The actions for Jurisdiction Type are:

[DISPLAY]

Display Auto-Scroll List from *Jurisdiction Type* with *Jurisdiction Type. Name*
Select *Jurisdiction Type. Name*
Display Selected *Jurisdiction Type* data

[PRINT]

(DELETE)
    Delete Selected *Jurisdiction Type* occurrence

(NEW)
    Display blank data fields for entry of new *Jurisdiction Type* data

[ACCEPT]

[RETURN]
    Close window and Return to <u>Data Protection Reference Set Task</u>

[HELP]
    Open <u>Help Message View</u>
    Display Jurisdiction Type Help Message

Legal Regulation Type

Legal Regulation Type is opened from Data Protection Reference Set Task. The actions for Legal Regulation Type are:

[DISPLAY]
    Display Auto-Scroll List from *Legal Regulation Type* with *Legal Regulation Type. Name*
    Select *Legal Regulation Type. Name*
    Display Selected *Legal Regulation Type* data

[PRINT]

(DELETE)
    Delete Selected *Legal Regulation Type* occurrence

(NEW)
    Display blank data fields for entry of new *Legal Regulation Type* data

[ACCEPT]

[RETURN]
    Close window and Return to <u>Data Protection Reference Set Task</u>

[HELP]

Open <u>Help Message View</u>
Display Legal Regulation Type Help Message

DATA PROTECTION REPORTS

Data Protection Reports contains the reports for the Data Protection Function. It is opened from Data Protection Function. Only a few examples of reports are shown. Many additional reports could be developed based on an organization's needs and added to the Data Resource Guide.

The specific reports and actions to obtain those reports are:

[Jurisdiction Name]
　　Display Each *Jurisdiction. Legal Name*

　　[PRINT]

　　[RETURN]
　　　　Close report and Return to <u>Data Protection Reports</u>

[Jurisdiction Detail]
　　Display Each *Jurisdiction* data

　　[PRINT]

　　[RETURN]
　　　　Close report and Return to <u>Data Protection Reports</u>

[Jurisdiction Name ^ Legal Regulation Title]
　　Display Each *Jurisdiction. Legal Name*
　　　　Display Each *Legal Regulation. Title*

　　[PRINT]

　　[RETURN]
　　　　Close report and Return to <u>Data Protection Reports</u>

[Jurisdiction Name ^ Legal Regulation Detail]
　　Display Each *Jurisdiction. Legal Name*
　　　　Display Each *Legal Regulation* data

　　[PRINT]

　　[RETURN]
　　　　Close report and Return to <u>Data Protection Reports</u>

[Selected Jurisdiction Name ^ Legal Regulation Detail]
　　Display Auto-Scroll List from *Jurisdiction* with *Jurisdiction. Legal Name*

Select Jurisdiction. Legal Name
Display Each *Legal Regulation* data within Selected *Jurisdiction*

[PRINT]

[RETURN]
Close report and Return to <u>Data Protection Reports</u>

[Jurisdiction Name ^ Legal Regulation Title ^ Data Privacy Regulation
Detail]
Display Each *Jurisdiction. Legal Name*
Display Each *Legal Regulation. Title*
Display Each *Data Privacy Regulation* data

[PRINT]

[RETURN]
Close report and Return to <u>Data Protection Reports</u>

[Selected Jurisdiction Name ^ Legal Regulation Title ^ Data Privacy
Regulation]
Display Auto-Scroll List from *Jurisdiction* with *Jurisdiction. Legal
Name*
Select *Jurisdiction. Legal Name*
Display Each *Legal Regulation. Title* within Selected *Jurisdiction*
Display Each *Data Privacy Regulation* data

[PRINT]

[RETURN]
Close report and Return to <u>Data Protection Reports</u>

[Jurisdiction Type Detail]
Display Each *Jurisdiction Type* data

[PRINT]

[RETURN]
Close report and Return to <u>Data Protection Reports</u>

[Legal Regulation Type Detail]
Display Each *Legal Regulation Type* data

[PRINT]

[RETURN]
Close report and Return to <u>Data Protection Reports</u>

[RETURN]

Close window and Return to <u>Data Protection Function</u>

[HELP]
   Open <u>Help Message View</u>
   Display Data Protection Reports Help Message

Chapter 9

DATA ACCESS

Data Access Function includes Business Process Task, Business Process Steward Task, Data Product Process Task, and Data Access Reports, as shown in Figure 9.1. It is opened from Data Resource Guide Edit / View.

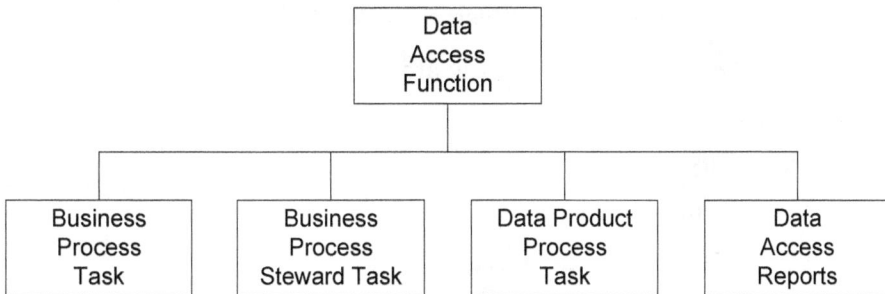

```
                    ┌─────────────┐
                    │    Data     │
                    │   Access    │
                    │  Function   │
                    └──────┬──────┘
        ┌──────────────┬───┴──────┬──────────────┐
 ┌──────┴──────┐┌──────┴──────┐┌──┴──────────┐┌──┴──────────┐
 │  Business   ││  Business   ││Data Product ││    Data     │
 │  Process    ││  Process    ││  Process    ││   Access    │
 │    Task     ││Steward Task ││    Task     ││   Reports   │
 └─────────────┘└─────────────┘└─────────────┘└─────────────┘
```

Figure 9.1. Data Access Function.

The actions for Data Access Function are:

[BUSINESS PROCESS TASK]
Open Business Process Task

[BUSINESS PROCESS STEWARD TASK]
Open Business Process Steward Task

[DATA PRODUCT PROCESS TASK]
Open Data Product Set Process Task

[DATA ACCESS REPORTS]
Open Data Access Reports

[RETURN]
Close window and Return to Data Resource Guide Edit / View

[HELP]
Open Help Message View
Display Data Access Function Help Message

BUSINESS PROCESS TASK

Business Process Task includes Business Process and Business Process

Type, as shown in Figure 9.2. It is opened from Data Access Function.

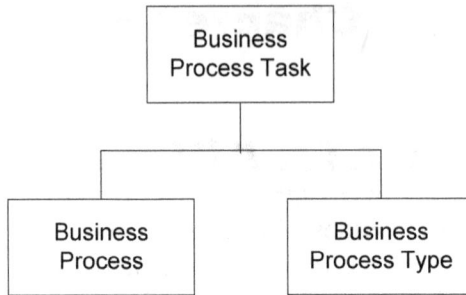

```
        ┌─────────────────┐
        │    Business     │
        │  Process Task   │
        └─────────────────┘
                 │
       ┌─────────┴─────────┐
┌──────────────┐    ┌──────────────┐
│   Business   │    │   Business   │
│   Process    │    │ Process Type │
└──────────────┘    └──────────────┘
```

Figure 9.2. Business Process Task.

The actions for Business Process Task are:

[BUSINESS PROCESS]
> Open <u>Business Process</u>

[BUSINESS PROCESS TYPE]
> Open <u>Business Process Type</u>

[RETURN]
> Close window and Return to <u>Data Access Function</u>

[HELP]
> Open <u>Help Message View</u>
> Display Business Process Task Help Message

Business Process

Business Process is opened from Business Process Task. The actions for Business Process are:

[DISPLAY]
> Display Auto-Scroll List from *Business Process* with *Business Process. Name*
> Select *Business Process. Name*
> Display Selected *Business Process* data

[PRINT]

(DELETE)
> Delete Selected *Business Process* occurrence

(NEW)
> Display blank data fields for entry of new *Business Process* data

Display Auto-Scroll List from *Business Process Steward* with
  Business Process Steward. Name Complete
Select *Business Process Steward. Name Complete*

Display Auto-Scroll List from *Business Process Type* with *Business
  Process Type. Name*
Select *Business Process Type. Name*

Display Auto-Scroll List from *Business Process* with *Business
  Process. Name*
Select *"Parent" Business Process. Name*

[ACCEPT]

[RETURN]
  Close Window and Return to <u>Business Process Task</u>

[HELP]
  Open <u>Help Message View</u>
  Display Business Process Help Message

Business Process Type

Business Process Type is opened from Business Process Task. The actions
for Business Process Type are:

[DISPLAY]
  Display Auto-Scroll List from *Business Process Type* with *Business
    Process Type. Name*
  Select *Business Process Type. Name*
  Display Selected *Business Process Type* data

  [PRINT]

  (DELETE)
    Delete Selected *Business Process Type* occurrence

(NEW)
  Display blank data fields for entry of new *Business Process Type*
  data

  [ACCEPT]

[RETURN]
  Close window and Return to <u>Business Process Task</u>

[HELP]
  Open <u>Help Message View</u>

163

Display Business Process Type Help Message

BUSINESS PROCESS STEWARD TASK

Business Process Steward Task includes Business Process Steward and Organization Unit, as shown in Figure 9.3. It is opened from Data Access Function.

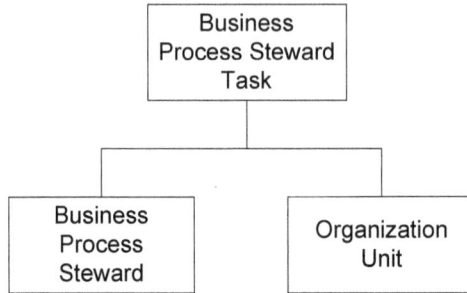

Figure 9.3. Business Process Steward Task.

The actions for Business Process Steward Task are:

[BUSINESS PROCESS STEWARD]
   Open Business Process Steward

[ORGANIZATION UNIT]
   Open Organization Unit

[RETURN]
   Close window and Return to Data Access Function

[HELP]
   Open Help Message View
   Display Business Process Steward Task Help Message

Business Process Steward

Business Process Steward is opened from Business Process Task. The actions for Business Process Steward are:

[DISPLAY]
   Display Auto-Scroll List from *Business Process Steward* with
      Business Process Steward. Name Complete
   Select *Business Process Steward. Name Complete*
   Display Selected *Business Process Steward* data

[PRINT]

(DELETE)
> Delete Selected *Business Process Steward* occurrence

(NEW)
> Display blank data fields for entry of new *Business Process Steward* data

> Display Auto-Scroll List from *Organization Unit* with *Organization Unit. Name*
> Select *Business Organization Unit. Name*

> [ACCEPT]

[RETURN]
> Close Window and Return to <u>Business Process Steward Task</u>

[HELP]
> Open <u>Help Message View</u>
> Display Business Process Steward Help Message

Organization Unit

Organization Unit is opened from Business Process Steward Task. The actions for Organization Unit are provided in the Data Responsibility Chapter.

DATA PRODUCT PROCESS TASK

Data Product Process Task includes Data Product Set Process and Data Product Unit Process, as shown in Figure 9.4. It is opened from Data Access Function.

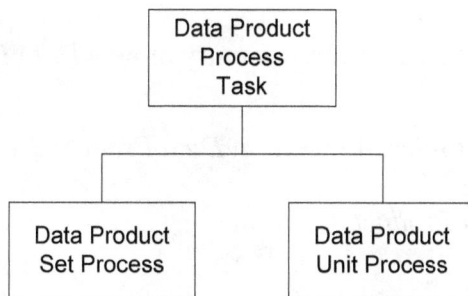

Figure 9.4. Data Product Process Task.

The actions for Data Product Process Task are:

[DATA PRODUCT SET PROCESS]
> Open <u>Data Product Set Process</u>

[DATA PRODUCT UNIT PROCESS]
>Open <u>Data Product Unit Process</u>

[RETURN]
>Close window and Return to <u>Data Access Function</u>

[HELP]
>Open <u>Help Message View</u>
>Display Data Product Process Task Help Message

Data Product Set Process

Data Product Set Process is opened from Data Product Process Task. The actions for Data Product Set Process are:

>Display Auto-Scroll List from *Business Process* with *Business Process. Name Complete*
>Select *Business Process. Name Complete*

[DISPLAY]
>Display Scroll List from *Data Process Set Process* within Selected *Business Process* with *Data Product Set Process. Comment, Data Product Set. Name, Business Process. Name*
>Select *Data Product Set Process*
>Display Selected *Data Product Set Process* data

>[PRINT]

>(DELETE)
>>Delete Selected *Data Product Set Process* occurrence

(NEW)
>Display blank data fields for entry of new *Data Product Set Process* data

>Display Auto-Scroll List from *Data Product Set* with *Data Product Set. Name*
>Select *Data Product Set. Name*

>[ACCEPT]

[RETURN]
>Close Window and Return to <u>Data Product Process Task</u>

[HELP]
>Open <u>Help Message View</u>
>Display Data Product Set Process Help Message

166

Data Product Unit Process

Data Product Unit Process is opened from Data Product Process Task. The actions for Data Product Unit Process are:

Display Auto-Scroll List with *Business Process. Name Complete*
Select *Business Process. Name Complete*

[DISPLAY]
  Display Scroll List from *Data Product Unit Process* within
    Selected *Business Process* with *Data Product Unit Process.*
    Comment, Data Product Unit. Name, Business Process. Name
  Select *Data Product Unit Process*
  Display Selected *Data Product Unit Process* data

  [PRINT]

  (DELETE)
    Delete Selected *Data Product Unit Process* occurrence

(NEW)
  Display blank data fields for entry of new *Data Product Unit*
    Process data

  Display Auto-Scroll List from *Data Product Unit* with *Data*
    Product Unit. Name
  Select *Data Product Unit. Name*

  [ACCEPT]

[RETURN]
  Close Window and Return to Data Product Process Task

[HELP]
  Open Help Message View
  Display Data Product Unit Process Help Message

DATA ACCESS REPORTS

Data Access Reports contains the reports for the Data Access Function. It is opened from Data Access Function. Only a few examples of reports are shown. Many additional reports could be developed based on an organization's needs and added to the Data Resource Guide.

[Business Process Name]
  Display Each *Business Process. Name*

  [PRINT]

[RETURN]
>   Close report and Return to <u>Data Access Reports</u>

[Business Process Detail]
>   Display Each *Business Process* data

>   [PRINT]

>   [RETURN]
>   >   Close report and Return to <u>Data Access Reports</u>

[Business Process Type]
>   Display Each *Business Process Type* data

>   [PRINT]

>   [RETURN]
>   >   Close report and Return to <u>Data Access Reports</u>

[Business Process Name ^ Data Product Set Name]
>   Display Each *Business Process. Name*
>   >   Display Each *Data Product Set. Name*

>   [PRINT]

>   [RETURN]
>   >   Close report and Return to <u>Data Access Reports</u>

[Business Process Name ^ Data Product Set Detail]
>   Display Each *Business Process. Name*
>   >   Display Each *Data Product Set* data

>   [PRINT]

>   [RETURN]
>   >   Close report and Return to <u>Data Access Reports</u>

[Selected Business Process Name ^ Data Product Set Detail]
>   Display Auto-Scroll List from *Business Process* with *Business Process. Name*
>   Select *Business Process Name*
>   Display Each *Data Product Set* data within Selected *Business Process*

>   [PRINT]

>   [RETURN]
>   >   Close report and Return to <u>Data Access Reports</u>

[Business Process Name ^ Data Product Unit Name]
 Display Each *Business Process. Name*
  Display Each *Data Product Unit. Name*

[PRINT]

[RETURN]
 Close report and Return to <u>Data Access Reports</u>

[Business Process Name ^ Data Product Unit Detail]
 Display Each *Business Process. Name*
  Display Each *Data Product Unit* data

[PRINT]

[RETURN]
 Close report and Return to <u>Data Access Reports</u>

[Selected Business Process Name ^ Data Product Unit Detail]
 Display Auto-Scroll List from *Business Process* with *Business Process. Name*
 Select *Business Process Name*
 Display Each *Data Product Unit* data within Selected *Business Process*

[PRINT]

[RETURN]
 Close report and Return to <u>Data Access Reports</u>

[Data Product Set Name ^ Business Process Name]
 Sort *Data Product Set Process* by *Data Product Set. Name* ^ *Business Process. Name*
 Display from Sort Each Unique *Data Product Set. Name*
  Display Each *Business Process. Name*

[PRINT]

[RETURN]
 Close report and Return to <u>Data Access Reports</u>

[Data Product Unit Name ^ Business Process Name]
 Sort *Data Product Unit Process* by *Data Product Unit. Name* ^ *Business Process. Name*
 Display from Sort Each Unique *Data Product Unit. Name*
  Display Each *Business Process. Name*

[PRINT]

[RETURN]
Close report and Return to <u>Data Access Reports</u>

[RETURN]
Close window and Return to <u>Data Access Function</u>

[HELP]
Open <u>Help Message View</u>
Display Data Access Reports Help Message

Chapter 10

DATA PROVENANCE

The Data Provenance Function includes Data Track Task, Data Step Task, and Data Provenance Reports, as shown in Figure 10.1. It is opened from Data Resource Guide Edit / View.

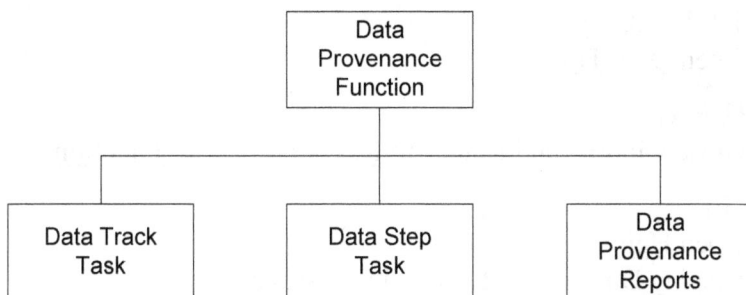

Figure 10.1. Data Provenance Function.

The actions for Data Provenance Function are:

[DATA TRACK TASK]
    Open Data Track Task

[DATA STEP TASK]
    Open Data Step Task

[DATA PROVENANCE REPORTS]
    Open Data Provenance Reports

[RETURN]
    Close window and Return to Data Resource Guide Edit / View

[HELP]
    Open Help Message View
    Display Data Provenance Function Help Message

DATA TRACK TASK

Data Track Task includes Data Track, as shown in Figure 10.2 It is opened from Data Provenance Function.

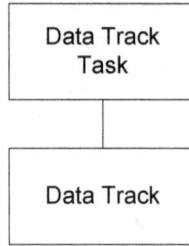

Figure 10.2. Data Track Task.

The actions for Data Track Task are:

[DATA TRACK]
Open <u>Data Track</u>

[RETURN]
Close window and Return to <u>Data Provenance Function</u>

[HELP]
Open <u>Help Message View</u>
Display Data Track Task Help Message

Data Track

Data Track is opened from Data Track Task. The actions for Data Track are:

[DISPLAY]
Display Auto-Scroll List from *Data Track* with *Data Track. Name*
Select *Data Track. Name*
Display Selected *Data Track* data

[PRINT]

(DELETE)
Delete Selected *Data Track* occurrence

(NEW)
Display blank data fields for entry of new *Data Track* data

[ACCEPT]

[RETURN]
Close window and Return to <u>Data Track Task</u>

[HELP]
Open <u>Help Message View</u>
Display Data Track Help Message

172

DATA STEP TASK

Data Step Task includes Data Step, as shown in Figure 10.3 It is opened from Data Provenance Function.

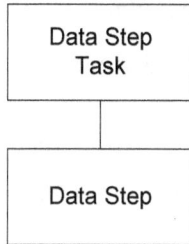

Figure 10.3. Data Step Task.

The actions for Data Step Task are:

[DATA STEP]
Open Data Step

[RETURN]
Close window and Return to Data Provenance Function

[HELP]
Open Help Message View
Display Data Step Task Help Message

Data Step

Data Step is opened from Data Step Task. Only the Data Product Unit is used because the physical data are tracked. The actions for Data Step are:

[DISPLAY]
Display Scroll List from *Data Step* with *"Incoming" Data Product Unit. Name*, *"Outgoing" Data Product Unit. Name*
Select *Data Step*
Display Selected *Data Step* data

[PRINT]

(DELETE)
Delete Selected *Data Step* occurrence

(NEW)
Display blank data fields for entry of new *Data Step* data

Display Auto-Scroll List from *Data Product* with *Data Product. Name*

173

Select *Data Product. Name*

Display Auto-Scroll List from *Data Product Set* within Selected
Data Product with *Data Product Set. Name*
Select *Data Product Set. Name*

Display Auto-Scroll List from *Data Product Unit* within Selected
Data Product Set with *Data Product Unit. Name*
Select *"Incoming" Data Product Unit. Name*

Display Auto-Scroll List from *Data Product* with *Data Product. Name*
Select *Data Product. Name*

Display Auto-Scroll List from *Data Product Set* within Selected
Data Product with *Data Product Set. Name*
Select *Data Product Set. Name*

Display Auto-Scroll List from *Data Product Unit* within Selected
Data Product Set with *Data Product Unit. Name*
Select *"Outgoing" Data Product Unit. Name*

[ACCEPT]

[RETURN]
Close window and Return to Data Step Task

[HELP]
Open Help Message View
Display Data Step Help Message

DATA PROVENANCE REPORTS

Data Provenance Reports contains the reports for the Data Provenance
Function. It is opened from Data Provenance Function. Only a few
examples of reports are shown. Many additional reports could be developed
based on an organization's needs and added to the Data Resource Guide.

[Data Track Name]
Display Each *Data Track. Name*

[PRINT]

[RETURN]
Close report and Return to Data Provenance Reports

[Data Track Detail]
Display Each *Data Track* data

174

[PRINT]

[RETURN]
>   Close report and Return to <u>Data Provenance Reports</u>

[Data Track Name ^ Data Step Detail]
>   Display Each *Data Track. Name*
>>   Display Each *Data Step* data

[PRINT]

[RETURN]
>   Close report and Return to <u>Data Provenance Reports</u>

[Data Track Detail ^ Data Step Detail]
>   Display Each *Data Track* data
>>   Display Each *Data Step* data

[PRINT]

[RETURN]
>   Close report and Return to <u>Data Provenance Reports</u>

[Selected Data Track Name ^ Data Step Detail
>   Display Auto-Scroll List from *Data Track* with *Data Track. Name*
>   Select *Data Track Name*
>   Display Each *Data Step* data within Selected *Data Track*

[PRINT]

[RETURN]
>   Close report and Return to <u>Data Provenance Reports</u>

[RETURN]
>   Close window and Return to <u>Data Provenance Function</u>

[HELP]
>   Open <u>Help Message View</u>
>   Display Data Provenance Reports Help Message

Chapter 11

DATA SHARING

Data Sharing Function includes Data Clearinghouse Topic Task, Data Clearinghouse Author Task, Spatial Area Task, Data Clearinghouse Item Task, Data Project Task, and Data Sharing Reports, as shown in Figure 11.1. It is opened from Data Resource Guide Edit / View.

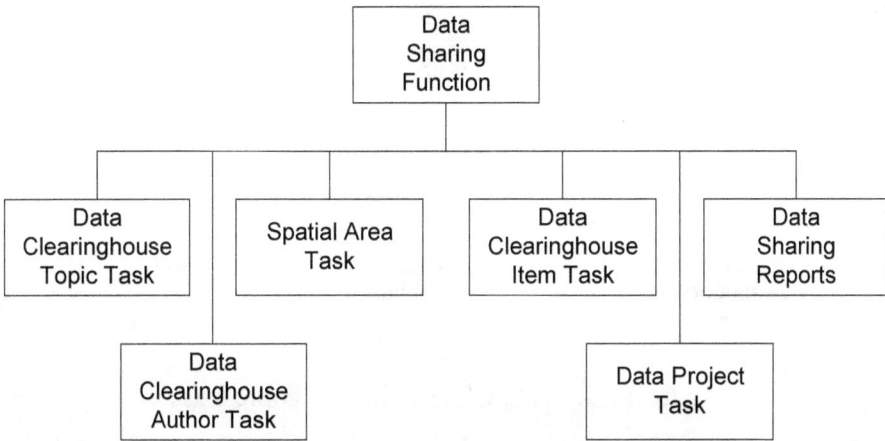

Figure 11.1. Data Sharing Function.

The actions for Data Sharing Function are:

[DATA CLEARINGHOUSE TOPIC TASK]
Open Data Clearinghouse Topic Task

[DATA CLEARINGHOUSE AUTHOR TASK]
Open Data Clearinghouse Author Task

[SPATIAL AREA TASK]
Open Spatial Area Task

[DATA CLEARINGHOUSE ITEM TASK]
Open Data Clearinghouse Item Task

[DATA PROJECT TASK]
Open Data Project Task

[DATA SHARING REPORTS]

177

Open Data Sharing Reports

[RETURN]
Close window and Return to Data Resource Guide Edit / View

[HELP]
Open Help Message View
Display Data Sharing Function Help Message

DATA CLEARINGHOUSE TOPIC TASK

Data Clearinghouse Topic Task includes Data Clearinghouse Topic, Data Clearinghouse Keyword, and Data Clearinghouse Topic Keyword, as shown in Figure 11.2. It is opened from Data Sharing Function

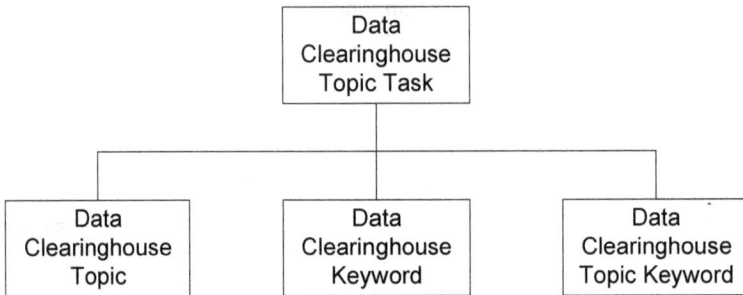

```
            ┌─────────────────┐
            │      Data       │
            │  Clearinghouse  │
            │   Topic Task    │
            └─────────────────┘
      ┌──────────────┼──────────────┐
┌───────────┐  ┌───────────┐  ┌───────────┐
│   Data    │  │   Data    │  │   Data    │
│Clearinghouse│ │Clearinghouse│ │Clearinghouse│
│   Topic   │  │  Keyword  │  │Topic Keyword│
└───────────┘  └───────────┘  └───────────┘
```

Figure 11.2. Data Clearinghouse Topic Task.

The actions for Data Clearinghouse Topic Task are:

[DATA CLEARINGHOUSE TOPIC]
Open Data Clearinghouse Topic

[DATA CLEARINGHOUSE KEYWORD]
Open Data Clearinghouse Keyword

[DATA CLEARINGHOUSE TOPIC KEYWORD]
Open Data Clearinghouse Topic Keyword

[RETURN]
Close window and Return to Data Sharing Function

[HELP]
Open Help Message View
Display Data Clearinghouse Topic Task Help Message

Data Clearinghouse Topic

Data Clearinghouse Topic is opened from Data Clearinghouse Topic Task.

The actions for Data Clearinghouse Topic are:

[DISPLAY]
> Display Auto-Scroll List from *Data Clearinghouse Topic* with *Data Clearinghouse Topic. Phrase*
> Select *Data Clearinghouse Topic. Phrase*
> Display Selected *Data Clearinghouse Topic* data

> [PRINT]

> (DELETE)
>> Delete Selected *Data Clearinghouse Topic* occurrence

(NEW)
> Display blank data fields for entry of new *Data Clearinghouse Topic* data

> [ACCEPT]

[RETURN]
> Close window and Return to <u>Data Clearinghouse Topic Task</u>

[HELP]
> Open <u>Help Message View</u>
> Display Data Clearinghouse Topic Help Message

Data Clearinghouse Keyword

Data Clearinghouse Keyword is opened from Data Clearinghouse Topic Task. The actions for Data Clearinghouse Keyword are:

[DISPLAY]
> Display Auto-Scroll List from *Data Clearinghouse Keyword* with *Data Clearinghouse Keyword. Phrase*
> Select *Data Clearinghouse Keyword. Phrase*
> Display Selected *Data Clearinghouse Keyword* data

> [PRINT]

> (DELETE)
>> Delete Selected *Data Clearinghouse Keyword* occurrence

(NEW)
> Display blank data fields for entry of new *Data Clearinghouse Keyword* data

> [ACCEPT]

[RETURN]
>Close window and Return to <u>Data Clearinghouse Topic Task</u>

[HELP]
>Open <u>Help Message View</u>
>Display Data Clearinghouse Keyword Help Message

Data Clearinghouse Topic Keyword

Data Clearinghouse Topic Keyword is opened from Data Clearinghouse Topic Task. The actions for Data Clearinghouse Topic Keyword are:

[DISPLAY]
>Display Scroll List from *Data Clearinghouse Topic Keyword* with *Data Clearinghouse Topic. Phrase*, *Data Clearinghouse Keyword. Phrase*
>Select *Data Clearinghouse Topic Keyword*
>Display Selected *Data Clearinghouse Topic Keyword* data

[PRINT]

(DELETE)
>Delete Selected *Data Clearinghouse Topic Keyword* occurrence

(NEW)
>Display blank data fields for entry of new *Data Clearinghouse Topic Keyword* data

>Display Auto-Scroll List from *Data Clearinghouse Topic* with *Data Clearinghouse Topic. Phrase*
>Select *Data Clearinghouse Topic. Phrase*

>Display Auto-Scroll List from *Data Clearinghouse Keyword* with *Data Clearinghouse Keyword. Phrase*
>Select *Data Clearinghouse Keyword. Phrase*

[ACCEPT]

[RETURN]
>Close window and Return to <u>Data Clearinghouse Topic Task</u>

[HELP]
>Open <u>Help Message View</u>
>Display Data Clearinghouse Topic Keyword Help Message

DATA CLEARINGHOUSE AUTHOR TASK

Data Clearinghouse Author Task includes Data Clearinghouse Author, as shown in Figure 11.3. It is opened from Data Sharing Function.

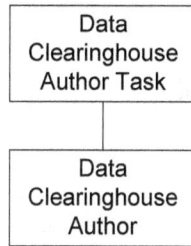

```
┌──────────────┐
│     Data     │
│ Clearinghouse│
│ Author Task  │
└──────┬───────┘
       │
┌──────┴───────┐
│     Data     │
│ Clearinghouse│
│    Author    │
└──────────────┘
```

Figure 11.3. Data Clearinghouse Author Task.

The actions for Data Clearinghouse Author Task are:

[DATA CLEARINGHOUSE AUTHOR]
    Open Data Clearinghouse Author

[RETURN]
    Close window and Return to Data Sharing Function

[HELP]
    Open Help Message View
    Display Data Clearinghouse Author Task Help Message

Data Clearinghouse Author

Data Clearinghouse Author is opened from Data Clearinghouse Author Task. The actions for Data Clearinghouse Author are:

[DISPLAY]
    Display Scroll List from *Data Clearinghouse Author* with *Data Clearinghouse Author. Family Name, Data Clearinghouse Author. Individual Name*
    Select *Data Clearinghouse Author*
    Display Selected *Data Clearinghouse Author* data

    [PRINT]

    (DELETE)
        Delete Selected *Data Clearinghouse Author* occurrence

(NEW)
    Display blank data fields for entry of new *Data Clearinghouse Author* data

181

[ACCEPT]

[RETURN]
Close window and Return to Data Clearinghouse Author Task

[HELP]
Open Help Message View
Display Data Clearinghouse Author Help Message

SPATIAL AREA TASK

Spatial Area Task includes Spatial Area and Spatial Area Type, as shown in Figure 11.4. It is opened from Data Sharing Function

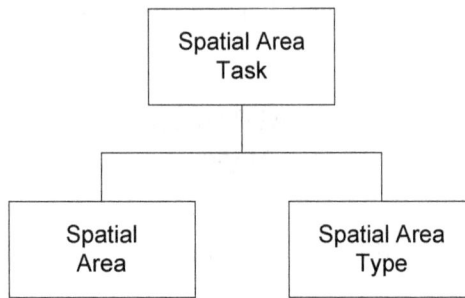

Figure 11.4. Spatial Area Task.

The actions for Spatial Area Task are:

[SPATIAL AREA]
Open Spatial Area

[SPATIAL AREA TYPE]
Open Spatial Area Type

[RETURN]
Close window and Return to Data Sharing Function

[HELP]
Open Help Message View
Display Spatial Area Task Help Message

Spatial Area

Spatial Area is opened from Spatial Area Task. The actions for Spatial Area are:

[DISPLAY]

Display Auto-Scroll List from *Spatial Area* with *Spatial Area.
Name*
Select *Spatial Area. Name*
Display Selected *Spatial Area* data

[PRINT]

(DELETE)
Delete Selected *Spatial Area* occurrence

(NEW)
Display blank data fields for entry of new *Spatial Area* data

Display Auto-Scroll List from *Spatial Area Type* with *Spatial Area
Type. Name*
Select *Spatial Area Type. Name*

[ACCEPT]

[RETURN]
Close window and Return to <u>Spatial Area Task</u>

[HELP]
Open <u>Help Message View</u>
Display Spatial Area Help Message

Spatial Area Type

Spatial Area Type is opened from Spatial Area Task. The actions for Spatial
Area Type are:

[DISPLAY]
Display Auto-Scroll List from *Spatial Area Type* with *Spatial Area
Type. Name*
Select *Spatial Area Type. Name*
Display Selected *Spatial Area Type* data

[PRINT]

(DELETE)
Delete Selected *Spatial Area Type* occurrence

(NEW)
Display blank data fields for entry of new *Spatial Area Type* data

[ACCEPT]

[RETURN]

Close window and Return to <u>Spatial Area Task</u>

[HELP]
Open <u>Help Message View</u>
Display Spatial Area Type Help Message

DATA CLEARINGHOUSE ITEM TASK

Data Clearinghouse Item Task includes Data Clearinghouse Item, Data Clearinghouse Item Topic, Data Clearinghouse Item Author, Data Clearinghouse Item Area, Data Clearinghouse Item Type, Data Steward, and Organization Unit as shown in Figure 11.5. It is opened from Data Sharing Function.

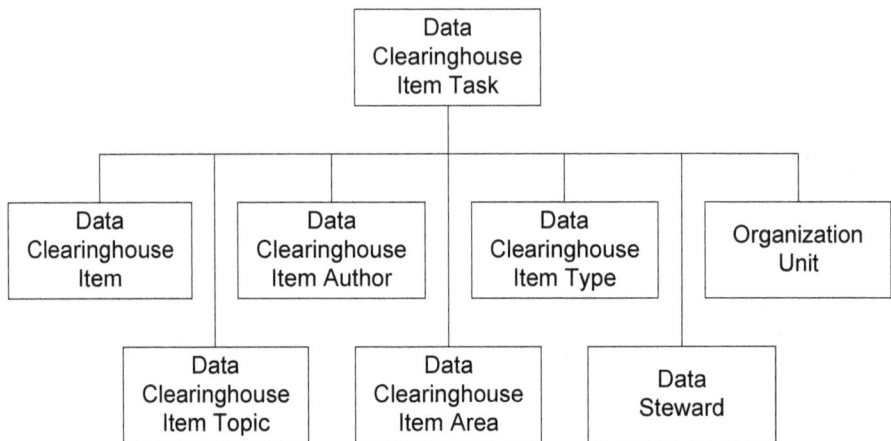

Figure 11.5. Data Clearinghouse Item Task.

The actions for Data Clearinghouse Item Task are:

[DATA CLEARINGHOUSE ITEM]
Open <u>Data Clearinghouse Item</u>

[DATA CLEARINGHOUSE ITEM TOPIC]
Open <u>Data Clearinghouse Item Topic</u>

[DATA CLEARINGHOUSE ITEM AUTHOR]
Open <u>Data Clearinghouse Item Author</u>

[DATA CLEARINGHOUSE ITEM AREA]
Open <u>Data Clearinghouse Item Area</u>

[DATA CLEARINGHOUSE ITEM TYPE]
Open <u>Data Clearinghouse Item Type</u>

[DATA STEWARD]

Open <u>Data Steward</u>

[ORGANIZATION UNIT]
Open <u>Organization Unit</u>

[RETURN]
Close window and Return to <u>Data Sharing Function</u>

[HELP]
Open <u>Help Message View</u>
Display Data Clearinghouse Item Task Help Message

Data Clearinghouse Item

Data Clearinghouse Item is opened from Data Clearinghouse Item Task.
The actions for Data Clearinghouse Item are:

[DISPLAY]
Display Auto-Scroll List from *Data Clearinghouse Item* with *Data
Clearinghouse Item. Name Complete*
Select *Data Clearinghouse Item. Name Complete*
Display Selected *Data Clearinghouse Item* data

[PRINT]

(DELETE)
Delete Selected *Data Clearinghouse Item* occurrence

(NEW)
Display blank data fields for entry of new *Data Clearinghouse Item*
data

Display Auto-Scroll List from *Data Clearinghouse Item Type* with
Data Clearinghouse Item Type. Name
Select *Data Clearinghouse Item Type. Name*

Display Auto-Scroll List from *Data Steward* with *Data Steward.
Name Complete*
Select *Data Steward. Name Complete*

[ACCEPT]

[RETURN]
Close window and Return to <u>Data Clearinghouse Item Task</u>

[HELP]
Open <u>Help Message View</u>
Display Data Clearinghouse Item Help Message

Data Clearinghouse Item Topic

Data Clearinghouse Item Topic is opened from Data Clearinghouse Item Task.[3] The actions for Data Clearinghouse Item Topic are:

[DISPLAY]
> Display Scroll List from *Data Clearinghouse Item Topic* with *Data Clearinghouse Topic. Phrase, Data Clearinghouse Item. Name Complete*
> Select *Data Clearinghouse Item Topic*
> Display Selected *Data Clearinghouse Item Topic* data

[PRINT]

(DELETE)
> Delete Selected *Data Clearinghouse Item Topic* occurrence

(NEW)
> Display blank data fields for entry of new *Data Clearinghouse Item Topic* data

> Display Auto-Scroll List from *Data Clearinghouse Item* with *Data Clearinghouse Item Name Complete*
> Select *Data Clearinghouse Item. Name Complete*

> Display Auto-Scroll List from *Data Clearinghouse Topic* with *Data Clearinghouse Topic. Phrase*
> Select *Data Clearinghouse Topic. Phrase*

[ACCEPT]

[RETURN]
> Close window and Return to <u>Data Clearinghouse Item Task</u>

[HELP]
> Open <u>Help Message View</u>
> Display Data Clearinghouse Item Topic Help Message

Data Clearinghouse Item Author

Data Clearinghouse Item Author is opened from Data Clearinghouse Item Task[4]. The actions for Data Clearinghouse Item Author are:

---

[3] Correction: *Data Clearinghouse Item Topic. Phrase* (R) on Page 100 of *Data Resource Understanding* is erroneous and should not be there.

[4] Correction: Foreign data characteristics for *Data Clearinghouse Author*

[DISPLAY]

> Display Scroll List from *Data Clearinghouse Item Author* with *Data Clearinghouse Author. Individual Name, Data Clearinghouse Author. Family Name, Data Clearinghouse Item. Name Complete*
> Select *Data Clearinghouse Item Author*
> Display Selected *Data Clearinghouse Item Author* data

[PRINT]

(DELETE)

> Delete Selected *Data Clearinghouse Item Author* occurrence

(NEW)

> Display blank data fields for entry of new *Data Clearinghouse Item Author* data
>
> Display Auto-Scroll List from *Data Clearinghouse Item* with *Data Clearinghouse Item Name Complete*
> Select *Data Clearinghouse Item. Name Complete*
>
> Display Scroll List from *Data Clearinghouse Author* with *Data Clearinghouse Author. Individual Name, Data Clearinghouse Author. Family Name. Phrase*
> Select *Data Clearinghouse Author*

[ACCEPT]

[RETURN]

> Close window and Return to Data Clearinghouse Item Task

[HELP]

> Open Help Message View
> Display Data Clearinghouse Item Author Help Message

Data Clearinghouse Item Area

Data Clearinghouse Item Area is opened from Data Clearinghouse Item Task. The actions for Data Clearinghouse Item Area are:

[DISPLAY]

---

on Page 99 of *Data Resource Understanding* should be *Data Clearinghouse Author. Individual Name* and *Data Clearinghouse Author. Family Name. Data Clearinghouse Author. System Identifier* should be removed.

Display Scroll List from *Data Clearinghouse Item Area* with
Spatial Area. Name, Data Clearinghouse Item. Name Complete
Select *Data Clearinghouse Item Area*
Display Selected *Data Clearinghouse Item Area* data

[PRINT]

(DELETE)
Delete Selected *Data Clearinghouse Item Area* occurrence

(NEW)
Display blank data fields for entry of new *Data Clearinghouse Item
Area* data

Display Auto-Scroll List from *Data Clearinghouse Item* with *Data
Clearinghouse Item Name Complete*
Select *Data Clearinghouse Item. Name Complete*

Display Scroll List from *Spatial Area* with *Spatial Area. Name*
Select *Spatial Area. Name*

[ACCEPT]

[RETURN]
Close window and Return to Data Clearinghouse Item Task

[HELP]
Open Help Message View
Display Data Clearinghouse Item Area Help Message

Data Clearinghouse Item Type

Data Clearinghouse Item Type is opened from Data Clearinghouse Item
Task. The actions for Data Clearinghouse Item Type are:

[DISPLAY]
Display Auto-Scroll List from *Data Clearinghouse Item Type* with
Data Clearinghouse Item Type. Name
Select *Data Clearinghouse Item Type. Name*
Display Selected *Data Clearinghouse Item Type* data

[PRINT]

(DELETE)
Delete Selected *Data Clearinghouse Item Type* occurrence

(NEW)

Display blank data fields for entry of new *Data Clearinghouse Item Type a* data

[ACCEPT]

[RETURN]
Close window and Return to <u>Data Clearinghouse Item Task</u>

[HELP]
Open <u>Help Message View</u>
Display Data Clearinghouse Item Type Help Message

Data Steward

Data Steward is opened from Data Clearinghouse Item Task. The actions for Data Steward are provided in the Data Responsibility Chapter.

Organization Unit

Organization Unit is opened from Data Clearinghouse Item Task. The actions for Organization Unit are provided in the Data Responsibility Chapter.

DATA PROJECT TASK

Data Project Task includes Data Project, Data Project Status, Data Project Topic, Data Project Type, Data Steward, and Organization Unit, as shown in Figure 11.6. It is opened from Data Sharing Function.

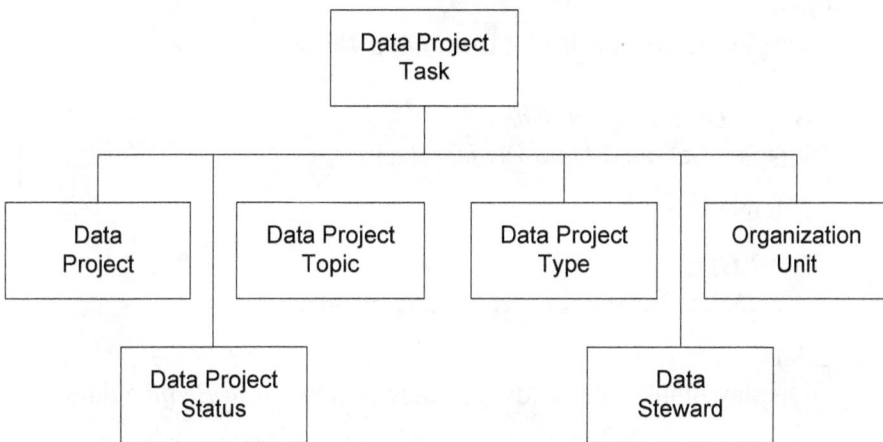

Figure 11.6. Data Project Task.

The actions for Data Project Task are:

[DATA PROJECT]

Open <u>Data Project</u>

[DATA PROJECT STATUS]
Open <u>Data Project Status</u>

[DATA PROJECT TOPIC]
Open <u>Data Project Topic</u>

[DATA PROJECT TYPE]
Open <u>Data Project Type</u>

[DATA STEWARD]
Open <u>Data Steward</u>

[ORGANIZATION UNIT]
.Open <u>Organization Unit</u>

[RETURN]
Close window and Return to <u>Data Sharing Function</u>

[HELP]
Open <u>Help Message View</u>
Display Data Project Task Help Message

Data Project

Data Project is opened from Data Project Task. The actions for Data Project
are:

[DISPLAY]
Display Auto-Scroll List from *Data Project* with *Data Project.
Name*
Select *Data Project. Name*
Display Selected *Data Project* data

[PRINT]

(DELETE)
Delete Selected *Data Project* occurrence

(NEW)
Display blank data fields for entry of new *Data Project* data

Display Auto-Scroll List from *Data Steward* with *Data Steward.
Name Complete*
Select *Data Steward. Name Complete*

Display Auto-Scroll List from *Organization Unit* with
  Organization Unit. Name
Select *Organization Unit. Name*

Display Auto-Scroll List from *Data Project Status* with *Data
  Project Status. Name*
Select *Data Project Status. Name*

Display Auto-Scroll List from *Data Project Topic* with *Data
  Project Topic. Name*
Select *Data Project Topic. Name*

Display Auto-Scroll List from *Data Project Type* with *Data Project
  Type. Name*
Select *Data Project Type. Name*

[ACCEPT]

[RETURN]
  Close window and Return to <u>Data Project Task</u>

[HELP]
  Open <u>Help Message View</u>
  Display Data Project Help Message

Data Project Status

Data Project Status is opened from Data Project Task. The actions for Data
Project Status are:

[DISPLAY]
  Display Auto-Scroll List from *Data Project Status* with *Data
    Project Status. Name*
  Select *Data Project Status. Name*
  Display Selected *Data Project Status* data

[PRINT]

(DELETE)
  Delete Selected *Data Project Status* occurrence

(NEW)
  Display blank data fields for entry of new *Data Project Status* data

[ACCEPT]

[RETURN]
  Close window and Return to <u>Data Project Task</u>

[HELP]
Open <u>Help Message View</u>
Display Data Project Status Help Message

Data Project Topic

Data Project Topic is opened from Data Project Task. The actions for Data Project Topic are:

[DISPLAY]
Display Auto-Scroll List from *Data Project Topic* with *Data Project Topic. Name*
Select *Data Project Topic. Name*
Display Selected *Data Project Topic* data

[PRINT]

(DELETE)
Delete Selected *Data Project Topic* occurrence

(NEW)
Display blank data fields for entry of new *Data Project Topic* data

[ACCEPT]

[RETURN]
Close window and Return to <u>Data Project Task</u>

[HELP]
Open <u>Help Message View</u>
Display Data Project Topic Help Message

Data Project Type

Data Project Type is opened from Data Project Task. The actions for Data Project Type are:

[DISPLAY]
Display Auto-Scroll List from *Data Project Type* with *Data Project Type. Name*
Select *Data Project Type. Name*
Display Selected *Data Project Type* data

[PRINT]

(DELETE)
Delete Selected *Data Project Type* occurrence

(NEW)
>   Display blank data fields for entry of new *Data Project Type* data

[ACCEPT]

[RETURN]
>   Close window and Return to <u>Data Project Task</u>

[HELP]
>   Open <u>Help Message View</u>
>   Display Data Project Type Help Message

Data Steward

Data Steward is opened from Data Project Task. The actions for Data Steward are provided in the Data Responsibility Chapter.

Organization Unit

Organization Unit is opened from Data Project Task. The actions for Organization Unit are provided in the Data Responsibility Chapter.

DATA SHARING REPORTS

Data Sharing Reports contains reports for the Data Sharing Function. It is opened from Data Sharing Function. Only a few examples of reports are shown. Many additional reports could be developed based on an organization's needs and added to the Data Resource Guide.

[Data Clearinghouse Topic Phrase]
>   Display Each *Data Clearinghouse Topic. Phrase*

[PRINT]

[RETURN]
>   Close report and Return to <u>Data Sharing Reports</u>

[Data Clearinghouse Topic Detail]
>   Display Each *Data Clearinghouse Topic* data

[PRINT]

[RETURN]
>   Close report and Return to <u>Data Sharing Reports</u>

[Data Clearinghouse Keyword Phrase]
>   Display Each *Data Clearinghouse Keyword. Phrase*

[PRINT]

[RETURN]
>Close report and Return to <u>Data Sharing Reports</u>

[Data Clearinghouse Keyword Detail]
>Display Each *Data Clearinghouse Keyword* data

[PRINT]

[RETURN]
>Close report and Return to <u>Data Sharing Reports</u>

[Data Clearinghouse Topic Phrase ^ Keyword Phrase]
>Sort *Data Clearinghouse Topic Keyword* by *Data Clearinghouse Topic. Phrase ^ Data Clearinghouse Keyword. Phrase*
>Display from Sort Each Unique *Data Clearinghouse Topic. Phrase*
>>Display Each *Data Clearinghouse Keyword. Phrase, Data Clearinghouse Topic Keyword. Comment*

[PRINT]

[RETURN]
>Close report and Return to <u>Data Sharing Reports</u>

[Data Clearinghouse Keyword Phrase ^ Topic Phrase]
>Sort *Data Clearinghouse Topic Keyword* by *Data Clearinghouse Keyword. Phrase ^ Data Clearinghouse Keyword. Phrase*
>Display from Sort Each Unique *Data Clearinghouse Keyword. Phrase*
>>Display Each *Data Clearinghouse Topic. Phrase, Data Clearinghouse Topic Keyword. Comment*

[PRINT]

[RETURN]
>Close report and Return to <u>Data Sharing Reports</u>

[Data Clearinghouse Author Name]
>Display Each *Data Clearinghouse Author. Family Name, Data Clearinghouse Author. Individual Name*

[PRINT]

[RETURN]
>Close report and Return to <u>Data Sharing Reports</u>

[Data Clearinghouse Author Detail]

Sort *Data Clearinghouse Author* by *Data Clearinghouse Author.*
Family Name, Data Clearinghouse Author. Individual Name
Display from Sort Each *Data Clearinghouse Author* data

[PRINT]

[RETURN]
  Close report and Return to Data Sharing Reports

[Spatial Area Name]
  Display *Each Spatial Area. Name*

[PRINT]

[RETURN]
  Close report and Return to Data Sharing Reports

[Spatial Area Detail]
  Display Each *Spatial Area* data

[PRINT]

[RETURN]
  Close report and Return to Data Sharing Reports

[Selected Spatial Area Detail]
  Display Auto-Scroll List from *Spatial Area* with *Spatial Area.*
  Name
  Select *Spatial Area. Name*
  Display Selected *Spatial Area* data

[PRINT]

[RETURN]
  Close report and Return to Data Sharing Reports

[Spatial Area Type Name]
  Display Each *Spatial Area Type. Name*

[PRINT]

[RETURN]
  Close report and Return to Data Sharing Reports

[Spatial Area Type Detail]
  Display Each *Spatial Area Type* data

[PRINT]

[RETURN]

Close report and Return to <u>Data Sharing Reports</u>

[Data Clearinghouse Item Name]
Display Each *Data Clearinghouse Item. Name Complete*

[PRINT]

[RETURN]
Close report and Return to <u>Data Sharing Reports</u>

[Data Clearinghouse Item Detail]
Display Each *Data Clearinghouse Item* data

[PRINT]

[RETURN]
Close report and Return to <u>Data Sharing Reports</u>

[Selected Data Clearinghouse Item Detail]
Display Auto-Scroll List from *Data Clearinghouse Item* with *Data
Clearinghouse Item. Name Complete*
Select *Data Clearinghouse Item. Name Complete*
Display Selected *Data Clearinghouse Item* data

[PRINT]

[RETURN]
Close report and Return to <u>Data Sharing Reports</u>

[Data Clearinghouse Item Name ^ Topic Phrase]
Sort *Data Clearinghouse Item Topic* by *Data Clearinghouse Item.
Name Complete ^ Data Clearinghouse Topic. Phrase*
Display from Sort Each Unique *Data Clearinghouse Item. Name
Complete*
Display Each *Data Clearinghouse Topic. Phrase, Data
Clearinghouse Item Topic. Comment*

[PRINT]

[RETURN]
Close report and Return to <u>Data Sharing Reports</u>

[Selected Data Clearinghouse Item Name ^ Topic Phrase]
Display Auto-Scroll List from *Data Clearinghouse Item* with *Data
Clearinghouse Item. Name Complete*
Select *Data Clearinghouse Item. Name Complete*
Display Selected *Data Clearinghouse Item* data

Sort *Data Clearinghouse Item Topic* within Selected *Data Clearinghouse Item* by *Data Clearinghouse Topic. Phrase*
Display from Sort Each *Data Clearinghouse Topic. Phrase*

[PRINT]

[RETURN]
    Close report and Return to <u>Data Sharing Reports</u>

[Data Clearinghouse Topic Phrase ^ Item Name]
    Sort *Data Clearinghouse Item Topic* by *Data Clearinghouse Topic. Phrase ^ Data Clearinghouse Item. Name Complete*
    Display from Sort Each Unique *Data Clearinghouse Topic Phrase*
        Display Each *Data Clearinghouse Item. Name Complete, Data Clearinghouse Item Topic. Comment*

[PRINT]

[RETURN]
    Close report and Return to <u>Data Sharing Reports</u>

[Selected Data Clearinghouse Topic Phrase ^ Item Name]
    Display Auto-Scroll List from *Data Clearinghouse Topic* with *Data Clearinghouse Topic. Phrase*
    Select *Data Clearinghouse Topic. Phrase*

    Display Selected *Data Clearinghouse Topic* data
    Sort *Data Clearinghouse Item Topic* within Selected *Data Clearinghouse Topic* by *Data Clearinghouse Item. Name Complete*
    Display from Sort Each *Data Clearinghouse Item. Name Complete*

[PRINT]

[RETURN]
    Close report and Return to <u>Data Sharing Reports</u>

[Data Clearinghouse Item Name ^ Author Name]
    Display Each *Data Clearinghouse Item. Name*
        Display Each *Data Clearinghouse Author. Name*

[PRINT]

[RETURN]
    Close report and Return to <u>Data Sharing Reports</u>

[Data Clearinghouse Item Detail ^ Author Detail]
    Display Each *Data Clearinghouse Item* data

197

       Display Each *Data Clearinghouse Author* data

[PRINT]

[RETURN]
       Close report and Return to <u>Data Sharing Reports</u>

[Selected Data Clearinghouse Item Detail ^ Author Detail]
       Display Auto-Scroll List from *Data Clearinghouse Item* with *Data Clearinghouse Item. Name Complete*
       Select *Data Clearinghouse Item. Name Complete*
       Display Selected *Data Clearinghouse Item* data
           Display Each *Data Clearinghouse Author* data

[PRINT]

[RETURN]
       Close report and Return to <u>Data Sharing Reports</u>

[Data Clearinghouse Author Name ^ Item Name]
       Display Each *Data Clearinghouse Author. Family Name, Data Clearinghouse Author. Individual Name*
           Display Each *Data Clearinghouse Item. Name Complete*

[PRINT]

[RETURN]
       Close report and Return to <u>Data Sharing Reports</u>

[Data Clearinghouse Author Detail ^ Item Detail]
       Display Each *Data Clearinghouse Author* data
           Display Each *Data Clearinghouse Item* data

[PRINT]

[RETURN]
       Close report and Return to <u>Data Sharing Reports</u>

[Selected Data Clearinghouse Author Detail ^ Item Detail]
       Display Scroll List from *Data Clearinghouse Author* with *Data Clearinghouse Author. Family Name, Data Clearinghouse Author. Individual Name*
       Select *Data Clearinghouse Author*
       Display Selected *Data Clearinghouse Author* data
           Display Each *Data Clearinghouse Item* data

[PRINT]

[RETURN]
    Close report and Return to <u>Data Sharing Reports</u>

[Data Clearinghouse Item Name ^ Spatial Area Name]
    Display Each *Data Clearinghouse Item. Name Complete*
        Display Each *Spatial Area. Name*

[PRINT]

[RETURN]
    Close report and Return to <u>Data Sharing Reports</u>

[Data Clearinghouse Item Detail ^ Spatial Area Detail]
    Display Each *Data Clearinghouse Item* data
        Display Each *Spatial Area* data

[PRINT]

[RETURN]
    Close report and Return to <u>Data Sharing Reports</u>

[Selected Data Clearinghouse Item Detail ^ Spatial Area Detail]
    Display Auto-Scroll List from *Data Clearinghouse Item* with *Data*
        Clearinghouse Item. Name Complete
    Select *Data Clearinghouse Item. Name Complete*
    Display Selected *Data Clearinghouse* data
        Display Each *Spatial Area* data

[PRINT]

[RETURN]
    Close report and Return to <u>Data Sharing Reports</u>

[Spatial Area Name ^ Data Clearinghouse Item Name]
    Display Each *Spatial Area. Name*
        Display Each *Data Clearinghouse Item. Name Complete*

[PRINT]

[RETURN]
    Close report and Return to <u>Data Sharing Reports</u>

[Spatial Area Detail ^ Data Clearinghouse Item Detail]
    Display Each *Spatial Area* data
        Display Each *Data Clearinghouse Item* data

[PRINT]

[RETURN]

Close report and Return to <u>Data Sharing Reports</u>

[Selected Spatial Area Detail ^ Data Clearinghouse Item Detail]
Display Auto-Scroll List from *Spatial Area* with *Spatial Area.
Name*
Select *Spatial Area. Name*
Display Selected *Spatial Area* data
Display Each *Data Clearinghouse Item* data

[PRINT]

[RETURN]
Close report and Return to <u>Data Sharing Reports</u>

[Data Clearinghouse Item Type Name]
Display Each *Data Clearinghouse Item Type. Name*

[PRINT]

[RETURN]
Close report and Return to <u>Data Sharing Reports</u>

[Data Clearinghouse Item Type Detail]
Display Each *Data Clearinghouse Item Type* data

[PRINT]

[RETURN]
Close report and Return to <u>Data Sharing Reports</u>

[Data Project Name]
Display Each *Data Project. Name*

[PRINT]

[RETURN]
Close report and Return to <u>Data Sharing Reports</u>

[Data Project Detail]
Display Each *Data Project* data

[PRINT]

[RETURN]
Close report and Return to <u>Data Sharing Reports</u>

[Selected Data Project Detail]
Display Auto-Scroll List from *Data Project* with *Data Project.
Name*

Select *Data Project. Name*
Display Selected *Data Project* data

[PRINT]

[RETURN]
Close report and Return to <u>Data Sharing Reports</u>

[Data Project Status Name]
Display Each *Data Project Status. Name*

[PRINT]

[RETURN]
Close report and Return to <u>Data Sharing Reports</u>

[Data Project Status Detail]
Display Each *Data Project Status* data

[PRINT]

[RETURN]
Close report and Return to <u>Data Sharing Reports</u>

[Data Project Topic Name]
Display Each Data Project Topic. Name

[PRINT]

[RETURN]
Close report and Return to <u>Data Sharing Reports</u>

[Data Project Topic Detail]
Display Each *Data Project Topic* data

[PRINT]

[RETURN]
Close report and Return to <u>Data Sharing Reports</u>

[Data Project Type Name]
Display Each *Data Project Type. Name*

[PRINT]

[RETURN]
Close report and Return to <u>Data Sharing Reports</u>

[Data Project Type Detail]
Display Each *Data Project Type* data

[PRINT]

[RETURN]
    Close report and Return to <u>Data Sharing Reports</u>

[RETURN]
    Close window and Return to <u>Data Sharing Function</u>

[HELP]
    Open <u>Help Message View</u>
    Display Data Sharing Reports Help Message

Chapter 12

DERIVED DATA

Derived Data Function includes Data Subject Contributor Task, Foreign Data Characteristic Task, Data Set Hierarchy Task, and Derived Data Reports, as shown in Figure 12.1. It is opened from Data Resource Guide Edit / View.

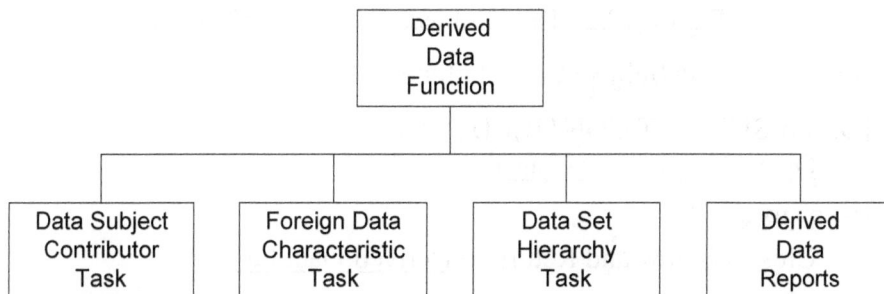

Figure 12.1. Derived Data Function.

The actions for Derived Data Function are:

[DATA SUBJECT CONTRIBUTOR TASK]
    Open Data Subject Contributor Task

[FOREIGN DATA CHARACTERISTIC TASK]
    Open Foreign Data Characteristic Task

[DATA SET HIERARCHY TASK]
    Open Data Set Hierarchy Task

[DERIVED DATA REPORTS]
    Open Derived Data Reports

[RETURN]
    Close window and Return to Data Resource Guide Edit / View

[HELP]
    Open Help Message View
    Display Derived Data Function Help Message

DATA SUBJECT CONTRIBUTOR TASK

Data Subject Contributor Task includes Data Subject Contributor, as shown in Figure 12.2.

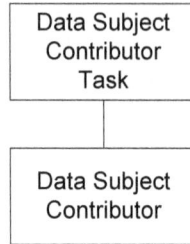

```
┌─────────────────┐
│  Data Subject   │
│   Contributor   │
│      Task       │
└────────┬────────┘
         │
┌────────┴────────┐
│  Data Subject   │
│   Contributor   │
└─────────────────┘
```

Figure 12.2. Data Subject Contributor Task.

The actions for Data Subject Contributor Task are:

[DATA SUBJECT CONTRIBUTOR]
Open Data Subject Contributor

[RETURN]
Close window and Return to Derived Data Function

[HELP]
Open Help Message View
Display Data Subject Contributor Task Help Message

Data Subject Contributor

Data Subject Contributor is opened from Data Subject Contributor Task. The actions for Data Subject Contributor are:

[DISPLAY]
Display Scroll List from *Data Subject Contributor* with *"Contributor" Data Subject. Name Complete*, *"Derived" Data Subject. Name Complete*
Select *Data Subject Contributor*
Display Selected *Data Subject Contributor* data

[PRINT]

(DELETE)
Delete Selected *Data Subject Contributor* occurrence

(NEW)
Display blank data fields for entry of new *Data Subject Contributor* data

Display Auto-Scroll List from *Data Subject* with *Data Subject.*
  Name Complete
Select *"Derived" Data Subject*

Display Auto-Scroll List from *Data Subject* with *Data Subject.*
  Name Complete
Select *"Contributor" Data Subject*

[ACCEPT]

[RETURN]
  Close window and Return to <u>Derived Subject Contributor Task</u>

[HELP]
  Open <u>Help Message View</u>
  Display Data Subject Contributor Help Message

FOREIGN DATA CHARACTERISTIC TASK

Foreign Data Characteristic Task includes Foreign Data Characteristic Assignment, as shown in Figure 12.3.

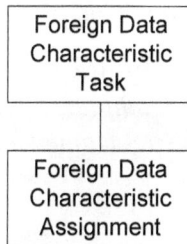

Figure 12.3. Foreign Data Characteristic Task.

The actions for Foreign Data Characteristic Task are:

[FOREIGN DATA CHARACTERISTIC ASSIGNMENT]
  Open Foreign Data Characteristic Assignment

[RETURN]
  Close window and Return to <u>Derived Data Function</u>

[HELP]
  Open <u>Help Message View</u>
  Display Foreign Data Characteristic Task Help Message

Foreign Data Characteristic Assignment

Foreign Data Characteristic Assignment is opened from Foreign Data Characteristic Task. The actions for Foreign Data Characteristic Assignment are:

[DISPLAY]

Display Scroll List from *Foreign Data Characteristic Assignment* with *Data Subject. Name Complete*, *Data Characteristic. Name Complete*
Select *Foreign Data Characteristic Assignment*
Display Selected *Foreign Data Characteristic Assignment* data

[PRINT]

(DELETE)

Delete Selected *Foreign Data Characteristic Assignment* occurrence

(NEW)

Display blank data fields for entry of new *Foreign Data Characteristic Assignment* data

Display Auto-Scroll List from *Data Subject* with *Data Subject. Name Complete*
Select *Data Subject. Name Complete*

Display Auto-Scroll List from *Data Characteristic* with *Data Characteristic. Name Complete*
Select *Data Characteristic. Name Complete*

[ACCEPT]

[RETURN]

Close window and Return to <u>Foreign Data Characteristic Task</u>

[HELP]

Open <u>Help Message View</u>
Display Foreign Data Characteristic Assignment Help Message

DATA SET HIERARCHY TASK

Data Set Hierarchy Task includes Data Set Hierarchy, Data Subject Set, and Data Subject Set Characteristic, as shown in Figure 12.4

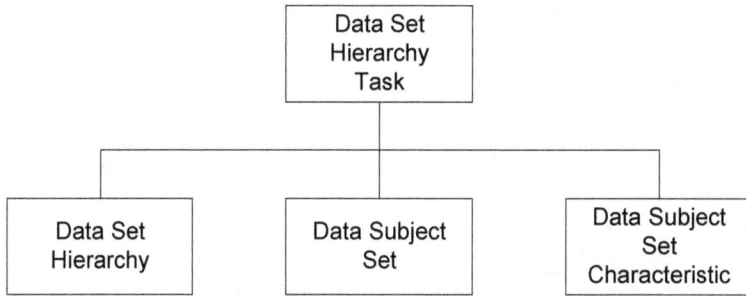

Figure 12.4. Data Set Hierarchy Task

The actions for Data Set Hierarchy Task are:

[DATA SET HIERARCHY]
>   Open <u>Data Set Hierarchy</u>

[DATA SUBJECT SET]
>   Open <u>Data Subject Set</u>

[DATA SUBJECT SET CHARACTERISTIC]
>   Open <u>Data Subject Set Characteristic</u>

[RETURN]
>   Close window and Return to <u>Derived Data Function</u>

[HELP]
>   Open <u>Help Message View</u>
>   Display Data Set Hierarchy Task Help Message

Data Set Hierarchy

Data Set Hierarchy is opened from Data Set Hierarchy Task. The actions for Data Set Hierarchy are:

[DISPLAY]
>   Display Auto-Scroll List from *Data Set Hierarchy* with *Data Set Hierarchy. Name*
>   Select *Data Set Hierarchy. Name*
>   Display Selected *Data Set Hierarchy* data

>   [PRINT]

>   (DELETE)
>>   Delete Selected *Foreign Data Characteristic Assignment* occurrence

(NEW)

207

Display blank data fields for entry of new *Data Set Hierarchy* data

[ACCEPT]

[RETURN]
Close window and Return to Data Set Hierarchy Task

[HELP]
Open Help Message View
Display Data Set Hierarchy Help Message

Data Subject Set

Data Subject Set is opened from Data Set Hierarchy Task[5]. The actions for Data Subject Set are:

Display Auto-Scroll List from *Data Set Hierarchy* with *Data Set Hierarchy. Name*
Select *Data Set Hierarchy. Name*

[DISPLAY]
Display Scroll List from *Data Subject Set* within Selected *Data Set Hierarchy* with *"Parent Set" Data Subject. Name Complete*, *"Child Set" Data Subject. Name Complete*
Select *Data Subject Set*
Display Selected *Data Subject Set* data

[PRINT]

(DELETE)
Delete Selected *Data Subject Set* occurrence

(NEW)
Display blank data fields for entry of new *Data Subject Set* data

Display Auto-Scroll List from *Data Subject* with *Data Subject. Name Complete*
Select *"Parent Set" Data Subject. Name Complete*

Display Auto-Scroll List from *Data Subject* with *Data Subject. Name Complete*
Select *"Child Set" Data Subject. Name Complete*

---

[5] Correction: Data Subject Set on Page 114 of *Data Resource Understanding* should not have *Data Set Hierarchy. System Identifier* in the data characteristic list. *Data Set Hierarchy. Name* should be added to the data characteristic list.

[ACCEPT]

[RETURN]
> Close window and Return to Data Set Hierarchy Task

[HELP]
> Open Help Message View
> Display Data Subject Set Help Message

Data Subject Set Characteristic

Data Subject Set Characteristic is opened from Data Set Hierarchy Task.[6] The actions for Data Subject Set Characteristic are:

> Display Auto-Scroll List from *Data Set Hierarchy* with *Data Set Hierarchy. Name*
> Select *Data Set Hierarchy. Name*

> Display Scroll List from *Data Subject Set* within Selected *Data Set Hierarchy* with *"Parent Set' Data Subject. Name Complete, "Child Set" Data Subject. Name Complete*
> Select *Data Subject Set*

[DISPLAY]
> Display Scroll List from *Data Subject Set Characteristic* within Selected *Data Subject Set* with *Data Characteristic. Name Complete*
> Select *Data Subject Set Characteristic*
> Display Selected *Data Subject Set Characteristic* data

[PRINT]

(DELETE)
> Delete Selected *Data Subject Set Characteristic* occurrence

(NEW)
> Display blank data fields for entry of new *Data Subject Set Characteristic* data

---

[6] **Correction**: Data Subject Set Characteristics listed on Page 115 of *Data Resource Understanding* should not have *Data Subject Set. System Identifier* in the data characteristic list. *Data Set Hierarchy. Name, "Parent Set" Data Subject. Name Complete* and *"Child Set" Data Subject. Name Complete* should be added to the data characteristic list.

Display Auto-Scroll List from *Data Characteristic* with *Data Characteristic. Name Complete*
Select *Data Characteristic. Name Complete*

[ACCEPT]

[RETURN]
Close window and Return to <u>Data Set Hierarchy Task</u>

[HELP]
Open <u>Help Message View</u>
Display Data Subject Set Characteristic Help Message

DERIVED DATA REPORTS

Derived Data Reports contains reports for the Derived Data Function. It is opened from Derived Data Function. Only a few examples of reports are shown. Many additional reports could be developed based on an organization's needs and added to the Data Resource Guide.

[Data Set Hierarchy Name]
Display Each *Data Set Hierarchy. Name*

[PRINT]

[RETURN]
Close report and Return to <u>Derived Data Reports</u>

[Data Set Hierarchy Detail]
Display Each *Data Set Hierarchy* data

[PRINT]

[RETURN]
Close report and Return to <u>Derived Data Reports</u>

[Data Set Hierarchy Name ^ Data Subject Set Detail]
Display Each *Data Set Hierarchy. Name*
Display Each *Data Subject Set* data

[PRINT]

[RETURN]
Close report and Return to <u>Derived Data Reports</u>

[Selected Data Set Hierarchy Detail ^ Data Subject Set Detail]
Display Auto-Scroll List from *Data Set Hierarchy* with *Data Set Hierarchy. Name*

Select *Data Set Hierarchy. Name*
Display Selected *Data Set Hierarchy* data
    Display Each *Data Subject Set* data within Selected *Data Set Hierarchy*

[PRINT]

[RETURN]
    Close report and Return to <u>Derived Data Reports</u>

[Data Set Hierarchy Name ^ Data Subject Set Detail ^ Data Subject Set Characteristic Detail]
    Display Each *Data Set Hierarchy. Name*
        Display Each *Data Subject Set* data
            Display Each *Data Subject Set Characteristic* data

[PRINT]

[RETURN]
    Close report and Return to <u>Derived Data Reports</u>

[Selected Data Set Hierarchy ^ Data Subject Set ^ Data Subject Set Characteristic Detail]
    Display Auto-Scroll List from *Data Set Hierarchy* with *Data Set Hierarchy. Name*
    Select *Data Set Hierarchy. Name*
    Display Each *Data Subject Set* data within *Selected Data Set Hierarchy*
        Display Each *Data Subject Set Characteristic* data

[PRINT]

[RETURN]
    Close report and Return to <u>Derived Data Reports</u>

[Data Subject ^ Data Subject Contributor Detail]
    Display Each *Data Subject. Name Complete*
        Display Each *Data Subject Contributor* data

[PRINT]

[RETURN]
    Close report and Return to <u>Derived Data Reports</u>

[Selected Data Subject ^ Data Subject Contributor Detail]
    Display Auto-Scroll List from *Data Subject* with *Data Subject. Name Complete*

211

Select *Data Subject. Name Complete*
Display Each *Data Subject Contributor* data within Selected *Data Subject*

[PRINT]

[RETURN]
    Close report and Return to <u>Derived Data Reports</u>

[Data Subject Name ^ Foreign Data Characteristic Assignment Detail]
    Display Each *Data Subject. Name Complete*
        Display Each *Foreign Data Characteristic Assignment* data

[PRINT]

[RETURN]
    Close report and Return to <u>Derived Data Reports</u>

[Selected Data Subject Name ^ Foreign Data Characteristic Assignment Detail]
    Display Auto-Scroll List from *Data Subject* with *Data Subject. Name Complete*
    Select *Data Subject. Name Complete*
    Display Each *Foreign Data Characteristic Assignment* data within Selected *Data Subject*

[PRINT]

[RETURN]
    Close report and Return to <u>Derived Data Reports</u>

[Data Characteristic Name ^ Foreign Data Characteristic Assignment Detail]
    Display Each *Data Subject. Name Complete*
        Display Each *Data Characteristic. Name Complete*
            Display Each *Foreign Data Characteristic Assignment* data

[PRINT]

[RETURN]
    Close report and Return to <u>Derived Data Reports</u>

[Selected Data Characteristic Name ^ Foreign Data Characteristic Assignment Detail]
    Display Auto-Scroll List from *Data Subject* with *Data Subject. Name Complete*

Select *Data Subject. Name Complete*

Display Auto-Scroll List from *Data Characteristic* within Selected *Data Subject* with Data Characteristic. Name Complete

Select *Data Characteristic. Name Complete*

Display Each *Foreign Data Characteristic Assignment* data within Selected *Data Characteristic*

[PRINT]

[RETURN]
> Close report and Return to <u>Derived Data Reports</u>

[RETURN]
> Close window and Return to <u>Derived Data Function</u>

[HELP]
> Open <u>Help Message View</u>
> Display Derived Data Reports Help Message

Chapter 13

PREFERRED DATA

Preferred Data Function includes Preferred Common Data Task, Preferred Data Lexicon Task, Preferred Data Product Data Task, and Preferred Data Reports, as shown in Figure 13.1. It is opened from Data Resource Guide Edit / View. However, only persons authorized to edit the data can enter preferred data indicators. Anyone can view the Preferred Data Reports.

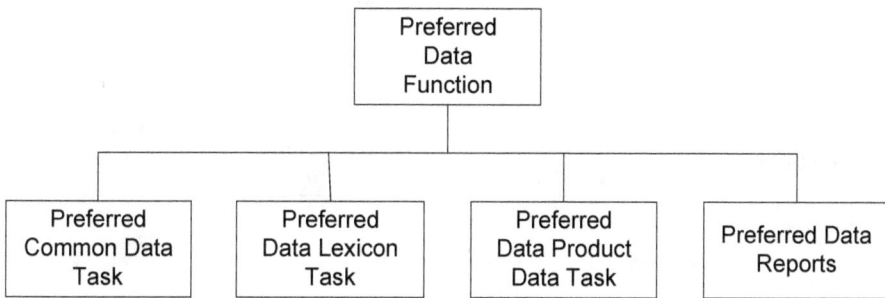

```
                        +-------------+
                        |  Preferred  |
                        |    Data     |
                        |  Function   |
                        +-------------+
                               |
     +-------------+-----------+-----------+-------------+
     |             |                       |             |
+-----------+ +-----------+         +-----------+ +---------------+
| Preferred | | Preferred |         | Preferred | | Preferred Data|
|Common Data| |Data Lexicon|        |Data Product| |    Reports    |
|   Task    | |   Task    |         | Data Task | +---------------+
+-----------+ +-----------+         +-----------+
```

Figure 13.1. Preferred Data Function.

The actions for Preferred Data Function are:

[PREFERRED COMMON DATA TASK]
    Open Preferred Common Data Task

[PREFERRED DATA LEXICON TASK]
    Open Preferred Data Lexicon Task

[PREFERRED DATA PRODUCT DATA TASK]
    Open Preferred Data Product Data Task

[PREFERRED DATA REPORTS]
    Open Preferred Data Reports

[RETURN]
    Close window and Return to Data Resource Guide Edit / View

[HELP]
    Open Help Message View
    Display Preferred Data Function Help Message

PREFERRED COMMON DATA TASK

Preferred Common Data Task includes Preferred Data Subject, Preferred Data Characteristic, Preferred Data Characteristic Variation, Preferred Data Reference Set Variation, Preferred Data Reference Item, Preferred Primary Key, and Preferred Foreign Key, as shown in Figure 13.2. These routines only cover the actions for setting Preferred Indicators and Common Data Status. The Preferred Indicators and Common Data Status could also be set as provided in the Common Data Chapter, but are included in the Preferred Common Data Task for convenience.

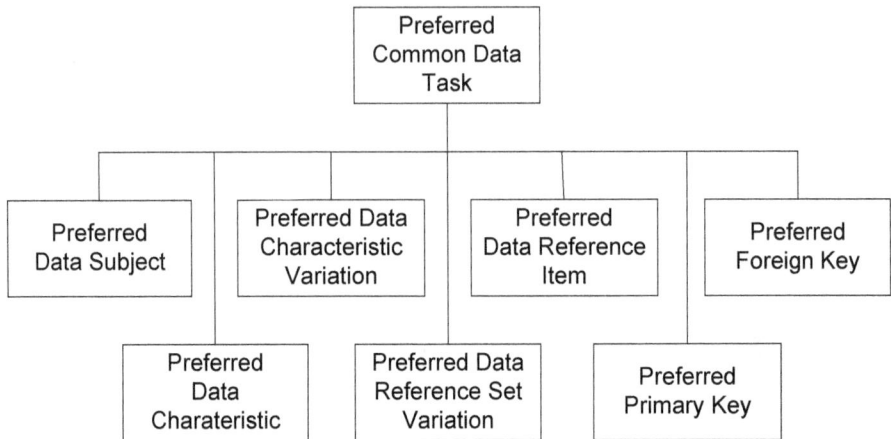

Figure 13.2. Preferred Common Data Task.

The Preferred Common Data Task actions do not include preparing preferred data definitions or preferred data integrity rules, or changing dates and status codes. Those actions are provided in the Common Data Chapter. However, the reports provided in the Preferred Data Function show the data definitions and data integrity rules from the Data Product Data and from subordinate Common Data that can be used to help prepare the preferred data definitions and data integrity rules.

The actions for Preferred Common Data Task are:

> [PREFERRED DATA SUBJECT]
>> Open <u>Preferred Data Subject</u>

> [PREFERRED DATA CHARACTERISTIC]
>> Open <u>Preferred Data Characteristic</u>

> [PREFERRED DATA CHARACTERISTIC VARIATION]
>> Open <u>Preferred Data Characteristic Variation</u>

> [PREFERRED DATA REFERENCE SET VARIATION]

Open Preferred Data Reference Set Variation

[PREFERRED DATA REFERENCE ITEM]
Open Preferred Data Reference Item

[PREFERRED PRIMARY KEY]
Open Preferred Primary Key

[PREFERRED FOREIGN KEY]
Open Preferred Foreign Key

[RETURN]
Close window and Return to Preferred Data Function

[HELP]
Open Help Message View
Display Preferred Common Data Task Help Message

Preferred Data Subject

Preferred Data Subject is opened from Preferred Common Data Task. The actions for Preferred Data Subject are:

[DISPLAY]
Display from *Data Subject* Each *Data Subject. Name Complete,
Data Subject. Definition, Data Subject. Comment, Common Data
Status. Name*

(STATUS)
Display Auto-Scroll List from *Common Data Status* with
Common Data Status. Name
Select *Common Data Status. Name*

[ACCEPT]

[NEXT]
Display Next *Data Subject* occurrence

[BACK]
Display Previous *Data Subject* occurrence

[RETURN]
Close window and Return to Preferred Common Data Task

[HELP]
Open Help Message View
Display Preferred Data Subject Help Message

Preferred Data Characteristic

Preferred Data Characteristic is opened from Preferred Common Data Task. The actions for Preferred Data Characteristic are:

[DISPLAY]
>Display Auto-Scroll List from *Data Subject* with *Data Subject. Name Complete*
>Select *Data Subject. Name Complete*
>Display from *Data Characteristic* within *Selected Data Subject* Each *Data Characteristic. Name Complete*, *Data Characteristic. Definition*, *Data Characteristic. Comment*, *Common Data Status. Name*

>(STATUS)
>>Display Auto-Scroll List from *Common Data Status* with *Common Data Status. Name*
>>Select *Common Data Status. Name*

>[ACCEPT]

>[NEXT]
>>Display Next *Data Characteristic* occurrence

>[BACK]
>>Display Previous *Data Characteristic* occurrence

[RETURN]
>Close window and Return to <u>Preferred Common Data Task</u>

[HELP]
>Open <u>Help Message View</u>
>Display Preferred Data Characteristic Help Message

Preferred Data Characteristic Variation

Preferred Data Characteristic Variation is opened from Preferred Common Data Task. The actions for Preferred Data Characteristic Variation are:

>Display Auto-Scroll List from *Data Subject* with *Data Subject. Name Complete*
>Select *Data Subject. Name Complete*

>Display Auto-Scroll List from *Data Characteristic* within Selected *Data Subject* with *Data Characteristic. Name Complete*
>Select *Data Characteristic. Name Complete*

>[DISPLAY]

Display from *Data Characteristic Variation* within Selected *Data Characteristic* Each *Data Characteristic Variation. Name Complete, Data Characteristic Variation Definition. Data Characteristic Variation. Comment, Data Characteristic Variation. Preferred Indicator, Common Data Status. Name*

(YES)

Set *Data Characteristic Variation. Preferred Indicator* >< 'Yes'

(NO)

Set *Data Characteristic Variation. Preferred Indicator* >< 'No'

(STATUS)

Display Auto-Scroll List from *Common Data Status* with *Common Data Status. Name*
Select *Common Data Status. Name*

[ACCEPT]

[NEXT]

Display Next *Data Characteristic Variation* occurrence

[BACK]

Display Previous *Data Characteristic Variation* occurrence

[RETURN]

Close window and Return to Preferred Common Data Task

[HELP]

Open Help Message View
Display Preferred Data Characteristic Variation Help Message

Preferred Data Reference Set Variation

Preferred Data Reference Set Variation is opened from Preferred Common Data Task. The actions for Preferred Data Reference Set Variation are:

Display Auto-Scroll List from *Data Subject* with *Data Subject. Name Complete* When *Data Subject. Data Reference Set. Indicator* >< 'Yes'
Select *Data Subject. Name Complete*

[DISPLAY]

Display from *Data Reference Set Variation* within Selected *Data Subject* Each *Data Reference Set Variation. Name Complete, Data Reference Set Variation Definition. Data Reference Set Variation.*

Comment, *Data Reference Set Variation. Preferred Indicator,*
Common Data Status. Name

(YES)

Set *Data Reference Set Variation. Preferred Indicator* ><
'Yes'

(NO)

Set Data Reference Set Variation. Preferred Indicator >< 'No'

(STATUS)

Display Auto-Scroll List from *Common Data Status* with
Common Data Status. Name
Select *Common Data Status. Name*

[ACCEPT]

[NEXT]

Display Next *Data Reference Set Variation* occurrence

[BACK]

Display Previous *Data Reference Set Variation* occurrence

[RETURN]

Close window and Return to <u>Preferred Common Data Task</u>

[HELP]

Open <u>Help Message View</u>
Display Preferred Data Reference Set Variation Help Message

Preferred Data Reference Item

Preferred Data Reference Item is opened from Preferred Common Data
Task. The actions for Preferred Data Reference Item are:

Display Auto-Scroll List from *Data Subject* with *Data Subject. Name*
Complete When *Data Subject. Data Reference Set Indicator* >< 'Yes'
Select *Data Subject. Name Complete*

Display Auto-Scroll List from *Data Reference Set Variation* within
Selected *Data Subject* with *Data Reference Set Variation. Name*
Complete
Select *Data Reference Set Variation. Name Complete*

[DISPLAY]

Display from *Data Reference Item* within Selected *Data Reference*
Set Variation Each *Data Reference Item. Name, Data Reference*

Item. Code, Data Reference Item Definition. Data Reference Set Variation. Comment, Common Data Status. Name

(STATUS)
>   Display Auto-Scroll List from *Common Data Status* with
>   *Common Data Status. Name*
>   Select *Common Data Status. Name*

[ACCEPT]

[NEXT]
>   Display Next *Data Reference Set Variation* occurrence

[BACK]
>   Display Previous *Data Reference Set Variation* occurrence

[RETURN]
>   Close window and Return to <u>Preferred Common Data Task</u>

[HELP]
>   Open <u>Help Message View</u>
>   Display Preferred Data Reference Item Help Message

Preferred Primary Key

Preferred Primary Key is opened from Preferred Common Data Task. The actions for Preferred Primary Key are:

Display Auto-Scroll List from *Data Subject* with *Data Subject. Name*
Select *Data Subject. Name*

[DISPLAY]
>   Display from *Primary Key* within Selected *Data Subject* Each
>   *Primary Key. Comment, Primary Key. Preferred Indicator,*
>   *Common Data Status. Name*
>>   Display from *Primary Key Characteristic* Each *Primary Key*
>>   *Characteristic. Comment, Data Characteristic. Name*
>>   *Complete*

(YES)
>   Set *Primary Key. Preferred Indicator* >< 'Yes'

(NO)
>   Set *Primary Key. Preferred Indicator* >< 'No'

(STATUS)

221

Display Auto-Scroll List from *Common Data Status* with
Common Data Status. Name
Select *Common Data Status. Name*

[ACCEPT]

[NEXT]
Display Next *Primary Key* occurrence

[BACK]
Display Previous *Primary Key* occurrence

[RETURN]
Close window and Return to <u>Preferred Common Data Task</u>

[HELP]
Open <u>Help Message View</u>
Display Preferred Primary Key Help Message

Preferred Foreign Key

Preferred Foreign Key is opened from Preferred Common Data Task. The
actions for Preferred Foreign Key are:

Display Auto-Scroll List from *Data Subject* with *Data Subject. Name*
Select *Data Subject. Name*

[DISPLAY]
Display from *Foreign Key* within Selected *Data Subject* Each
*Foreign Key. Comment, Foreign Key. Preferred Indicator,
"Local" Data Subject. Name Complete, "Parent" Data Subject.
Name Complete* from *Foreign Key, Common Data Status. Name*

(YES)
Set *Foreign Primary Key. Preferred Indicator* >< 'Yes'

(NO)
Set *Foreign Key. Preferred Indicator* >< 'No'

(STATUS)
Display Auto-Scroll List from *Common Data Status* with
Common Data Status. Name
Select *Common Data Status. Name*

[ACCEPT]

[NEXT]
Display Next *Foreign Key* occurrence

[BACK]
>Display Previous *Foreign Key* occurrence

[RETURN]
>Close window and Return to <u>Preferred Common Data Task</u>

[HELP]
>Open <u>Help Message View</u>
>Display Preferred Foreign Key Help Message

PREFERRED DATA LEXICON TASK

Preferred Data Lexicon Task includes Preferred Data Name Abbreviation and Preferred Business Glossary Item, as shown in Figure 13.3.

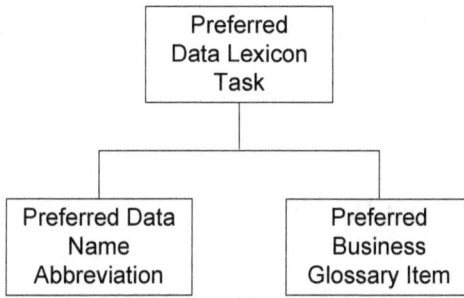

Figure 13.3. Preferred Data Lexicon Task.

The actions for Preferred Data Lexicon Task are:

[PREFERRED DATA NAME ABBREVIATION]
>Open <u>Preferred Data Name Abbreviation</u>

[PREFERRED BUSINESS GLOSSARY ITEM]
>Open <u>Preferred Business Glossary Item</u>

[RETURN]
>Close window and Return to <u>Preferred Data Function</u>

[HELP]
>Open <u>Help Message View</u>
>Display Preferred Data Lexicon Task Help Message

Preferred Data Name Abbreviation

Preferred Data Name Abbreviation is opened from Preferred Data Lexicon Task. Preferred Data Name Abbreviation is intended for rapid review of Name and Description for Data Name Abbreviation Scheme, and setting the

Preferred Indicator. It is not intended for entering or editing Data Name Abbreviation Scheme data. Those tasks are performed as described in the Data Lexicon Chapter. The actions for Preferred Data Name Lexicon are:

[DISPLAY]
> Display Each *Data Name Abbreviation Scheme. Name, Data Name Abbreviation Scheme. Description, Data Name Abbreviation Scheme. Preferred Indicator* from *Data Name Abbreviation Scheme*

(YES)
> Set *Data Name Abbreviation Scheme. Preferred Indicator* >< 'Yes'

(NO)
> Set *Data Name Abbreviation Scheme. Preferred Indicator* >< 'No'

[ACCEPT]

[NEXT]
> Display Next *Data Name Abbreviation Scheme* occurrence

[BACK]
> Display Previous *Data Name Abbreviation Scheme* occurrence

[RETURN]
> Close window and Return to <u>Preferred Data Lexicon Task</u>

[HELP]
> Open <u>Help Message View</u>
> Display Preferred Data Name Abbreviation Help Message

Preferred Business Glossary Item

Preferred Business Glossary Item is opened from Preferred Data Lexicon Task. Preferred Business Glossary Item is intended for rapid review of the Phrase and Definition, and setting the Preferred Indicator. It is not intended for entering or editing Business Glossary Item data. Those tasks are performed as described in the Data Lexicon Chapter. The actions for Preferred Data Name Lexicon are:

[DISPLAY]
> Display Auto-Scroll List from *Business Glossary* with *Business Glossary. Name*
> Select *Business Glossary. Name*

Display Each *Business Glossary Item. Phrase, Business Glossary Item. Definition, Business Glossary Item. Preferred Indicator* from *Business Glossary Item* within Selected *Business Glossary*

(YES)
Set *Business Glossary Item. Preferred Indicator* >< 'Yes'

(NO)
Set *Business Glossary Item. Preferred Indicator* >< 'No'

[ACCEPT]

[NEXT]
Display Next *Business Glossary Item* occurrence

[BACK]
Display Previous *Business Glossary Item* occurrence

[RETURN]
Close window and Return to Preferred Data Lexicon Task

[HELP]
Open Help Message View
Display Preferred Business Glossary Help Message

PREFERRED DATA PRODUCT DATA TASK

Preferred Data Product Data Task includes Preferred Data Product, Preferred Data Product Set, Preferred Data Product Unit, and Preferred Data Product Code, as shown in Figure 13.4. These routines only cover the actions for setting the Preferred Common Indicators and Preferred Source Indicators. The Preferred Common Indicators and Preferred Source Indicators could also be set as provided in the Data Inventory Chapter, but are included in the Preferred Data Product Data Task for convenience.

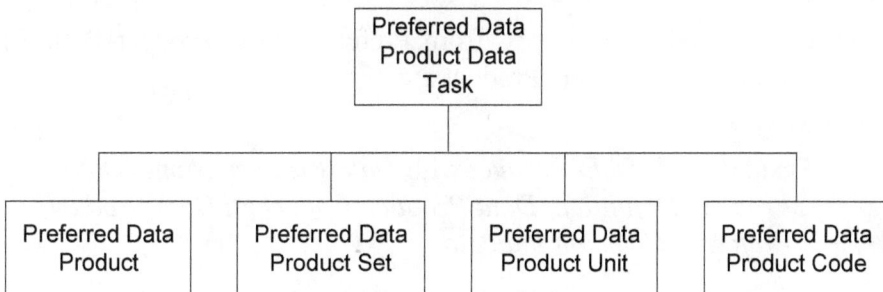

Figure 13.4. Preferred Data Product Data Task.

The creation of preferred Data Product Data resulting from the formal

225

denormalization of the preferred Common Data is done as provided in the Data Inventory Chapter and in *Data Resource Understanding*.

The Preferred Data Product Data resulting from formal denormalization of the preferred Common Data do not include any Data Product Set Variation, Data Product Unit Variation, or Data Product Code Variation because the situations resulting in those variations do not exist in the Preferred Common Data.

The Preferred Data Product Data Task actions do not include adding new Preferred Data Product Data or editing existing Preferred Data Product Data. Those actions are provided in the Data Inventory Chapter.

The actions for Preferred Data Product Data Task are:

[PREFERRED DATA PRODUCT]
    Open Preferred Data Product

[PREFERRED DATA PRODUCT SET]
    Open Preferred Data Product Set

[PREFERRED DATA PRODUCT UNIT]
    Open Preferred Data Product Unit

[PREFERRED DATA PRODUCT CODE]
    Open Preferred Data Product Code

[RETURN]
    Close window and Return to Preferred Data Function

[HELP]
    Open Help Message View
    Display Preferred Data Product Data Task Help Message

Preferred Data Product

Preferred Data Product is opened from Preferred Data Product Data Task. The actions for Preferred Data Product are:

[DISPLAY]
    Display Each *Data Product* with *Data Product. Name, Data Product. Definition, Data Product. Comment, Data Product. Preferred Common Indicator*

(YES)
    Set *Data Product. Preferred Common Indicator* >< 'Yes'

(NO)

Set *Data Product. Preferred Common Indicator* >< 'No'

[ACCEPT]

[NEXT]
Display Next *Data Product* occurrence

[BACK]
Display Previous *Data Product* occurrence

[RETURN]
Close window and Return to <u>Preferred Data Product Data Task</u>

[HELP]
Open <u>Help Message View</u>
Display Preferred Data Product Help Message

Preferred Data Product Set

Preferred Data Product Set is opened from Preferred Data Product Data Task. The actions for Preferred Data Product Set are:

Display Auto-Scroll List from *Data Product* with *Data Product. Name*
Select *Data Product. Name*

[DISPLAY]
Display Each *Data Product Set* within Selected *Data Product* with *Data Product Set. Name, Product Set. Definition, Data Product Set. Comment, Data Product Set. Preferred Common Indicator*

(YES)
Set *Data Product Set. Preferred Common Indicator* >< 'Yes'

(NO)
Set *Data Product Set. Preferred Common Indicator* >< 'No'

[ACCEPT]

[NEXT]
Display Next *Data Product Set* occurrence

[BACK]
Display Previous *Data Product Set* occurrence

[RETURN]
Close window and Return to <u>Preferred Data Product Data Task</u>

[HELP]
Open <u>Help Message View</u>

227

Display Preferred Data Product Set Help Message

Preferred Data Product Unit

Preferred Data Product Unit is opened from Preferred Data Product Data Task. The actions for Preferred Data Product Unit are:

Display Auto-Scroll List from *Data Product* with *Data Product. Name*
Select *Data Product. Name*

Display Auto-Scroll List from *Data Product Set* within *Selected Data Product* with *Data Product Set. Name*
Select *Data Product Set. Name*

[DISPLAY]
Display Each *Data Product Unit* within Selected *Data Product Set* with *Data Product Unit. Name, Data Product Unit. Mnemonic, Data Product Unit. Definition, Data Product Unit. Comment, Data Product Unit. Preferred Common Indicator, Data Product Unit. Preferred Source Indicator*

(COMMON YES)
Set *Data Product Unit. Preferred Common Indicator* >< 'Yes'

(COMMON NO)
Set *Data Product Unit. Preferred Common Indicator* >< 'No'

(SOURCE YES)
Set *Data Product Unit. Preferred Source Indicator* >< 'Yes'

(SOURCE NO)
Set *Data Product Unit. Preferred Source Indicator* >< 'No'

[ACCEPT]

[NEXT]
Display Next *Data Product Unit* occurrence

[BACK]
Display Previous *Data Product Unit* occurrence

[RETURN]
Close window and Return to <u>Preferred Data Product Data Task</u>

[HELP]
Open <u>Help Message View</u>
Display Preferred Data Product Unit Help Message

Preferred Data Product Code

Preferred Data Product Code is opened from Preferred Data Product Data Task. The actions for Preferred Data Product Code are:

Display Auto-Scroll List from *Data Product* with *Data Product. Name*
Select *Data Product. Name*

Display Auto-Scroll List from *Data Product Set* within *Selected Data Product* with *Data Product Set. Name*
Select *Data Product Set. Name*

Display *Auto-Scroll List* from *Data Product Unit* within *Selected Data Product Set* with *Data Product Unit. Name*
Select *Data Product Unit. Name*

[DISPLAY]
Display Each *Data Product Code* within Selected *Data Product Unit* with *Data Product Code. Name, Data Product Code. Definition, Data Product Code. Comment, Data Product Code. Preferred Common Indicator*

(YES)
Set *Data Product Code. Preferred Common Indicator* >< 'Yes'

(NO)
Set *Data Product Code. Preferred Common Indicator* >< 'No'

[ACCEPT]

[NEXT]
Display Next *Data Product Code* occurrence

[BACK]
Display Previous *Data Product Code* occurrence

[RETURN]
Close window and Return to <u>Preferred Data Product Data Task</u>

[HELP]
Open <u>Help Message View</u>
Display Preferred Data Product Code Help Message

PREFERRED DATA REPORTS

Preferred Data Reports contains reports for the Preferred Data Function. It is opened from Preferred Data Function. Only a few examples of reports are shown. Many additional reports could be developed based on an organization's needs and added to the Data Resource Guide.

[Extract Data Product Set Definitions by Data Subject]
Display Auto-Scroll List from *Data Subject* with *Data Subject. Name Complete*
Select *Data Subject. Name Complete*
Display for Each *Data Product Set | Data Product Set Variation* v Selected *Data Subject* with *Data Product. Name ^ Data Product Set. Name, Data Product Set. Definition (^ Data Product Set Variation. Name, Data Product Set Variation. Definition* When Present)

[PRINT]

[RETURN]
Close report and Return to <u>Preferred Data Reports</u>

[Extract Data Product Unit Definitions by Data Characteristic Variation]
Display Auto-Scroll List from *Data Subject* with *Data Subject. Name Complete*
Select *Data Subject. Name Complete*

Display Auto-Scroll List from *Data Characteristic* within Selected *Data Subject* with *Data Characteristic. Name Complete*
Select *Data Characteristic Name Complete*

Display Auto-Scroll List from *Data Characteristic Variation* within Selected *Data Characteristic* with *Data Characteristic Variation. Name Complete*
Select *Data Characteristic Variation. Name Complete*

Display for Each *Data Product Unit | Data Product Unit Variation* v Selected *Data Characteristic Variation* with *Data Product. Name ^ Data Product Set. Name, (^ Data Product Set Variation. Name* When Present) *^ Data Product Unit. Name, Data Product Unit. Mnemonic, Data Product Unit. Definition (^ Data Product Unit Variation. Name, Data Product Unit Variation. Mnemonic, Data Product Unit Variation. Definition* When Present)

[PRINT]

[RETURN]
Close report and Return to <u>Preferred Data Reports</u>

[Extract Data Product Code Definitions by Data Reference Set Variation]

230

Display Auto-Scroll List from *Data Subject* with *Data Subject. Name Complete*
Select *Data Subject. Name Complete*

Display Auto-Scroll List from *Data Reference Set Variation* within Selected *Data Subject* with *Data Reference Set Variation. Name*
Select *Data Reference Set Variation. Name*

Display for Each *Data Product Code* | *Data Product Code Variation* v Selected *Data Reference Set Variation* with *Data Product. Name* ^ *Data Product Set. Name* (^ *Data Product Set Variation. Name* When Present) ^ *Data Product Unit. Name*, Data Product Unit. Mnemonic (^ *Data Product Unit Variation. Name*, *Data Product Unit Variation. Mnemonic* When Present) ^ *Data Product Code. Name, Data Product Code. Value, Data Product Code. Definition* (^ *Data Product Code Variation. Name, Data Product Code Variation. Value, Data Product Code Variation. Definition* When Present)

[PRINT]

[RETURN]
    Close report and Return to <u>Preferred Data Reports</u>

[Extract Data Characteristic Definitions by Data Subject]
    Display Auto-Scroll List from *Data Subject* with *Data Subject. Name Complete*
    Select *Data Subject. Name Complete*
    Display Selected *Data Subject. Definition*
    Display from Each *Data Characteristic* within Selected *Data Subject* with *Data Characteristic. Name, Data Characteristic. Definition*
    [PRINT]

    [RETURN]
        Close report and Return to <u>Preferred Data Reports</u>

[Extract Data Reference Set Variation Definitions by Data Subject]
    Display Auto-Scroll List from *Data Subject* with *Data Subject. Name Complete* When *Data Subject. Data Reference Set Indicator* >< 'Yes'
    Select *Data Subject. Name Complete*

    Display Selected *Data Subject. Definition*

231

Display from *Data Reference Set Variation* within Selected *Data Subject* Each *Data Reference Set Variation. Name, Data Reference Set Variation. Definition* within Selected *Data Subject*

[PRINT]

[RETURN]
Close report and Return to <u>Preferred Data Reports</u>

[Extract Data Characteristic Variation Definitions by Data Characteristic]
Display Auto-Scroll List from *Data Subject* with *Data Subject. Name Complete*
Select *Data Subject. Name Complete*

Display Auto-Scroll List from *Data Characteristic* within Selected *Data Subject* with *Data Characteristic. Name Complete*
Select *Data Characteristic. Name Complete*

Display Selected *Data Characteristic. Definition*
Display from *Data Characteristic Variation* within Selected *Data Characteristic* Each *Data Characteristic Variation. Name, Data Characteristic Variation. Definition*

[PRINT]

[RETURN]
Close report and Return to <u>Preferred Data Reports</u>

[Extract Data Item Definitions by Data Reference Set *Variation]*
Display Auto-Scroll List from Data Subject with Data Subject. Name Complete When *Data Subject. Data Reference Set Indicator* >< 'Yes'
Select *Data Subject. Name Complete*

Display Auto-Scroll List from *Data Reference Set Variation* within Selected *Data Subject* with *Data Reference Set Variation. Name Complete*
Select *Data Reference Set Variation. Name Complete*

Display Selected *Data Reference Set Variation. Definition*
Display from *Data Reference Item* within Selected *Data Reference Set Variation* Each *Data Reference Item. Name, Data Reference Item. Value, Data Reference Item. Definition*

[PRINT]

[RETURN]
    Close report and Return to <u>Preferred Data Reports</u>

[Extract Data Product Set Integrity Rules by Data Subject]
    Display Auto-Scroll List from *Data Subject* with *Data Subject.*
    Name Complete
    Select *Data Subject. Name Complete*

    Display for Each *Data Product Set | Data Product Set Variation* ∨
    Selected *Data Subject* with *Data Product. Name* ^ *Data Product
    Set. Name, Data Product Set. Data Integrity Rules* (^ *Data
    Product Set Variation. Name, Data Product Set Variation. Data
    Integrity Rules* When Present)

    [PRINT]

    [RETURN]
        Close report and Return to <u>Preferred Data Reports</u>

[Extract Data Product Unit Integrity Rules by Data Characteristic
    Variation]
    Display Auto-Scroll List from *Data Subject* with *Data Subject.*
    Name Complete
    Select *Data Subject. Name Complete*

    Display Auto-Scroll List from *Data Characteristic* within Selected
    Data Subject with *Data Characteristic. Name Complete*
    Select *Data Characteristic Name Complete*

    Display Auto-Scroll List from *Data Characteristic Variation* within
    Selected *Data Characteristic* with *Data Characteristic Variation.*
    Name Complete
    Select *Data Characteristic Variation. Name Complete*

    Display for Each *Data Product Unit | Data Product Unit Variation*
    ∨ Selected *Data Characteristic Variation* with *Data Product.
    Name* ^ *Data Product Set. Name,* (^ *Data Product Set Variation.
    Name* When Present) ^ *Data Product Unit. Name, Data Product
    Unit. Mnemonic, Data Product Unit. Data Integrity Rules* (^ *Data
    Product Unit Variation. Name, Data Product Unit Variation.
    Mnemonic, Data Product Unit Variation. Data Integrity Rules*
    When Present)

    [PRINT]

    [RETURN]

Close report and Return to <u>Preferred Data Reports</u>

[Extract Data Characteristic Integrity Rules by Data Subject]
Display Auto-Scroll List from *Data Subject* with *Data Subject.
Name Complete*
Select *Data Subject. Name Complete*

Display Selected *Data Subject. Integrity Rules*
Display from Each *Data Characteristic* within Selected *Data
Subject* with *Data Characteristic. Name, Data Characteristic.
Integrity Rules*

[PRINT]

[RETURN]
Close report and Return to <u>Preferred Data Reports</u>

[Extract Data Characteristic Variation Integrity Rules by Data
Characteristic]
Display Auto-Scroll List from *Data Subject* with *Data Subject.
Name Complete*
Select *Data Subject. Name Complete*

Display Auto-Scroll List from *Data Characteristic* within Selected
Data Subject with *Data Characteristic. Name Complete*
Select *Data Characteristic. Name Complete*

Display Selected *Data Characteristic. Data Integrity Rules*
Display from Each *Data Characteristic Variation* within Selected
Data Characteristic with *Data Characteristic Variation. Name,
Data Characteristic Variation. Data Integrity Rules*

[PRINT]

[RETURN]
Close report and Return to <u>Preferred Data Reports</u>

[Preferred Data Product]
Display Each *Data Product. Name, Data Product. Preferred
Common Indicator* When *Data Product. Preferred Common
Indicator* >< 'Yes'

[PRINT]

[RETURN]
Close report and Return to <u>Preferred Data Reports</u>

[Preferred Data Product - Non-Preferred Data Product Set]

Display Each *Data Product. Name* When *Data Product. Common Data Indicator* >< 'Yes'
> Display Each *Data Product Set. Name* When *Data Product Set. Common Data Indicator* >< 'No'

[PRINT]

[RETURN]
> Close report and Return to <u>Preferred Data Reports</u>

[Preferred Data Product Set – Non-Preferred Data Product Unit]
Display Each *Data Product. Name* When *Data Product. Common Data Identifier* >< 'Yes'
> Display Each *Data Product Set. Name* When *Data Product Set. Common Data Identifier* >< 'Yes'
> > Display Each *Data Product Unit. Name* When *Data Product Unit. Common Data Identifier* >< 'No'

[PRINT]

[RETURN]
> Close report and Return to <u>Preferred Data Reports</u>

[Preferred Data Product Unit – Non-Preferred Data Product Code]
Display Each *Data Product. Name* When *Data Product. Common Data Identifier* >< 'Yes'
> Display Each *Data Product Set. Name* When *Data Product Set. Common Data Identifier* >< 'Yes'
> > Display Each *Data Product Unit. Name* When *Data Product Unit. Common Data Identifier* >< 'Yes'
> > > Display Each *Data Product Code. Name, Data Product Code. Value* When *Data Product Code. Common Data Indicator* >< 'No'

[PRINT]

[RETURN]
> Close report and Return to <u>Preferred Data Reports</u>

[Preferred Data Reference Set Variation]
Display Each *Data Subject. Name Complete* When *Data Subject. Data Reference Set Indicator* >< 'Yes' & When *Common Data Status. Name* >< 'Preferred'
> Display Each *Data Reference Set Variation. Name* within Selected *Data Subject* When *Common Data Status. Name* >< 'Preferred'

[PRINT]

[RETURN]
   Close report and Return to <u>Preferred Data Reports</u>

[Preferred Data Characteristic Variation]
   Display Auto-Scroll List from *Data Subject* with *Data Subject.*
      Name Complete When *Common Data Status. Name* >< 'Preferred
   Select *Data Subject. Name Complete*
   Display Auto-Scroll List from *Data Characteristic* within Selected
      Data Subject with *Data Characteristic. Name Complete* When
      Common Data Status. Name >< 'Preferred
   Select *Data Characteristic. Name Complete*

   Display from Each *Data Characteristic Variation* within Selected
      Data Characteristic with *Data Characteristic Variation. Name*
      When *Common Data Status. Name* >< 'Preferred'

[PRINT]

[RETURN]
   Close report and Return to <u>Preferred Data Reports</u>

[Preferred Data Name Abbreviation Scheme]
   Display from *Data Name Abbreviation Scheme* Each *Data Name*
      Abbreviation Scheme. Name When *Data Name Abbreviation*
      Scheme. Preferred Indicator >< 'Yes'

[PRINT]

[RETURN]
   Close report and Return to <u>Preferred Data Reports</u>

[Selected Business Glossary – Preferred Business Glossary Item]
   Display Auto-Scroll List from *Business Glossary* with *Business*
      Glossary. Name
   Select *Business Glossary. Name*

   Display from Each *Business Glossary Item* within Selected
      Business Glossary with *Business Glossary Item. Phrase* When
      Business Glossary Item. Preferred Indicator >< 'Yes'

[PRINT]

[RETURN]
   Close report and Return to <u>Preferred Data Reports</u>

236

[Selected Data Subject – Preferred Primary Key Status]
  Display Auto-Scroll List from *Data Subject* with *Data Subject. Name Complete*
  Select *Data Subject. Name Complete*

  Each *Primary Key* within Selected *Data Subject* When *Common Data Status. Name* >< 'Preferred'
    Display from Each *Primary Key Characteristic* with *Data Characteristic. Name Complete*

  [PRINT]

  [RETURN]
    Close report and Return to <u>Preferred Data Reports</u>

[Selected Data Subject - Preferred Foreign Key Status]
  Display Auto-Scroll List from *Data Subject* with *Data Subject. Name Complete*
  Select *Data Subject. Name Complete*

  Display from Each *Foreign Key* within Selected *Data Subject* with *'Local" Data Subject. Name Complete, "Parent" Data Subject. Name Complete* When *Common Data Status. Name* >< 'Yes'
    Display from Each *Foreign Key Characteristic* with *Data Characteristic. Name Complete*

  [PRINT]

  [RETURN]
    Close report and Return to <u>Preferred Data Reports</u>

[Preferred Data Subject Status]
  Display from Each *Data Subject* with *Data Subject. Name* When *Common Data Status. Name* >< 'Preferred'

  [PRINT]

  [RETURN]
    Close report and Return to <u>Preferred Data Reports</u>

[Selected Data Subject – Preferred Data Characteristic Status]
  Display Auto-Scroll List from *Data Subject* with *Data Subject. Name Complete* When *Common Data Status. Name* >< 'Preferred'
  Select *Data Subject. Name Complete*

Display from Each *Data Characteristic* within Selected *Data Subject* with *Data Characteristic. Name Complete* When *Common Data Status. Name* >< 'Preferred'

[PRINT]

[RETURN]
    Close report and Return to <u>Preferred Data Reports</u>

[Selected Data Subject – Preferred Data Characteristic Variation Status]
    Display Auto-Scroll List from *Data Subject* with *Data Subject. Name Complete* When *Common Data Status. Name* >< 'Preferred'
Select *Data Subject. Name Complete*

Display from Each *Data Characteristic* within Selected *Data Subject* with *Data Characteristic. Name Complete* When *Common Data Status. Name* >< 'Preferred'
Select *Data Characteristic. Name Complete*

Display from Each *Data Characteristic Variation* within Selected *Data Characteristic* with *Data Characteristic Variation. Name Complete* When *Common Data Status. Name* >< 'Preferred'

[PRINT]

[RETURN]
    Close report and Return to <u>Preferred Data Reports</u>

[Selected Data Subject – Preferred Data Reference Set Variation Status]
    Display Auto-Scroll List from *Data Subject* with *Data Subject. Name Complete* When *Common Data Status. Name* >< 'Preferred'
Select *Data Subject. Name Complete*

Display from Each *Data Reference Set Variation* within Selected *Data Subject* with *Data Reference Set Variation. Name Complete* When *Common Data Status. Name* >< 'Preferred'

[PRINT]

[RETURN]
    Close report and Return to <u>Preferred Data Reports</u>

[Selected Data Subject – Preferred Data Reference Item Status]

Display Auto-Scroll List from *Data Subject* with *Data Subject.*
Name Complete When *Common Data Status. Name* ><
'Preferred'
Select *Data Subject. Name Complete*

Display Auto-Scroll List from Each *Data Reference Set Variation*
within Selected *Data Subject* with *Data Reference Set Variation.*
Name Complete When *Common Data Status. Name* ><
'Preferred'
Select *Data Reference Set Variation. Name*

Display from Each *Data Reference Item* within Selected *Data*
Reference Set Variation with *Data Reference Item. Name* When
Common Data Status. Name >< 'Preferred'

[PRINT]

[RETURN]
Close report and Return to <u>Preferred Data Reports</u>

[RETURN]
Close window and Return to <u>Preferred Data Function</u>

[HELP]
Open <u>Help Message View</u>
Display Preferred Data Reports Help Message

Chapter 14

DATA TRANSFORMATION

Data Transformation Function includes Data Translation Task, Data Transformation Task, and Data Transformation Reports, as shown in Figure 14.1. It is opened from Data Resource Guide Edit / View.

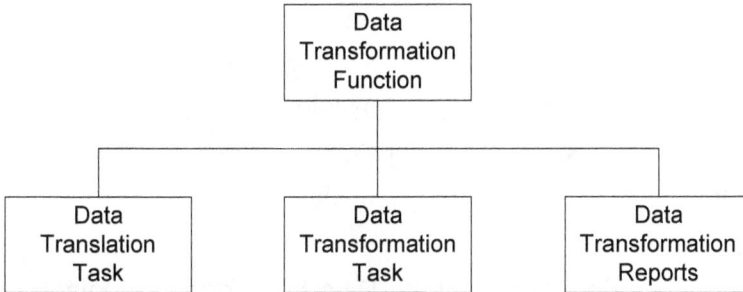

```
                    ┌─────────────────┐
                    │      Data       │
                    │ Transformation  │
                    │    Function     │
                    └─────────────────┘
                             │
        ┌────────────────────┼────────────────────┐
┌───────────────┐   ┌───────────────┐   ┌───────────────┐
│     Data      │   │     Data      │   │     Data      │
│  Translation  │   │ Transformation│   │ Transformation│
│     Task      │   │     Task      │   │    Reports    │
└───────────────┘   └───────────────┘   └───────────────┘
```

Figure 14.1. Data Transformation Function.

The actions for Data Transformation Function are:

[DATA TRANSLATION TASK]
Open Data Translation Task

[DATA TRANSFORMATION TASK]
Open Data Transformation Task

[DATA TRANSFORMATION REPORTS]
Open Data Transformation Reports

[RETURN]
Close window and Return to Data Resource Guide Edit / View

[HELP]
Open Help Message View
Display Data Transformation Function Help Message

DATA TRANSLATION TASK

Data Translation Task includes Data Characteristic Translation and Data Reference Item Translation, as shown in Figure 14.2. It is opened from Data Transformation Function.

```
                    ┌─────────────┐
                    │    Data     │
                    │ Translation │
                    │    Task     │
                    └──────┬──────┘
            ┌──────────────┴──────────────┐
    ┌───────┴────────┐            ┌────────┴───────┐
    │     Data       │            │     Data       │
    │ Characteristic │            │ Reference tem  │
    │  Translation   │            │  Translation   │
    └────────────────┘            └────────────────┘
```

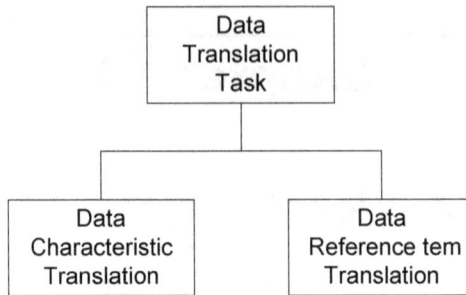

Figure 14.2. Data Translation Task.

The actions for Data Translation Task are:

[DATA CHARACTERISTIC TRANSLATION]
   Open <u>Data Characteristic Translation</u>

[DATA REFERENCE ITEM TRANSLATION]
   Open <u>Data Reference Item Translation</u>

[RETURN]
   Close window and Return to <u>Data Transformation Function</u>

[HELP]
   Open <u>Help Message View</u>
   Display Data Translation Task Help Message

Data Characteristic Translation

Data Characteristic Translation is opened from Data Translation Task. The actions for Data Characteristic Translation are:

[DISPLAY SOURCE]
   Display Auto-Scroll List from *Data Subject* with *Data Subject. Name Complete*
   Select *Data Subject. Name Complete*

   Display Auto-Scroll List from *Data Characteristic* within Selected *Data Subject* with *Data Characteristic. Name Complete*
   Select *Data Characteristic. Name Complete*

   Display Auto-Scroll List from *Data Characteristic Variation* within Selected *Data Characteristic* with *Data Characteristic Variation. Name Complete*
   Select *Data Characteristic Variation. Name*

242

Display *Data Characteristic Translation* data When *"Source" Data Characteristic Variation. Name Complete* >< Selected *Data Characteristic Variation. Name Complete*

[PRINT]

(DELETE)
    Delete Selected *Data Characteristic Translation* occurrence

[DISPLAY TARGET]
    Display Auto-Scroll List from *Data Subject* with *Data Subject. Name Complete*
    Select *Data Subject. Name Complete*

    Display Auto-Scroll List from *Data Characteristic* within Selected *Data Subject* with *Data Characteristic. Name Complete*
    Select *Data Characteristic. Name Complete*

    Display Auto-Scroll List from *Data Characteristic Variation* within Selected *Data Characteristic* with *Data Characteristic Variation. Name Complete*
    Select *Data Characteristic Variation. Name*

    Display *Data Characteristic Translation* data Where *"Target" Data Characteristic Variation. Name Complete* >< Selected *Data Characteristic Variation. Name Complete*

[PRINT]

(DELETE)
    Delete Selected *Data Characteristic Translation* occurrence

(NEW)
    Display blank data fields for entry of new *Data Characteristic Translation* data

    Display Auto-Scroll List from *Data Subject* with *Data Subject. Name Complete*
    Select *Data Subject. Name Complete*

    Display Auto-Scroll List from *Data Characteristic* within Selected Data Subject with *Data Characteristic. Name Complete*
    Select *Data Characteristic. Name Complete*

    Display Auto-Scroll List from *Data Characteristic Variation* within Selected *Data Characteristic*
    Select *"Source" Data Characteristic Variation. Name Complete*

Display Auto-Scroll List from *Data Subject* with *Data Subject. Name Complete*
Select *Data Subject. Name Complete*

Display Auto-Scroll List from *Data Characteristic* within Selected *Data Subject* with *Data Characteristic. Name Complete*
Select *Data Characteristic. Name Complete*

Display *Auto-Scroll List* from *Data Characteristic Variation* within Selected *Data Characteristic*
Select *"Target" Data Characteristic Variation. Name Complete*

Display Scroll List from *Data Characteristic Translation* with *"Source" Data Characteristic Variation. Name Complete*, *"Target" Data Characteristic Variation. Name Complete*
Select *"Reference" Data Characteristic Translation*

[ACCEPT]

[RETURN]
Close window and Return to Data Translation Task

[HELP]
Open Help Message View
Display Data Characteristic Translation Help Message

Data Reference Item Translation

Data Reference Item Translation is opened from Data Translation Task. The actions for Data Reference Item Translation are:

[DISPLAY SOURCE]
Display Auto-Scroll List from *Data Subject* with *Data Subject. Name Complete*
Select *Data Subject. Name Complete*

Display Auto-Scroll List from *Data Reference Set Variation* within Selected *Data Subject* with *Data Reference Set Variation. Name Complete*
Select *Data Reference Set Variation. Name Complete*

Display Scroll List from *Data Reference Item* within Selected *Data Reference Set Variation* with *Data Reference Item. Name, Data Reference Item. Code*
Select *Data Reference Item*

Display *Data Reference Item Translation* data When *"Source"*
Data Reference Item. Name >< Selected *Data Reference Item.*
Name

[PRINT]

(DELETE)
Delete Selected *Data Reference Item Translation* occurrence

[DISPLAY TARGET]
Display Auto-Scroll List from *Data Subject* with *Data Subject.*
Name Complete
Select *Data Subject. Name Complete*

Display Auto-Scroll List from *Data Reference Set Variation* within
Selected *Data Subject* with *Data Reference Set Variation. Name*
Complete
Select *Data Reference Set Variation. Name Complete*

Display Scroll List from *Data Reference Item* within Selected *Data*
Reference Set Variation with *Data Reference Item. Name, Data*
Reference Item. Code
Select *Data Reference Item*

Display *Data Reference Item Translation* data Where *"Target"*
Data Reference Item. Name >< Selected *Data Reference Item.*
Name

[PRINT]

(DELETE)
Delete Selected *Data Reference Item Translation* occurrence

(NEW)
Display blank data fields for entry of new *Data Reference Item*
Translation data

Display Auto-Scroll List from *Data Subject* When *Data Subject.*
Data Reference Set Indicator >< "Yes' with *Data Subject. Name*
Complete
Select *Data Subject. Name Complete*

Display Auto-Scroll List from *Data Reference Set Variation* within
Selected *Data Subject* with *Data Reference Set Variation. Name*
Complete
Select *Data Reference Set Variation. Name Complete*

Display Scroll List from *Data Reference Item* within Selected *Data Reference Set Variation* with *Data Reference Item. Name*, *Data Reference Item. Code*
Select *"Source" Data Reference Item. Name*

Display Auto-Scroll List from *Data Subject* When Data Subject. Data Reference Set Indicator >< 'Yes' with *Data Subject. Name Complete*
Select *Data Subject. Name Complete*

Display Auto-Scroll List from *Data Reference Set Variation* within Selected *Data Subject* with *Data Reference Set Variation. Name Complete*
Select *Data Reference Set Variation. Name Complete*

Display Scroll List from *Data Reference Item* within Selected *Data Reference Set Variation* with *Data Reference Item. Name*, *Data Reference Item. Code*
Select *"Target" Data Reference Item. Name*

Display Scroll List from *Data Reference Item Translation* with *"Source" Data Reference Item. Name* , *"Target" Data Reference Item. Name*
Select *"Reference" Data Reference Item Translation*

[ACCEPT]

[RETURN]
Close window and Return to <u>Data Translation Task</u>

[HELP]
Open <u>Help Message View</u>
Display Data Reference Item Translation Help Message

DATA TRANSFORMATION TASK

Data Transformation Task includes Data Transform Task, Data Transform Step, Data Transform Unit, Organization Unit, and Data Steward, as shown in Figure 14.3.

246

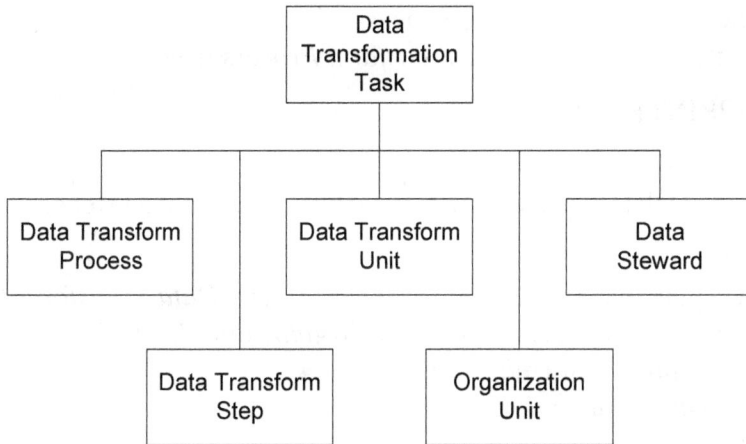

Figure 14.3. Data Transformation Task.

The actions for Data Transformation Task are:

[DATA TRANSFORM PROCESS]
Open <u>Data Transform Process</u>

[DATA TRANSFORM STEP]
Open <u>Data Transform Step</u>

[DATA TRANSFORM UNIT]
Open <u>Data Transform Unit</u>

[ORGANIZATION UNIT]
Open <u>Organization Unit</u>

[DATA STEWARD]
Open <u>Data Steward</u>

[RETURN]
Close window and Return to <u>Data Transformation Function</u>

[HELP]
Display <u>Help Message View</u>
Display Data Transformation Task Help Message

Data Transform Process

Data Transform Process is opened from Data Transformation Task. The actions for Data Transform Process are:

[DISPLAY]
Display Auto-Scroll List from *Data Transform Process* with *Data Transform Process. Name*

247

Select *Data Transform Process. Name*
Display Selected *Data Transform Process* data

[PRINT]

(DELETE)
    Delete Selected *Data Transform Process* occurrence

(NEW)
    Display blank data fields for entry of new *Data Transform Process*
    Display Auto-Scroll List from *Organization Unit* with
      Organization Unit. Name
    Select *Organization Unit. Name*

    Display Auto-Scroll List from *Data Steward* with *Data Steward.*
      Name Complete
    Select *Data Steward. Name Complete*

    [ACCEPT]

[RETURN]
    Close window and Return to <u>Data Transformation Task</u>

[HELP]
    Open <u>Help Message View</u>
    Display Data Transform Process Help Message

Data Transform Step

Data Transform Step is opened from Data Transformation Task. The actions for Data Transform Step are:

Display Auto-Scroll List from *Data Transform Process* with *Data
    Transform Process. Name*
Select *Data Transform Process. Name*

[DISPLAY]
    Display Auto-Scroll List from *Data Transform Step* within Selected
      Data Transform Process with *Data Transform Step. Name*
    Select *Data Transform Step. Name*
    Display Selected *Data Transform Step* data

    [PRINT]

    (DELETE)
      Delete Selected *Data Transform Step* occurrence

(NEW)

Display blank data fields for entry of new *Data Transform Step*

[ACCEPT]

[RETURN]
Close window and Return to <u>Data Transformation Task</u>

[HELP]
Open <u>Help Message View</u>
Display Data Transform Step Help Message

Data Transform Unit

Data Transform Unit is opened from Data Transformation Task. The actions for Data Transform Unit are:

Display Auto-Scroll List from *Data Transform Process* with *Data Transform Process. Name*
Select *Data Transform Process. Name*

Display *Auto-Scroll List* from *Data Transform Step* within Selected *Data Transform Process* with *Data Transform Step. Name*
Select *Data Transform Step. Name*

[DISPLAY]
Display Auto-Scroll List from *Data Transform Unit* within Selected *Data Transform Step* with *Data Transform Unit. Name*
Select *Data Transform Unit. Name*
Display Selected *Data Transform Unit* data

[PRINT]

(DELETE)
Delete Selected *Data Transform Unit* occurrence

(NEW)
Display blank data fields for entry of new *Data Transform Unit*

Display Auto-Scroll List from *Data Product* with *Data Product. Name*
Select *Data Product. Name*

Display Auto-Scroll List from *Data Product Set* within Selected *Data Product* with *Data Product Set. Name*
Select *Data Product Set. Name*

Display Auto-Scroll List from *Data Product Unit* with *Data Product Unit. Name*

249

Select *Data Product Unit. Name*

[ACCEPT]

[RETURN]
Close window and Return to <u>Data Transformation Task</u>

[HELP]
Open <u>Help Message View</u>
Display Data Transform Unit Help Message

Organization Unit

Organization Unit is opened from Data Transformation Task. The actions for Organization Unit are provided in the Data Responsibility Chapter.

Data Steward

Data Steward is opened from Data Transformation Task. The actions for Data Steward are provided in the Data Responsibility Chapter.

DATA TRANSFORMATION REPORTS

Data Transformation Reports contains reports for the Data Transformation Function. It is opened from Data Transformation Function. Only a few examples of reports are shown. Many additional reports could be developed based on an organization's needs and added to the Data Resource Guide.

[Data Characteristic Translation Name]
Display from Each *Data Characteristic Translation* with *"Source" Data Characteristic Variation. Name Complete, "Target" Data Characteristic Variation. Name Complete*

[PRINT]

[RETURN]
Close report and Return to <u>Data Transformation Reports</u>

[Data Characteristic Translation Detail]
Display Each *Data Characteristic Translation* data

[PRINT]

[RETURN]
Close report and Return to <u>Data Transformation Reports</u>

[Selected Source Data Characteristic Translation Detail]

Display Auto-Scroll List from *Data Subject* with *Data Subject. Name Complete*
Select *Data Subject. Name Complete*

Display Auto-Scroll List from *Data Characteristic* within Selected *Data Subject* with *Data Characteristic. Name Complete*
Select *Data Characteristic. Name Complete*

Display Auto-Scroll list from *Data Characteristic Variation* within Selected *Data Characteristic* with *Data Characteristic Variation. Name Complete*
Select *Data Characteristic Variation. Name Complete*

Display from Each *Data Characteristic Translation* When *"Source" Data Characteristic. Variation. Name Complete* >< Selected *Data Characteristic Variation. Name Complete* with *Data Characteristic Translation* data

[PRINT]

[RETURN]
   Close report and Return to <u>Data Transformation Reports</u>

[Selected Target Data Characteristic Translation Detail]
Display Auto-Scroll List from *Data Subject* with *Data Subject. Name Complete*
Select *Data Subject. Name Complete*

Display Auto-Scroll List from *Data Characteristic* within Selected *Data Subject* with *Data Characteristic. Name Complete*
Select *Data Characteristic. Name Complete*

Display Auto-Scroll list from *Data Characteristic Variation* within Selected *Data Characteristic* with *Data Characteristic Variation. Name Complete*
Select *Data Characteristic Variation. Name Complete*

Display from Each *Data Characteristic Translation* When *"Target" Data Characteristic. Variation. Name Complete* >< Selected *Data Characteristic Variation. Name Complete* with *Data Characteristic Translation* data

[PRINT]

[RETURN]
   Close report and Return to <u>Data Transformation Reports</u>

251

[Data Reference Item Translation Name]
    Display from Each *Data Reference Item Translation* with *"Source" Data Characteristic Variation. Name Complete*, *"Target" Data Characteristic Variation. Name Complete*

    [PRINT]

    [RETURN]
        Close report and Return to <u>Data Transformation Reports</u>

[Data Reference Item Translation Detail]
    Display Each *Data Reference Item Translation* data

    [PRINT]

    [RETURN]
        Close report and Return to <u>Data Transformation Reports</u>

[Selected Source Data Reference Item Detail]
    Display Auto-Scroll List from *Data Subject* with *Data Subject. Name Complete*
    Select *Data Subject. Name Complete*

    Display Auto-Scroll List from *Data Reference Set Variation* within Selected *Data Subject* with *Data Reference Set Variation. Name Complete*
    Select *Data Reference Set Variation. Name Complete*

    Display from Each *Data Reference Item Translation* When *"Source" Data Reference Item. Name* >< Selected *Data Reference Item. Name* with *Data Reference Item Translation* data

    [PRINT]

    [RETURN]
        Close report and Return to <u>Data Transformation Reports</u>

[Selected Target Data Reference Item Detail]
    Display Auto-Scroll List from *Data Subject* with *Data Subject. Name Complete*
    Select *Data Subject. Name Complete*

    Display Auto-Scroll List from *Data Reference Set Variation* within Selected *Data Subject* with *Data Reference Set Variation. Name Complete*
    Select *Data Reference Set Variation. Name Complete*

Display from Each *Data Reference Item Translation* When *"Target" Data Reference Item. Name* >< Selected *Data Reference Item. Name* with *Data Reference Item Translation* data

[PRINT]

[RETURN]
Close report and Return to <u>Data Transformation Reports</u>

[Data Transform Process Name]
Display from Each *Data Transform Process* with *Data Transform Process. Name*

[PRINT]

[RETURN]
Close report and Return to <u>Data Transformation Reports</u>

[Data Transform Process Detail]
Display from Each *Data Transform Process* with *Data Transform Process* data

[PRINT]

[RETURN]
Close report and Return to <u>Data Transformation Reports</u>

[Data Transform Process Name ^ Step Name]
Display Each *Data Transform Process. Name*
Display Each *Data Transform Step. Name*

[PRINT]

[RETURN]
Close report and Return to <u>Data Transformation Reports</u>

[Data Transform Process Detail ^ Step Detail]
Display Each *Data Transform Process* data
Display Each *Data Transform Step* data

[PRINT]

[RETURN]
Close report and Return to <u>Data Transformation Reports</u>

[Selected Data Transform Step Detail]
Display Auto-Scroll List from *Data Transform Process* with *Data Transform Process. Name*
Select *Data Transform Process. Name*

253

Display from Each *Data Transform Step* within Selected *Data Transform Process* with *Data Transform Step* data

[PRINT]

[RETURN]
Close report and Return to Data Transformation Reports

[Data Transform Unit Name]
Display Each *Data Transform Process. Name*
Display Each *Data Transform Step. Name*
Display Each *Data Transform Unit. Name*

[PRINT]

[RETURN]
Close report and Return to Data Transformation Reports

[Data Transform Unit Detail]
Display Each *Data Transform Process* data
Display Each *Data Transform Step* data
Display Each *Data Transform Unit* data

[PRINT]

[RETURN]
Close report and Return to Data Transformation Reports

[Selected Data Transform Unit Detail]
Display Auto-Scroll List from *Data Transform Process* with *Data Transform Process. Name*
Select *Data Transform Process. Name*

Display Auto-Scroll List from *Data Transform Step* within Selected *Data Transform Process* with *Data Transform Step. Name*
Select *Data Transform Step. Name*

Display from Each *Data Transform Unit* within Selected *Data Transform Step* with *Data Transform Unit* data

[PRINT]

[RETURN]
Close report and Return to Data Transformation Reports

[RETURN]
Close window and Return to Derived Transformation Function

[HELP]

Open <u>Help Message View</u>
Display Data Transformation Reports Help Message

Chapter 15

FUTURE ENHANCEMENTS

The concept behind the Data Resource Guide has been evolving for 30 years, and will continue to evolve as the concepts, principles, and techniques for managing data as a critical resource of the organization evolve. Eventually, today's relatively informal data management practices will evolve to become accepted formal data resource management practices.

The Data Resource Guide will evolve along with the evolution of data resource management in the five areas described below, including creating preferred Data Product Data, managing data understanding in very large organizations, data modeling software interfaces, existing Data Product Data inventory, and data name abbreviation.

PREFERRED DATA PRODUCT DATA

The preferred Data Product Data are created by denormalization of the preferred Common Data according to the formal data denormalization rules as adopted by an organization to suit their specific operating environment. The preferred Data Product Data can be created by manual or automated approaches as described below. When the preferred Data Product Data have been created and documented, the business activities and applications can be switched to use the preferred Data Product Data as described in *Data Resource Integration*.

Manual Denormalization

The preferred Common Data, as indicated by the Preferred Common Data status, can be manually denormalized according to formal data denormalization rules as adopted by an organization. The denormalized preferred Common Data can be entered into data modeling software, or can be entered directly into the Data Resource Guide as preferred Data Product Data. When the denormalized preferred Common Data are entered into data modeling software, they should also be entered into the Data Resource Guide as preferred Data Product Data so that the Data Resource Guide maintains complete documentation of the organization's data resource.

The process is relatively easy since the data denormalization process does not have to be encoded into software routines. However, it can be time consuming, particularly when the organization has a relatively large data architecture, and it is subject to human error and discretion.

The preferred Data Product Data may be cross-reference back to the Common Data through the Data Cross-Reference process at the organization's discretion. That cross-reference can be done to close the loop between preferred Common Data and preferred Data Product Data. However, that cross-reference is not required since the Preferred Common Indicators show that the Data Product Data represent the physical aspect of the preferred Common Data.

Automated Denormalization

The preferred Data Product Data can be automatically denormalized using data denormalization software routines. These software routines take the preferred Common Data, the organization's parameters for the data denormalization process, and use formal data denormalization rules for an organization's specific operating environment to create the preferred Data Product Data. The process is usually done incrementally as segments of the Common Data are finalized as preferred Common Data.

The approach efficiently uses the human resource, but requires the initial encoding of the formal data denormalization rules and the entry of parameters for the automated data denormalization process. The encoding process can be difficult, though not impossible, because the actions and decisions of people are involved. However, when the process has been encoded, it can be easily run whenever an organization desires to create preferred Data Product Data from the preferred Common Data.

VERY LARGE ORGANIZATIONS

In very large organizations, such as large multi-national private sector organizations or large public sector organizations, creating a single set of Common Data may be very difficult, though not impossible. Four approaches, separately or in combination, can be used to create a single set of Common Data for very large organizations, including interim Common Data sets, a recursive Common Data set, data steward coordination, and a Data Subject Thesaurus.

Interim Common Data Sets

Interim preferred Common Data sets can be developed for major segments of a very large organization. These interim preferred Common Data sets can then be integrated into a final preferred Common Data set for the entire organization. When interim preferred Common Data sets are completed, they are converted to Data Product Data sets. Those Data Product Data sets are then cross-referenced to a final Common Data set for the organization.

The conversion of an interim Common Data set to a Data Product Data set is done by creating a Data Product for the interim Common Data set representing a major segment of a very large organization. Each preferred Data Subject becomes a Data Product Set, each preferred Data Characteristic Variation becomes a Data Product Unit, and each preferred Data Reference Item becomes a Data Product Code with the Name, Value, and Definition entered under the Data Product Code. Name. Each preferred Primary Key can become a Data Product Primary Key and each preferred Foreign Key can become a Data Product Foreign Key, if they are relevant to the combination of interim Common Data sets.

Preferred Data Reference Set Variations are not converted to Data Product Data. Nor are all Data Characteristic Variations converted to Data Product Units, because those conversions would make the process unnecessarily complicated.

A Common Merge Indicator is added to Data Product, Data Product Set, Data Product Code, Data Product Primary Key, and Data Product Foreign Key to indicate that they represent the merging of interim preferred Common Data sets into a single preferred Common Data set. An Interim Merge Indicator and a Final Merge Indicator are added to Data Subject, Data Characteristic, Data Reference Set Variation, Primary Key, and Foreign Key to indicate that they represent interim and final Common Data sets respectively.

The Data Resource Data and the Data Resource Guide are enhanced to include these data additions, and the movement of the interim Common Data sets to Data Product Data.

The interim Common Data Sets approach requires additions to the Data Resource Data and the Data Resource Guide. It can be quite useful in situations where one or more preferred Common Data sets have already been established and the organizations desires to treat them as interim Common Data sets for the creation of a final preferred Common Data Set. However, the approach has only been implemented a few times because of the increased complexity of the Data Resource Data and the Data Resource Guide.

Recursive Common Data Set

A second approach is to keep the interim and final Common Data sets within

259

the Common Data by using recursive relationships. A recursive relationship is added to Data Subject, Data Characteristic, Data Reference Set Variation, Primary Key, and Foreign Key. An Interim Merge Indicator and a Final Merge Indicator are added to Data Subject, Data Characteristic, Data Reference Set Variation, Primary Key, and Foreign Key.

The recursive Common Data set approach requires additions to the Data Resource Data and the Data Resource Guide. The recursions can be difficult to manage, since many business professionals and some data management professionals are not familiar with handling recursions. Therefore, the approach is seldom used.

Data Stewards Coordination

A third approach is the use of the Tactical Data Stewards to readily share an evolving, single preferred Common Data set across the organization. Each project's Common Data for a segment of the organization complies with and/or enhances a single evolving preferred Common Data set for the entire organization. The Tactical Data Stewards have the primary responsibility for liaison efforts between segments of a very large organization, as described in *Data Resource Design*.

Data steward coordination is the easiest and simplest approach to creating a single Common Data set for a very large organization, particularly when projects are happening at roughly the same time, or when the data stewards become involved with the first project. It does not require any additions to the Data Resource Data or the Data Resource Guide. It is also the easiest and simplest approach when adding subsequent Common Data sets to an existing preferred Common Data set, although problems could arise with major discrepancies. However, most problems can be resolved with thought and cooperation, as described in *Data Resource Design*.

Data Subject Thesaurus

A fourth approach is the use of a Data Subject Thesaurus, particularly when disagreements arise with data names. Most data naming problems occur with data subject names and often the only difference in the data architectures is the data subject name. When the data subject names are established, the creation of data characteristic names and data reference item names is relatively easy.

Use of a Data Subject Thesaurus is coordinated by the data stewards and is kept current with the evolving Common Data sets. Maintenance of a very robust Data Subject Thesaurus resolves many existing data naming issues and problems, and prevents most future data naming issues and problems. It should be used with all projects that create Common Data.

DATA MODELING SOFTWARE INTERFACES

Data modeling software products, if allowed and accepted within an organization, can be a two-way street between the data models and the Data Resource Data. However, the common practice today is to keep data modeling software products independent of the Data Resource Data. In fact, the data modeling software products are often so independent that each data model contains its own data names, data definitions, data integrity rules, and so on. Coordination between data models within a single data modeling software product, and across multiple data modeling software products, seldom exists. That independence causes many problems associated with the redundant and inconsistent documentation of the organization's data resource, resulting in limited understanding, and ultimately a lower quality data resource.

Two approaches can be used for integrating data modeling software products and the Data Resource Guide, as described below.

Data Resource Guide Feeds Data Modeling Software

The Data Resource Guide should ideally feed all data modeling software products with existing Data Resource Data to ensure that the resulting data resource models are within a single organization wide data architecture. The Data Resource Guide feed ensures that data modeling software products and the resulting data resource models do not become disparate causing confusion and a lack of understanding about an organization's data resource architecture. The disparity in data resource models only leads to a disparate data resource and all the problems associated with a disparate data resource.

Use of the Data Resource Guide to feed data modeling software products can be expanded to include the creation of data resource models on demand, rather than storing data resource models in the Data Resource Guide or in an external location reference by the Data Resource Guide. Current data resource models can be produced when and where they are needed, which avoids one major aspect of the data resource model management process. Eliminating check-ins, check-outs, and ensuring the currentness of data resource models eliminates a huge workload from data management professionals and allows business professionals to become directly involved in the design and development of a data resource that supports their business activities.

261

Connecting the Data Resource Guide to data modeling software products can be problematic since most data modeling software products are quite proprietary. However, if data modeling software vendors would recognize the power of supporting a single organization wide data architecture and developing a high quality data resource, the proprietary problem could be easily resolved. In fact, the data modeling software vendors that move to integrate with a Data Resource Guide should have a distinct market advantage.

Data Modeling Software Feeds Data Resource Guide

Data modeling software products should feed the Data Resource Guide with any new Data Resource Data that are not already in the Data Resource Guide. Any new Data Resource Data that are created in a data resource model, that are not already in the Data Resource Guide, and have been approved and accepted, should be entered into the Data Resource Guide so that it remains current. Data Resource Data from new data resource models developed by data modeling software products should not have to be manually entered into the Data Resource Guide.

Data modeling software product feeds to the Data Resource Guide include both logical and physical data resource models. However, checks need to be made so that the logical data resource models and the physical data resource models are in synch. In other words, formal data denormalization rules should be followed when creating physical data resource models so that the preferred Data Product Data have a corresponding preferred Common Data.

Data Resource Data feeds from data modeling software products should include the removal of portions of the data resource model that were once approved and accepted, but were later removed. Since no Data Resource Data are deleted from the Data Resource Guide, the removed material should be listed as Obsolete with a corresponding comment as to why the data were removed.

When any Data Resource Data are to be removed from a data resource model, and those data are supporting current business activities, a warning should be raised that indicates a segment of the data architecture is being removed that currently supports business activities.

Planning and evaluation indicators can be added to data modeling software products that indicate the data resource model is being used for planning or evaluation purposes, and the Data Resource Guide should be updated accordingly. In other words, data modeling software products should make use of the Common Data Status codes that are available to indicate the status of any new Data Resource Data being entered into the Data Resource Guide.

Data modeling software product feeds to the Data Resource Guide are faced with the same proprietary concerns as feeds from the Data Resource Guide to the data modeling software products. Data modeling software vendors that include feeds to the Data Resource Guide are likely to have a distinct market advantage.

DATA PRODUCT DATA INVENTORY

One major hurdle for organizations implementing a Data Resource Guide is the huge volume of existing physical databases and data models that currently exist in the organization and need to be documented in the Data Resource Guide as Data Product Data. Two approaches can be used for inventorying database management systems and for inventorying data modeling software, as described below.

Database Management Systems

Existing database management systems can be automatically inventoried and the resulting Data Product Data entered into the Data Resource Guide. Many organizations have developed such routines for their unique environments. Since approximately 85 different database management systems exist today, many with their own unique design, writing even the generic detailed specifications is difficult. However, data management professionals in an organization that understand their environment and understand the Data Resource Guide can easily prepare automated data inventory routines.

In addition, since many databases in an organization are changed without a design that has been entered into the Data Resource Guide, routines can be developed that regularly re-inventory databases and enter any changes into the Data Resource Guide. Since Data Resource Data are not deleted from the Data Resource Guide, the Obsolete status is used with a corresponding comment for any data removed from a database.

Data Modeling Software

Existing data resource models developed from a variety of data modeling software can be automatically inventoried and the resulting Data Product Data entered into the Data Resource Guide. The approach is similar to that described above for data modeling software feeds to the Data Resource Guide, except that the data resource models already exist and some have existed for a long time.

The traditional approach has been to manually review the existing data resource models and enter the Data Resource Data into the Data Resource Guide. However, that process can be time consuming and subject to error. An automated inventory of existing data resource models would allow that time to be put to better advantage.

The problem with an automated inventory of data resource models is the proprietary nature of data modeling software products, as described above. Many data modeling software vendors are not willing to relinquish that proprietary design so that organizations can automatically inventory their existing data resource models to provide complete Data Resource Data about their data resource.

DATA NAME ABBREVIATION

Data name abbreviations have been a major problem for many years. The traditional approach has been to randomly abbreviate data names based on an individual's desire. The result is a loss of understanding about the data resource and is a major contributor to the creation of disparate data.

The preferred Data Name Abbreviation Scheme should be used to formally abbreviate physical data names based on the formal logical data name. In other words, the preferred Data Product Data name should be formally created from the preferred Common Data name according to the preferred Data Name Abbreviation Scheme.

The objective of the preferred Data Name Abbreviation Scheme is to formally abbreviate logical data names to physical data names, and to formally un-abbreviate physical data names to logical data names. That objective is seldom followed with random data name abbreviation.

Data names can be manually abbreviated and un-abbreviated using the preferred Data Name Abbreviation Scheme. However, that process is slow and time-consuming. A better approach is to automate the abbreviation and un-abbreviation of data names using the preferred Data Name Abbreviation Scheme.

Many organizations have written automated data name abbreviation and un-abbreviation routines. Those routines could easily be added to the Data Resource Guide so that the entry of a formal data name is automatically abbreviated to the formal abbreviated data name. Any data name words that do not have an abbreviation are flagged and appropriate abbreviations can be entered into preferred Data Name Abbreviation Scheme in the Data Resource Guide.

Chapter 16

MANAGING FOR QUALITY

Managing data as a critical resource of the organization has been a consistent theme for the past 30 years. That theme is carried out by thoroughly understanding all the data at an organization's disposal, developing a single organization-wide data architecture that supports the organization's perception of the business world where it operates, and integrating the existing disparate data within that architecture to provide a high quality comparate data resource. The result of that theme is a quality data resource that fully supports an organization's business activities.

COMMON DATA ARCHITECTURE

The Common Data Architecture paradigm has evolved over the last 30 years, although the roots of that evolution extend back much further. The evolution is briefly described with Basic Definitions, The Vision, The Hurdles, and The Challenge.

Basic Definitions

Achieving data resource quality is a difficult task, but it is far from an impossible task. The task begins by understanding a few basic definitions that are critical for developing a high quality data resource.

Data are the individual facts that are out of context, have no meaning, and are difficult to understand. They are often referred to as *raw data*. Data have historically been considered plural and must remain plural in order to establish a high quality data resource.

Data in context are individual facts that have meaning and can be readily understood. They are the raw facts wrapped with meaning. However, data in context are not yet information.

Information is a set of data in context, with relevance to one or more people at a point in time or for a period of time. Information is more than data in context – it must have relevance and a time frame. Information has historically been considered singular and must remain singular in order to establish a high quality data resource.

Data resource is a collection of data (facts), within a specific scope, that are of importance to the organization. It is one of the four critical resources in an organization, equivalent to the financial resource, the human resource, and real property. Data resource has historically been considered singular and must remain singular to establish a high quality data resource within a single organization wide data architecture.

The *business information demand* is an organization's continuously increasing, constantly changing, need for current, accurate, integrated information, often on short notice or very short notice, to support its business activities. It is a very dynamic demand for information to support a business that constantly changes.

Quality is a peculiar and essential character, the degree of excellence, being superior in kind. It has four virtues for clarity, elegance, simplicity, and value.

Data resource quality is a measure of how well the data resource supports the current and future business information demand of an organization. Ideally, the data resource must fully support both the current and the future business information demand to be considered a high quality data resource.

Data quality is a subset of data resource quality dealing with data values.

Ultimate data resource quality is a data resource that is stable across changing business and changing technology, so that it continues to support the current and future business information demand.

Information quality is how well the business information demand is met. It includes both the quality of the data used to produce the information and the quality of the information engineering process. It can be no better than the quality of the data used to produce that information, and may be worse depending on the information engineering process.

Umwelt means the environment or world around you. It's the world as perceived by an organism based on its cognitive and sensory powers. It's the environmental factors collectively that are capable of affecting an organism's behavior. It's a self-centered world where organisms can have different umwelten, even though they share the same environment. It's an organism's perception of the current surroundings and previous experiences which are unique to that organism. It's the world as perceived by a particular organism.

Changing 'organism' to 'organization' provides the *Organization Umwelt Principle* where each organization has a particular perception of the business world in which it operates based on previous experiences that are unique to that organization. Those experiences affect the organization's behavior in the business world, and determine how the organization adapts to a changing business world and operates in that business world.

The Vision

My data management career began in the late 1960s building simulation models for the growth and cutting patterns of about one million acres of State-owned forest land. Although the primary emphasis was building the simulation models, that effort required the acquisition of considerable quantities of data from a variety of different sources. The problem was understanding exactly what those data represented. The interpretation of any simulation model was directly dependent on the meaning of the data used in the simulation.

While struggling to thoroughly understand data, I began attending classes taught by Ken Orr pertaining to Data Structured System Development. He had the most advanced thoughts and ideas about systems development based on the data structure at that time. I began incorporating his thoughts and ideas in the work that I was doing, and began adding my thoughts and ideas about thoroughly understanding data.

In the early 1980s I started comparing the then prominent data design approaches, including those promoted by Ken Orr. I found that all approaches had strong and weak features, although Ken Orr's was among the strongest. The more I compared approaches, the more I began to see a better way to develop information systems based on well understood data. The result of that work was published in 1983 by Ken Orr and Associates as *Data Structured Information Systems*.

I continued to work on new data management concepts and began to realize that data and processes were orthogonal to each other, which was a major change in concept at that time. The data needed to be structured different from the structure of the information systems using the data! The result of that breakthrough was published in 1987 as *Developing Data Structured Databases*.

I continued to work on properly structuring data so that they would be well understood and could be used by multiple information systems, compared to having separate databases for each information system. Dr. E. F. "Ted" Codd's ground-breaking ideas began to emerge and become recognized as a way to design and develop physical databases. Dr. Peter Chen's ground-breaking ideas on entity-relationship modeling using a logical perspective from the business also began to emerge and become recognized. My thoughts about managing data at that time incorporating these ideas were published in 1990 as *Practical Data Design.*

For the next several years I worked on finding a way to thoroughly understand all data within some common context so that the same data could be used in multiple ways by many different information systems. In addition, those data needed to be thoroughly understood from the business perspective based on business activities. That was likely the biggest single breakthrough of my career and was published in 1994 as *Data Sharing Using A Common Data Architecture.*

One memorable and pivotal discussion I had was with Charlie Bachman at a presentation of his data re-engineering software application. His application took the physical data in one database management system and converted those data to another database management system. The details were, of course, proprietary. I explained by thoughts on understanding all data within a Common Data Architecture context and then converting disparate data to comparate data within that context. He listened very patiently to my explanation and when I was done he placed his hand on my shoulder and said "Young man, I have no idea how to do that. I wish you the very best." I had my career challenge!

I looked at many ways that a Common Data Architecture concept could be used to develop a data resource that would be used by multiple information systems in multiple disciplines. The result of that effort was published in 1996 as *The Data Warehouse Challenge.* The intended book title was along the lines of Implementing A Common Data Architecture, but was changed by the publisher without my knowledge to be more in line with the then emerging concept of data warehouses.

The theme that was unfolding through the years was quality. Quality data were thoroughly understood by the business, were not disparate, and could be used consistently across multiple information systems. The way to achieving that quality was through the Common Data Architecture paradigm. Those concepts were published in 2000 as *Data Resource Quality*, which became the theme for subsequent work.

Over the next ten years I consulted with many different public and private sector clients, gave numerous presentations, conducted numerous training classes, and wrote numerous articles. During that time I acquired tremendous insight as to the real problems with the data resource in most public and private sector organizations, and how those problems could be resolved. That effort led to the Simplexity series of six books with the current publisher.

Data Resource Simplexity, published in 2011, describes how data resource management concepts were producing a complex data resource, and how that complex data resource could be made simple with the Common Data Architecture paradigm. *Data Resource Integration*, published in early 2012, describes the wide variability in disparate data and how a disparate data resource could be converted to an integrated comparate data resource within the Common Data Architecture paradigm. *Data Resource Design,* published in late 2012, describes how to design a comparate data resource from the beginning and how avoid the whole disparate data fiasco. These three books form the Data Architecture Trilogy within the Simplexity series of books.

Data Resource Data, published in 2014, describes the meta-data fiasco and how that fiasco is resolved with the use of formal Data Resource Data within the Common Data Architecture paradigm. *Data Resource Understanding*, published in 2015, describes how to use the Data Resource Data to thoroughly understand an organization's data resource and create a comparate data resource that fully supports an organization's business information demand. The current *Data Resource Guide*, published in 2016, provides the design for software applications that have been used from the middle 1990s to the present to manage the Data Resource Data. These three books form the Data Understanding Trilogy within the Simplexity series of books.

The Common Data Architecture paradigm is not complete or perfect. It has evolved over the last 30 years as technology evolved and as people learned more about how to formally manage data as a critical resource. It will continue to evolve as technology evolves and as people learn more about managing data as a critical resource in a rapidly changing business environment.

The Hurdles

I encountered numerous hurdles along the way to achieving the vision. The first, and most difficult, was determining how to develop a new paradigm for formally managing data as a critical resource of an organization. What were the problems? How would those problems be resolved?

The first question was answered rather easily by working with a wide variety of public and private sector organizations and carefully observing their data problems. Documenting these problems provided the base for developing a new data resource management paradigm.

I have received a multitude of comments and suggestions from many individuals in public and private sector organizations about the problems they face with managing the data resource in their organization, and suggestions for resolving those problems. These problems and suggestions have provided a wealth of insight for developing the Common Data Architecture paradigm.

The second question was more difficult to answer and required going outside data management to establish basic concepts, principles, and techniques for formal data resource management. Considerable reading and study in other disciplines, including how they faced and resolved problems, provided the foundation for a new approach to formal data resource management. Considerable 'blue sky thinking' along with 'trial and error' led to achievement of the vision.

I tried talking to many chief scientists for software vendors. However, most declined, even bluntly refused, to talk with me because 1) they were worried I might learn their proprietary approach, and / or 2) they were intimidated by the ideas on formal data resource management that I was promoting, and / or 3) they were worried that their product might not hold up to my rigor. None seemed even remotely interested in learning my approach to formal data resource management.

I contacted several software vendors about developing commercial versions of the Data Resource Guide for managing the Data Resource Data. All declined with a variety of reasons, mainly along the lines of 1) it was not mainstream for supporting current hype, and /or 2) it did not fit their existing product line and revenue stream.

The first reason led to a look at what was meant by 'not being mainstream.' 'Not being mainstream' essentially means that an idea or approach does not follow or support current hype, is not part of The Agenda, does not support financial motivation, does not cater to personal agendas, is not covered by current standards, and so on. In other words, don't rock the boat because everything is fine just the way it is.

The second reason led to an understanding about the financial motivation that is driving most software vendors. Most software vendors develop a product line, keep the design of that product line proprietary, and promote their product line as the best approach for all solutions in order to achieve their financial motivation.

The Challenge

New data resource management concepts are often heavily rejected, just like most new scientific concepts. They are even ridiculed and suppressed for personal or financial reasons, before finally being proven and readily accepted. That scenario has certainly been true for development of the

Common Data Architecture paradigm.

I've had many personal attacks, public confrontation, private recriminations, scathing e-mails, and so on, about the new approaches to data resource management. All of those have been without substance, which has led to a philosophy that I continue to use. When a person cannot make a chink in the paradigm, then they make a personal attack on the promoter of that paradigm. The bottom line that I use when I receive a personal attack is – thank you very much for your support of the paradigm.

I've had many contacts 10 years or more after I've worked with people that didn't implement the Common Data Architecture paradigm saying that they wish that they had listened to me earlier. They would have saved countless resources and avoided considerable anxiety if they had simply followed the Common Data Architecture paradigm. Their organization's data resource, and its support to the business activities, would have been of much better quality.

I've also had many contacts 10 years or more after I've worked with people that did implement the Common Data Architecture paradigm for a segment of their data resource saying they wish that they had applied the paradigm to the organization's entire data resource. They would have had a much higher quality data resource and a much higher quality of support to the business.

The time has come for many organizations, and will come for many others, to manage their data as a critical resource of the organization, like the human resource, financial resource, and real property. Those resources went through their cycle of mismanagement, disparity, disasters, and recovery to formal management. Traditional data management will go through it's cycle and will eventually become formal data resource management.

BUSINESS MANAGEMENT

The Common Data Architecture paradigm is only one portion of the overall business architecture for an organization, as described below, including the Business Architecture Infrastructure, Business Architecture Management, and Data Resource Quality.

The Business Architecture Infrastructure

Architecture is the art, science, or profession of designing and building structures. It is the structure or structures as a whole, such as the frame, heating, plumbing, wiring, and so on, in a building. It's the style of structures and method of design and construction, such as Roman or Colonial architecture. It's the design of a system perceived by people, such

271

as the architecture of the Solar System.

Infrastructure is the underlying foundation or framework for a system or an organization. The term generally refers to basic installations and facilities for community development or military operations. However, the concept can be applied to an organization's business.

The Business Architecture Infrastructure, shown in Figure 16.1, consists of four separate architectures representing an organization's Business Activity Architecture, which is supported by the Data Resource Architecture and the Operating Platform Architecture, which is implemented through the Information System Architecture.

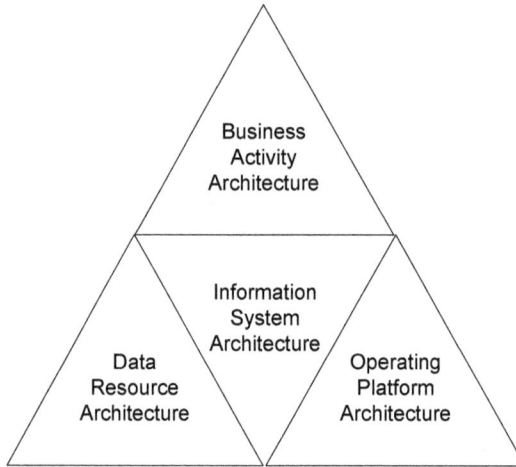

Figure 16.1. Business Architecture Infrastructure.

The Business Architecture Infrastructure was originally named the Information Technology Infrastructure. However, that name led to a technology oriented approach to managing an organization's business activities which resulted in many problems, such as disparity, high cost, poor performance, and so on. The name was changed to Business Architecture Infrastructure to promote an orientation toward managing the organization's business from a business perspective rather than from a technology perspective.

The Business Activity Architecture is a basic architecture that represents all of the business activities in an organization, whether manual or automated. The business activities may utilize the data resource and the operating platform, and may be performed by information systems.

The Data Resource Architecture is a basic architecture that represents all of the data available to the organization, whether developed by the organization or acquired from outside the organization. It is one of the four critical resources for an organization, equivalent to the human resource, financial resource, and real property.

The Operating Platform Architecture is a basic architecture that represents all of the hardware and system software at the organization's disposal, including storage, processing, and communications. The hardware and system software may be known and managed by the organization, or may be unknown to the organization, such as the various forms of distributed processing.

The Information System Architecture is a resultant architecture that is formed from the combination of business activities, using the data resource, and implemented on the operating platform.

The *Principle of Independent Architectures* states that each of the three basic architectures in the Business Architecture Infrastructure is independent of the other basic architectures in the Infrastructure. In other words, development of the Business Activity Architecture is independent of the Data Resource Architecture, which is independent of the Operating Platform Architecture.

The question is always asked if more than these four architectures exist. The answer is a resounding 'No.' Only three basic organization-wide architectures and one resultant organization-wide architecture exist in the Business Architecture Infrastructure. However, each of these four organization-wide architectures can be segmented into sub-architectures where each segment represents a specific topic of interest, such as the Human Resource Business Activity Architecture, the Water Resource Data Architecture, or the Central Office Operating Platform Architecture. Even though these segments may appear to be separate architectures, they are simply a segment of a larger architecture within the Business Architecture Infrastructure.

Business Architecture Management

Each public and private sector organization must develop a Business Architecture Infrastructure based on formal concepts, principles, and techniques if they are to be successful in their business endeavors.

That Business Architecture Infrastructure is developed through a Common Data Architecture paradigm, a Common Business Activity paradigm, a Common Operating Platform paradigm, and a Common Information System paradigm. Collectively, these paradigms form a Common Business Architecture paradigm. Each of these paradigms produces a single organization wide architecture, specifically a Common Data Architecture, a Common Business Activity Architecture, a Common Operating Platform Architecture, and a Common Information System Architecture. These four architectures collectively form the Business Architecture Infrastructure.

The Business Architecture Infrastructure is thoroughly understood through Data Resource Data, Business Activity Data, Operating Platform Data, and Information System Data. Collectively, these four sets of data form a comprehensive set of Business Architecture Data for thoroughly understanding the business.

That understanding is stored in a Data Resource Guide, a Business Activity Guide, an Operating Platform Guide, and an Information System Guide. Collectively, these four Guides form a comprehensive Business Architecture Guide that is readily available to anyone in the organization desiring to understand the business.

Disparity exists in all components of the Business Architecture Infrastructure in most public and private sector organizations. That disparity is resolved with data resource integration, business activity integration, operating platform integration, and information system integration. These separate integrations collectively become business architecture integration.

The components of the Business Architecture Infrastructure are managed through formal Data Resource Management, formal Business Activity Management, formal Operating Platform Management, and formal Information Systems Management, each consisting of concepts, principles, and techniques. These four management practices collectively become formal Business Architecture Management.

Quality is the ultimate goal of Business Architecture Management. Quality is achieved through data resource quality, business activity quality, operating platform quality, and information system quality, which collectively become business architecture quality. Business architecture management is the foundation for thoroughly understanding and formally managing all of the business activities in the organization. When all of the components of business architecture management are in place, then ultimate quality is achieved.

Data Resource Quality

Data resource quality is the goal of formal data resource management. Data resource quality directly supports business architecture quality. The higher the data resource quality, the higher the quality of support to the business. Similarly, the lower the data resource quality, the lower the quality of support to the business.

Traditional data management resulted in the massive quantities of disparate data that are seen in most public and private sector organizations today. Obviously, those disparate data do not provide high quality support to the business, and in many situations severely compromise the business. Only formal data resource management that manages data as a critical resource of the organization within the Common Data Architecture paradigm provides quality support to the business.

Emphasis on information management, and the improper term 'information resource management,' will not help improve quality and often decreases quality because information is not a resource. Data are the resource that becomes the raw material for producing information which is relevant and timely. Quality must begin with the raw material and be carried forward to the product based on that raw material. That fact becomes more obvious as the critical nature of data as a resource emerges.

Data resource quality is achieved by being both effective and efficient. Being effective is doing the right thing, which means thoroughly understanding the organization's Umwelt, formally developing a single organization wide data architecture to support that Umwelt, and ensuring business professional involvement in that development effort. Being efficient is doing the thing right, which means, using the proven concepts, principles, and techniques of the Common Data Architecture paradigm;

When the approach to managing data as a critical resource is not effective, then efficiency has no meaning. Efficiency only has meaning when the approach is effective. Being both effective and efficient means gaining understanding, and developing a high quality data resource with minimum effort and maximum benefit to the organization's business.

Each organization must build their data resource according to their particular Umwelt. In other words, a high quality data resource begins with the organization's Umwelt following the Umwelt Principle. When the data resource begins to deviate from that Umwelt, the quality declines. The greater the deviation, the greater the decline in quality.

An organization must not allow consultants or software vendors to force that organization's Umwelt into a foreign and unfamiliar data architecture. Some consultants and vendors have the general approach of 'We have the solution', followed by 'Now, what is your problem?', followed by warping the organization's problem into the consultant or vendor's solution without regard for the organization's Umwelt. When that happens, the quality is lost no matter what activities follow.

Data resource quality is the goal, the organization's Umwelt is the driver, the Common Data Architecture paradigm is the implementer, and the business is the recipient. The Data Resource Simplexity series of books, which include the Data Architecture Trilogy and the Data Understanding Trilogy, describe the Common Data Architecture paradigm as the foundation for formally managing data as a critical resource of the organization to provide a high quality data resource that fully supports an organization's business activities as well as the current and future business information demand.

A high quality data resource is often the driver for solving disparity in other components of the Business Architecture Infrastructure. Business activities are often more disparate than the data resource, and more difficult to integrate. Integrating the data resource and resolving data resource disparity often provides the incentive to integrate business activities and resolve business activity disparity.

The Common Data Architecture paradigm is available, and is proven. It just needs to be used and become a common practice. Take the initiative before the situation gets worse.

The choice is yours!

BIBLIOGRAPHY

Brackett, Michael H. *Developing Data Structured Information Systems.* Topeka, KS: Ken Orr and Associates, Inc., 1983.

_____. *Developing Data Structured Databases.* Englewood Cliffs, NJ: Prentice Hall, 1987.

_____. *Practical Data Design.* Englewood Cliffs, NJ: Prentice Hall, 1990.

_____. *Data Sharing Using a Common Data Architecture.* New York: John Wiley & Sons, Inc., 1994.

_____. *The Data Warehouse Challenge: Taming Data Chaos.* New York: John Wiley & Sons, Inc., 1996.

_____. *Data Resource Quality: Turning Bad Habits Into Good Practices.* New York: Addison-Wesley, 2000.

_____. *Data Resource Simplexity: How Organizations Choose Data Resource Success Or Failure.* New Jersey: Technics Publications, LLC, 2011.

_____. *Data Resource Integration: Understanding and Resolving a Disparate Data Resource.* New Jersey: Technics Publications, LLC, 2012.

_____. *Data Resource Design: Reality Beyond Illusion.* New Jersey: Technics Publications, LLC, 2012.

_____. *Data Resource Data: A Comprehensive Data Resource Understanding.* New Jersey: Technics Publications, LLC, 2014.

_____. *Data Resource Understanding: Utilizing the Data Resource Data.* New Jersey: Technics Publications, LLC, 2015.

_____. Monthly articles on Dataversity.net.

www.ingramcontent.com/pod-product-compliance
Lightning Source LLC
Chambersburg PA
CBHW061341210326
41598CB00035B/5844